# HEART SOUL FIRE

*The Journey of Paul Briggs*

# HEART SOUL FIRE

*The Journey of Paul Briggs*

**PAUL BRIGGS**
**and GREGOR SALMON**

HarperCollins*Publishers*

www.paulbriggs.com

**HarperCollins**_Publishers_

First published in Australia in 2005
by HarperCollins*Publishers* Pty Limited
ABN 36 009 913 517
A member of the HarperCollins*Publishers* (Australia) Pty Limited Group
www.harpercollins.com.au

Copyright © Paul Briggs and Gregor Salmon 2005

**HarperCollins**_Publishers_
25 Ryde Road, Pymble, Sydney, NSW 2073, Australia
31 View Road, Glenfield, Auckland 10, New Zealand
77–85 Fulham Palace Road, London, W6 8JB, United Kingdom
2 Bloor Street East, 20th floor, Toronto, Ontario M4W 1A8, Canada
10 East 53rd Street, New York NY 10022, USA

National Library of Australia Cataloguing-in-Publication data:

Briggs, Paul, 1975– .
   Heart soul fire: the journey of Paul Briggs.
   ISBN 0 7322 8190 3.
   1. Briggs, Paul, 1975– . 2. Boxers (Sports) – Australia –
   Biography. 3. Boxing. I. Salmon, Gregor. II. Title.
796.83092

Front cover images: Sport, The Library (top); Newspix (bottom)
Back cover image © ON Corporation
Cover and internal design by Matt Stanton, HarperCollins Design Studio
Typeset in 10.5/14pt Sabon by Kirby Jones
Printed and bound in Australia by Griffin Press on 79gsm Bulky Paperback White

5 4 3 2 1    05 06 07 08

*To the greatest teachers I'll ever know:*
*Isaiah and Aramea.*

# Contents

# 1

## A Mistake Becomes A Family

I came to Australia the infant son, grandson and nephew of Kiwi fighters. My family flew TAA from Christchurch, New Zealand, where my parents had lived for almost a decade, and I carried within me — so my father has taken to saying — the blood of the Romany people. Gypsies. Not the east Continental variety with their violins and dancing bears, but the Celtic type inclined to play music on people's heads — the kind of short-fused scrappers they had in that movie *Snatch*. Somewhere along the line a few had spilled into New Zealand, which I guess was as good a place as any for a bloke to make a buck with his fists, in and out of the ring.

But I know better than to believe everything my old man says. He's been a Christian, a Jew, a cowboy, a Celt, and far more besides than I'll ever know. Regardless, I'll buy his gypsy bloodline story; I accept that there's some truth in it. I've heard the stories of his mother and her black magic, her fatal spells. What I won't abide is the idea that I was born a fighter, that I'm part of a hair-trigger breed like some hard-wired pit dog.

I was born Paul Darius Briggs in the year 1975, seven minutes after my fraternal twin, Nathan, and the last of my parents' four children. I was born happy, innocent and of love, and with talents I could have applied well to other endeavours besides fighting.

True, I came into this world spirited, but it weren't genes that soured my cheek into malice, switched my anger so easily to violence and cast my life into hell. That was a process of acquisition, an education in things I never sought to learn, things that sparked within me a hatred of men that I cultivated darkly and doled out in increasingly vicious doses.

I'm not here to tell you I'm the victim of inflicted events — because I was my own greatest tormenter. I don't seek forgiveness for the wrongs I have done, because I have fought so hard to forgive and love myself. I had to drag myself upwards to allow me, a young man drowning in self-loathing, to gulp a lungful of clean air. I can say now with all my heart that I know what it means to be a man and it's not something to be found in the pub, that crucible of Aussie machismo. Nor is it a figure cast in the image of my father, a tough man who walked fearlessly among society's most fearsome men. As I said, there's so much of him I'll never know, so much of his life camouflaged by bullshit and held captive by his demons, and I don't expect that to change. That could well have been said of me if I hadn't sought to transform myself. It's something I still strive at daily. Yet for my son, my darling Isaiah, to know who I am, he must know who I was. And telling him won't be easy. I've done plenty of things most men couldn't do. I've been to plenty of places most men could never go to. But for all my hard and brutal experiences, I only really knew what it meant to be a man when I became a father, when I had to stand up and be responsible and support my family.

I'm a boxer, a contender for the world light heavyweight crown, but I'm defined by my family. I am defined by how I live my life every day in relation to them, not by winning fights and earning belts. I box for the self-mastery the sport offers. Boxing allows me to keep challenging myself, to find new lines I haven't yet crossed. And, let there be no doubt, I box because I love to fight. I am a warrior. When I'm in the ring I see no tomorrow, just forty-seven minutes of here and now. I direct my whole life into one little moment, and put all my passion, all my power and all my energy, all my love and all my sacrifice, and my children and my wife and everything they've given up as well, and everything that we've

2

battled through ... I channel this into one little moment. You could put an army of men in front of me and I swear to God that for forty-seven minutes they'd be in for the fight of their lives — never mind a solitary man who stands before me. Yes, like all boxers, I fight for the money — so burn me at the stake. There are no wages in boxing, no retirement plans, only paydays. That money happens to mean the livelihood of the three people I cherish beyond the power of words: Tasha, Isaiah and Aramea.

Right now, I'm still learning to be the best man, husband, father and boxer I can be. And I'd love to say this is what my old man taught me. But I can't. For as much as I have loved him deeply, I have wanted to see him deep in his grave. You could say we had our issues. God, did we have our issues.

My parents don't talk any more, but there's one thing they agree on: the minute they got married, they knew it was a mistake. Of course, this accord is the work of rueful hindsight. There was some real spark there to begin with. Enough for them to last twenty-nine years together.

Mum — Sharon — and her sister were dancers from Sydney who had decided to take a working holiday in New Zealand. Second day there they walked into a café in Wellington and sitting in a lounge booth was Dave Briggs, a young sailor whiling away some R and R with his mates by planning to stick up a bank. Purely as a training exercise, you understand; they'd leave the money on the doorstep of the nearby police station. Show them how it was all too easily done, spotlight their vulnerabilities. That sort of thing. All Dad and his buddies would get out of it would be a cheap thrill and a chuckle over what twits the cops were.

How scaring the shit out of civilians and soft-bellied bank clerks amounted to training I don't know, but my dad was no regular schemer. He was already accustomed to seeing everyone as a target, every situation as a threat. In his mind, even Big Bird could be fixing to smash you. When I was still a boy, he would conspiratorially pass this vital knowledge on to me as we ventured out to rent a video. I learnt you had to be vigilant and defensive, and to always size up your targets. Upon entering the store I'd take

*3*

stock of everyone, assess their potential threat and keep them on the radar of my peripheral vision, so that if they attacked I could swat them down like I'd seen it all coming. I'll give Dad this: it was one of the best lessons he ever taught me. Burnt into my brain was the rule that you never get into anything without an exit strategy. That has served me more valuably than he could have imagined. I owe my life to that tip.

My old man sometimes spoke of the action he saw during the Vietnam War. When he did he was usually pissed and ranting, so you never knew what was truth or fiction. We were all inclined to sway to the latter, given his tendency to use more imagination than fact when relating even modest adventures. Even so, I came to believe wholeheartedly that my father had been involved in military activity that far exceeded the modest and largely non-combative role the NZ Navy played in the conflict. I grew up convinced he was an 'I was there but I wasn't' soldier — you know, the secretive SAS type — who graduated into a veteran struggling to deal with the horrors of what he'd both seen and carried out, as well as the banality of a flat existence, one devoid of dire missions. My Mum reckons it's a crock, that if he had been in the Vietnam War there'd be records. None exist, she says. For me, the image of my father as a crack soldier is hard to shake. But the truth is, I really don't know what to believe. What is not in dispute, though, is that when she first met Seaman Briggs in that Wellington café, he rocked her world sideways. And she his.

Mum had a boyfriend at the time, a guy called Wayne. They'd been sweethearts for six years. That they were going to get married was a foregone conclusion for both their families. But Mum had never encountered a bloke like Dave Briggs before. And from the moment they met it was clear he was dead keen and she didn't mind a bit. Soon afterwards, Mum and her sister moved up to Auckland, where Dad was based, and, her loyalty to Wayne wearing through, she and Dad began to see each other. Mum felt deeply guilty about Wayne, of course, but the feelings she had for Dad were strong and irresistible. Both guys were eighteen, but Wayne was a boy in comparison with Briggs. Old Dave struck and excited Mum: he was worldly, romantic and a dead-set charmer.

Six months later, Mum and her sister moved down to Christchurch with the dancing troupe. Dad quit the Navy and followed her, moving back in with his parents and finding work. Meeting the Briggs family was a shock for Mum — they were poor rough-nuts who rorted and fought to put food on the table and beer down their gobs. But what really got Mum was the offensive way Dave's parents treated him. It really spurred the martyr in her, and she convinced herself that this downtrodden guy needed her more than any man on earth.

The news she'd agreed to marry Dave Briggs went down like strychnine back in Australia. Her parents flew into Christchurch on an intervention mission, but she stood her ground. And during their visit, while they were sitting with their daughter and her fiancé, Mr and Mrs Briggs walked in and introduced themselves. Old man Briggs wasn't one for idle chat: then and there he announced to everyone that he and his wife wouldn't be attending the wedding. When asked for a reason, he said, 'Because he shouldn't be marrying her. She's too good for him.' I believe Dad bore the scars of such comments the entire stretch of his life and marriage. He couldn't help but accept them. For shame — I can think of no other plausible reason — he has effectively ditched his whole family. To this day, I have met just one of his siblings, once. Ask him how many brothers and sisters he has and he seems uncertain — six or seven — as though it's some cryptic formula he put through the shredder long ago. The vagueness seems a deliberate act of putting things at a distance. Maybe that's what's best for him.

What Mum came to know of her fiancé only made her more determined to help him escape his past. She had optimism to burn and a tank on constant refill. She learnt that the authorities had sought to make Dad a ward of the state at age five. He'd bolted. They tried again when he was fourteen, but again he found a way to dodge the boys home: he signed up with the Navy.

I know little of Grandfather Briggs's record as a boxer. What I do know is that he used his wife and kids as punching bags. Between beatings, he gave his boys more formal lessons on how to handle themselves in the ring — enough for Dad and one of his brothers, Eric, to turn professional. It was also enough to give Dad the wherewithal to put his old man in his place. The last time they came to blows, Dad broke his father's back. The injury didn't cripple Briggs senior, but they didn't speak a word to each other for years afterwards. Their peace was eventually made on old Briggs's deathbed and he died before Dad got home from the hospital.

By that stage, though, Dad was making a new life for himself. He'd become a family man, and Christchurch was where he and Mum intended to raise their children. The two of them were committed Christians, and Dad — a Sunday School teacher at the local church — often took the kids out on camps. He never does things by halves, that's for sure.

It was a very positive time for them both. They lived by Christian standards and from their faith they forged their ideas on how they'd bring up their kids. It was a honeymoon period, in more ways than one. Up until they were married, Mum had only seen Dad sober. That is to say, she'd never had the misfortune of seeing Dave Briggs hit the piss. But that would come soon enough.

Since ditching Wayne, Mum hadn't wanted to return to Australia. She'd burnt him badly and had no desire to face the results of her handiwork. Not to mention seeing her parents. She knew their disapproval of Dad was as likely to soften as income tax was to be scrapped. It took the onset of her first child to get her back. I guess she figured it would be better to face the music at home than rely on the sorry-arsed Briggs family for support. So in 1969 my parents headed for Sydney, where my sister Leanne was, in time, born.

They spent five months there all up. But not long after they arrived, Wayne called Mum and told her that his parents wanted to meet her husband. She was, after all, like a daughter to them. This meeting caused no great stir that I'm aware of. In fact, Wayne's father gave Dad a job labouring for his concreting business. It was at Wayne's twenty-first birthday party that everyone — including Mum — first got an eyeful of Dad's darker side. Mum watched in horror as her sweet and God-fearing Dave downed drink after drink, corroding the lid he kept on his vast stores of anger and loathing. I'm not sure what spectacle he made of himself, but I have seen enough since to be able to imagine. And, as though mocked by the affluence surrounding him, he turned on Mum, saying, 'How could you give all this up for me?' She tried to reassure him — 'This is not me; this is not mine' — but I feel confident in saying that Dad couldn't allow himself to get past the contrast of their upbringings. Not then, nor ever. It might sound heartless to say this but it's the truth: this kind of display became Dad's thing. But it was nothing compared with what I would witness in later years. Plenty of times lay ahead when he would take a special occasion and guzzle it into a complete fucking nightmare.

Still, for the most part Dad stayed sober. He and Mum settled back in Christchurch and continued to align their lives with the gospel. Their next child was another daughter, whom they named Donna, and three years later came Nathan and me. Mum says that about six weeks into her pregnancy she believed she was carrying twin boys. Precedent supported her intuition: Dad's mum had given birth to three sets of identical twins — two sets of boys and one of girls, although one little girl had died at birth. And sure enough, on 13 August 1975, I followed Nathan into the light of the world, second out and, at six pounds six, lighter than my brother by three ounces shy of a pound. The doctors told Mum and Dad we were identical twins but when they saw that Nathan was jaundiced and I wasn't, they realised they were wrong. They discovered we even had different blood groups. So we are fraternal twins. Not that anyone gives a damn, but this is an important distinction. To most people, twins are those freaks who can finish each other's sentences and feel exactly what the other feels, those lucky bastards who can date the same chick without her catching on. This notion of twins stems from the identical version, siblings who have the exact same genetic make-up. They come from a single fertilised egg that divides into two. They are clones. Fraternal twins come from two different eggs fertilised by two different sperm. Nathan and I are no more genetic replicas than brothers born three years apart. Forgive the biology lesson, but to me Nathan has always been my brother, not my other self. This

7

seems to disappoint people — they want us to be inseparable mates. We were once, in our early years. But as we developed our own personalities, physiques, experiences and talents — as we diverged with age — we grew apart. And the process has been both painful and liberating.

But I'm getting ahead of myself.

For now, Dave Briggs had his first sons, a pair of them. And the first thing Mum said to him in regard to our upbringing was, 'Promise me they will never box.' Dad promised. To his credit, he kept his word. Mostly.

While Dad can't or won't put a bead on exactly how many siblings he has, I've always known about my uncle Eric. It stands to reason: he was a good boxer while the others were con men who may or may not have wound up in stir. Dad didn't have Eric's talent but he had enough to make boxing a sideline career that took him to England and America. He fought mostly at welterweight, moved up to junior middle and strung out a 200-fight journeyman's record.

Dad's mainstay earner was leatherwork and arabesque furniture. He was an excellent craftsman. Still is. He wasn't a jack of his trades: he mastered them. When he had a crack at something, he went at it full bore. In that sense he lived by his word, since he'd always tell us kids to do something right, whatever it was we chose to do. The thing was, he never consolidated. It was as if the proximity of success warded him off like an evil spirit. For, time and again, he'd walk away right when the next level beckoned. He'd set about clearing the decks and starting again. This was no healthy process of renewal — it was an act of self-sabotage, the most unfortunate craft he mastered. He could knock himself down better than anybody, damn it, but he always found the blame lying elsewhere.

Whatever his faults, Dad was initially a caring and devoted father. Whenever we woke during the night he was always there, never Mum. If we ever had a bad dream, Dad was the one who came to soothe us. He'd be there in a split second. As soon as we'd start crying Dad was in our room, there to cuddle us and comfort us.

It's funny, I had a flashback recently on a really hot night in the Los Angeles home my wife and I used to rent, and my little girl, Aramea, was crying. I came into the room and picked her up and she only had a nappy on. When I put her on my clammy chest, this shot of lucid memory hit me: I could smell my dad's scent and I could feel the tenderness of his care. Just for a split second I was straight back there, being lifted out of the cot to rest against his warm chest, the calming bed upon which I'd drift back to sleep. He was an amazing comforter and just loved us kids to death. We'd kiss him on the lips goodnight, right up until we were thirteen — he wouldn't let us go to bed without doing so. But this is the same man who held my infant brother, Nathan, aloft by the throat to castigate him for daring to wander from the dinner table as grace was being said.

In these early years my parents enjoyed a solid relationship and a growing business. By the time Nathan and I arrived, Dad had a shop specialising in leather jackets, with staff to help him stock it and fill orders for elsewhere. His hobby had become a fairly large enterprise requiring his full-time management. Then it began to unravel. Dad says the government came and stuck its nose in and told him he wasn't paying enough tax; Mum says he hated leaving the leatherwork to others. Both are probably telling the truth, but the upshot was that Dad shut down the whole thing. And before long they were looking to make a fresh start. They liked the idea of moving to Adelaide in South Australia because it sounded similar to Christchurch. Before settling down again, though, they decided to take a six-week break and visit Mum's mother and stepfather, who were living in Nhulunbuy, a small mining town on the Gove Peninsula in Arnhem Land. They put all their furniture into storage and left.

We never made it to Adelaide. For three years, this amazing, remote pocket of Australia became our home.

## II

## Thunder In Paradise

Good dreams will stay with you as long and as clearly as bad ones. From my experience, the same can't be said of memories. The highlights of my younger years, let alone those long stretches of idle contentment in between, seem flat and indistinct compared with the vivid jolts of my father's occasional rages. These are the things I snag on when I trawl back through my past. There is one period, though, that always surfaces from my memory banks as a gleaming treasure: the three years we spent in Nhulunbuy.

Mum and Dad fell in love with the place as soon as they arrived, and they ditched their plans for starting afresh in Adelaide when Dad was offered a job by Mum's stepfather, an industrial officer with Nabalco, the company that had built Nhulunbuy a few years earlier as a base for its bauxite mine. Mum and Dad shipped in our belongings from Christchurch and we settled into a home that defied the tropical heat with good air conditioning and stoically withstood the monsoonal storms. There were only around 4000 people in the entire community and we found a welcome place among them.

There were always stacks of kids around and as a gang we ran amok in one of the most spectacular parts of Australia, the Top End. We rode our bikes and scooters around the streets and ventured into the surrounding bush to go exploring and build tree houses, or else we'd muck around at the nearby beach. Plus there was a river we swam in that had strong undertows, and it was a kind of unwritten rule that we always swam with the dogs — I found out later that the idea was that the crocodiles would go for the dogs first.

The dangers of the environment were not something we felt as a close threat. One time when we were three, Nathan and I caught and killed a snake and waltzed into the police station with it dangling on a stick. The officer soberly informed us that we'd just killed a brown snake, one of the world's deadliest. We were chuffed.

My parents were just about the model couple then. They were openly affectionate, they did everything together, worked well together and were good friends. Often we would head away for weekend camping trips with a bunch of other families we'd befriended. We'd all pile into our cars and head for our favourite spot, a deserted beach where we'd have bonfires blazing at night and constant adventure during the days. Us kids would hang off the back of four-wheel drives as they burnt up and down the sand banks. We'd swim and go fishing — well, we'd watch Dad fish. Pointing at something he'd reeled in and asking what type of fish it was, that was about as hands-on as we got.

We could live without wetting a line, though. Dad was our hero, our god, and we were stoked just to hang around him, even though we seemed to bug him a little. That was the thing with Dad: while he could be affectionate, he was never what you'd call inclusive. His time, his experience, his knowledge were not things he could readily share. I think he had so many issues bound up tight that he didn't know how to let anything spill easily, even something as trivial as baiting a hook. The lighter the subject, the more he seemed inclined to disregard its worth, its purpose. If it wasn't deadly serious, if it didn't carry real consequence, he seemed to believe it was almost beneath him. Naturally, when he taught martial arts he was an excellent and committed teacher. Of course, I never dwelled on any of this back then. I'd simply spend as much time with him as he'd tolerate.

There was a lot Dad had to offer. He was a seeker back then —
still is — and on his travels he'd picked up a spectrum of martial
arts including karate, seibukan and tang soo do to add to his
boxing, hand-to-hand combat and knife-fighting skills. He was
your all-round action man — lethal weapon, hard to kill, die hard
and all that ... a freaking one-man army. One time, apparently, a
bloke bet a bunch of miners that his mate Dave could perform,
one-handed, double and a half the number of regular push-ups any
one of them could manage. Once they'd posted their highest tally,
away went Rocky Briggs, switching from one hand to the other, to
pocket some easy money.

Beneath Dad's formidable armour lay turbulent forces that too
often got the better of him. I don't mean to belittle the might of
what he was dealing with, but he tried more to accommodate
rather than overcome his problems. However, try he did. His
search for help was a deep quest that didn't stop at him knowing
the Bible well enough to teach it. And while he lived — or at least
strived to live — by the Christian word, he also took it upon
himself to read the Koran and learn the tenets of Buddhism. On
top of that, he was very proficient at yoga. This was the late 1970s,
remember, back in the days when probably the only other person
in Australia who was into yoga was that TV guru, Swami
Sarasvati. In many ways, Dad was New Age long before the old
one turned grey. He'd not duped my mother with tall stories back
in New Zealand; her bullshit radar was spot on — her Dave was
every inch a man of the world.

For as long as I can remember, Dad has been teaching one form
of self-defence or another. There was never a shortage of students.
He used to take classes out the front of our house and of course I
would watch and copy their moves. I must have observed pretty
closely, because by the age of four I could do a full *kata* — a
sequence of karate moves that demonstrates a wide range of skills.
Nathan and I were given boxing gloves around the same time and
in play fights we'd imitate Dad and his mates.

Every so often Dad would take off for a few days to go hunting
with some of the local Aborigines. As far as race relations went,
Nhulunbuy was just like any other Australian frontier town: the

whites held the blacks in contempt as useless, drunken bastards. Dad, though, had quite an affinity with the Kooris and believed there was a lot the Anglos could learn from them. Few shared his view.

One time he brought two Koori men back to our place for the night. They sat on the floor of our lounge room and I stared at them. They spooked me — they were so black and their faces seemed so old. I couldn't understand a word they spoke and they smelt. They were like strange spirits who had come to visit us. But I was intrigued too — they had an aura about them and an indifference to comforts such as chairs that made them seem above our world, or deliberately detached from it. Next day they were gone, entering the bush as though it were a portal to a place I could only wonder about.

Entertainment in Nhulunbuy was pretty thin on the ground, so most people took up sport. Mum and Dad played squash and were both very good. Dad also played a bit of rugby league. Every now and then, though, he'd put together a day of tent-show boxing. It was a boxing show in the old style. He'd set up a tarpaulin to shield boxers and spectators from the sun, provide two pairs of well-used gloves and referee the matches. They always happened on Anzac Day, as I recall, the only day of the year when two-up is deemed legal. I think Dad took advantage of the law's largesse to add fighting to the day's festivities, and gambling opportunities. The cops turned a blind eye — their chief was one of Dad's students.

So at the start of the dry season, when a thirst for a beer strikes not long after sunrise, all the menfolk of Nhulunbuy turned out for two-up and blues. As in the old days, the fighters were contained by a ring of spectators from which the square, raised platform got its name. I can't remember Dad fighting — I doubt many guys would have been prepared to step in with him, as his reputation preceded him — but he ran the whole show. Squeezing my way to the front through a forest of legs, I usually secured a ringside vantage point. And I loved what I saw. It may have been rough as guts to most people, but to me the spectacle of fighting was amazing. I was in the midst of an amped and boisterous crowd.

The spectators were so into the fights I often wondered what kept them from stepping in and having a crack themselves. What kudos the winner earnt, and even the loser walked away with respect. And there was my dad in the thick of it, stepping in to break up the fighters if they clinched, to count them out and raise a hand in victory. I was so keen to have a go myself; I couldn't have felt more excited and eager if a brand-new bike had appeared before me. To me, boxing simply seemed to be the best form of fun I'd ever seen.

Mum was very happy in Nhulunbuy. She was the full-on mother to us boys and she loved it. While Leanne and Donna were at school, we'd muck around in this big playroom, painting and drawing. We'd sleep after lunch, and then the girls would come home. Nathan and I would then wait for Dad to return, and we'd bolt down the cul du sac at the first sight of him and latch onto him. When the time came for us to go to school, Mum was devastated. The last of her children were old enough to leave her care, and she felt lost without us. To cope, she threw herself into squash, a sport she'd really enjoyed before she got married. And so she proceeded to spend her days playing squash. Dad played, too, but he wasn't as good as Mum and he'd just get pissed off all the time. Mum quickly became the top player in the club and would occasionally fly to Darwin to compete. And a major reason why she had so much time to play squash was because Dad didn't approve of her working.

Eventually, though, Mum decided she'd look for a job. Dad's reaction was typically negative. By his logic she could never hope to find employment — 'How could you get a job? You've never worked.' Ignoring Dad's put-downs, Mum got a job as a secretary at the local school. She then landed a second job at a bank. Dad was shocked. I'm no shrink, but I can take a stab at why he reacted like this — there's usually a pattern to human behaviour, and with Dad it was that every issue came down to one thing: him. Maybe it didn't look good — people might think a second income was needed in the Briggs household. The notion that work was a great channel for Mum's natural industry was lost on him. She wasn't exactly splitting the atom, yet her modest but quick success in the workforce prodded Dad's sense of failure. He continued to criticise her but Mum fended him off and went about her business. The demands of work, though, ate into her squash time and her game slipped to the point that she faced dropping down a grade. Dad reckoned that if she couldn't play at the top level she might as well give it away. I think this is the type of thing he must have screamed to himself all his life, carrying the baton from the fist of his father.

Despite the static over Mum working, these were our golden years. And the main reason for that was that Dad was healthy and sober, if not happy, a word that has never entirely fitted him. He was extremely fit: training all the time and developing a new martial art that incorporated the best elements of many. He and a friend refined their custom moves and one time, just to amuse themselves, they went into the pub and pretended to beat the bejesus out of each other. They hammed it up well enough to start a brawl, then left. Yep, life could be a little slow in Nhulunbuy.

They ended up starting a school together to teach their new style of self-defence. Again, Dad was building something entirely his own. However content he was at this time, us kids knew that his good moods were delicate things prone to vaporising with one gust of temper. However much we basked in his laughter or company or looked up to him, we were always on edge with a tension that never entirely dissipated. When would Dad lose it? We tried not to piss him off but it was an inexact science — there was simply no logic to the type of thing that could provoke him. He had a fuse so short we'd only see it flare the instant before the blast. Then we would know, only too late, that we'd done it. Suddenly, this boiling freak would be bearing down upon us and strike us boys as he would a man. *Bang!* He'd unleash a backhand and either Nathan or I would be flying across the room. There were no eggshells around him, only landmines, and submission was our only survival tactic; later we'd find out what lengths Dad would go to maintain his dominance. Anyway, the upshot here is that we mostly only had to deal with his temper. We rarely saw the drunken beast, but that was often enough.

Christmas didn't agree with Dad. And no matter how much our mother tried to get him to count his blessings, to look at his four children and see the abundance of love that was there to nourish him, he harboured a bitter and angry core. No wonders of the present could dispel the miseries of his past. Memories of his wretched childhood had him reaching for the bottle on occasion.

Mum did her utmost to support Dad staying sober. She kept the house dry and forewent the social pleasures of alcohol herself. Come Christmas Eve, though, Dad would be on one. A six-pack would do for starters, then he'd neck bottles of wine and anything else he could get his hands on. It was like he was trying to poison off a weed inside him but he only succeeded in making it thrive and quickly overrun him. Once he was blotto, something would go *click* and it would be 'see you later'. He'd just smash, crash and destroy, a terrible force lashing out at random targets, real or imagined.

Our time in Nhulunbuy ran out when my eldest sister, Leanne, neared the end of primary school. She was quite bright and made noises about wanting to be an architect. Local high school options were pretty limited. My parents had bought a small investment property in Brisbane, so they decided we'd move there. Problem was that Mum and Dad had purchased the house remotely and knew nothing about Woodridge, the area in which it was located. They found out soon enough when we arrived: our new home was a two-storey dump penned in by a chicken-wire fence and thick in the dregs of Brisbane suburbia. They were horrified. We all were. We'd given up our little piece of paradise to live in a lowlife-riddled clump of hovels. The plan to do the place up and sell immediately acquired a sense of urgency, a quest spurred on nightly by our neighbours' gutter-mouthed screaming.

The one noteworthy event of our time in Woodridge was seeing Dad fight professionally for the first and last time. The bout was held in Sydney, so we all watched it at home on *TV Ringside*, a boxing show long since axed. It was a confusing experience for me. I thought my dad was invincible, a man able to beat any man, yet here he was losing. Worse than that, he sat down. I just couldn't understand it — why would he give up? He was going so well and when he was down it was clear even to me he wasn't hurt. He dogged it, plain and simple. And it was kind of shattering to see his weakness laid bare. When I have asked him about it over the years the excuses have changed — the promoter wasn't paying him enough, he was sick, he was paid to throw the fight. Mum has always said, though, that whenever the going got tough in the ring, Dave Briggs would holler 'nuff. He didn't have the heart for it. This may sound unfair but it's not. As they say, there's nowhere to hide in the ring, and assessments of those who choose to enter are made in a harsh and pure light. A boxer can have all the skill in the world but without fierce intent — or go or mongrel — he will be found out as an impostor. He's not a real fighter, a man who would, if permitted, fight to his very last breath.

Believe me, my father is a freak when it comes to hand-to-hand combat. There have been situations in which his lack of fear has astounded me. He exhibits absolutely no nerves, no matter what the odds. Facing ten men, he would calmly remove his watch and his rings and put them in his pocket like he was readying himself for a hot bath — 'Okay, fellas; let's go.' He was so cool, calm and collected that it was shocking. So how could a guy who can tear just about anyone apart, regardless of whatever sort of skill or weapon they might be armed with, wind up cowering in the ring?

There's an enormous difference between fighting in the ring and on the street. What happens outside the ring is complete, unbridled terror: anything goes and you just let rip. You can't do that in the ring: calculated violence is required. You have to off-load in a measured way. If you completely let go, you'll tire and get smashed. You have to be extremely self-disciplined. And, though it's hard to generalise, that's what good fighters are: men who have mastered themselves.

Dad's boxing days were done long before that last fight. But he'd already set the next generation in train. At the age of six, he began holding up his hands as pads for us boys and we'd follow his call: left, right, left, left, right, keep your hands up. We thought it was fun, but Mum barely tolerated this kind of play. She didn't want us to get a taste for boxing. When my preschool complained to Mum that I'd bloodied a boy's lip in a play fight — an accident, truly — she put an end to it there and then. And Dad obeyed.

We were stuck in Woodridge for six months before Mum and Dad could sell the house. Spruced up, it was bought by the government for the housing commission. Says it all, really. The Briggs family, meantime, had found a 32-acre property in Park Ridge to occupy. Mum says it was Dad who suddenly had a thing for horses. By my recollection, she was half right. My sister Leanne was going through her *National Velvet* stage. Dad, who was smitten with his eldest daughter, figured he'd do more than buy the light of his life a pony; he was going to get her a ranch. Don't get me wrong, we were all up on the idea. But then we would have been up for anything to get clear of Woodridge. Man, was it good to see the back of that dive.

# III

# Black Christmas

Our new home in Park Ridge may have been a fibro shack but it was a castle to our kingdom. To us, 32 acres of property was a massive slab of uncharted territory awaiting exploration. Then there was the bush our land backed onto ... that was another world.

The house was at the end of a long driveway. At the street end stood an old letterbox, home to a family of huntsman spiders that made my trip to collect mail something to look forward to. They are big, hairy things, but placid and quite harmless. I thought they were really cool. I felt they were so amicable they'd just about pass the mail out to me.

Horses were the main concern of our acreage. The land was divided into paddocks and a breaking ring, Dad's new work station. Once we'd settled in, he immersed himself fully into cowboy mode. He claimed that handling horses was something he'd longed to do as a child; he'd make similar claims about other pursuits, but this did seem to be something of a calling. All of a sudden, with astonishing ease and no instruction, Dad turned himself into a horse breaker. He figured why buy a horse when there were plenty of brumbies — feral nags — roaming about in the bush. So off he went and caught them. In no time we had fourteen horses on the ranch trying to figure out where the heck their boundless space and forested shelter had gone. Dad thought he could make a nice earner selling his brumbies, and he wasn't wrong: Dave 'Breaker' Briggs found himself in steady business.

But Dad wasn't just any old breaker — he was the bloody Horse Whisperer. He had a truly splendid touch with horses, an affinity that tapped into a secret language between man and beast. While other breakers were all about domination, power and control, Dad was gentle and handled the horses with respect. I don't want to get all Man from Snowy River on you, but once there was a bastard of a horse roaming the bush that nobody could get near, let alone catch. Dad decided he'd have a crack. He saddled up and set off. He found the horse, rode it down, dismounted, spoke to it, handled it, bridled it, strapped a saddle to its back, then rode the bugger out and popped it in the float as though it were a trail-ride Shetland pony. If he deigned to tell you this story, he'd do so in an offhand way — an unsteady hybrid of modesty and pride. He'd want you to know how good he was but, really, what he did wasn't hard for anyone who really knew horses, unlike those other bullying idiots.

The truth, however, is that my old man was talented in everything he applied himself to. There was something very special about him; he was by many measures an extraordinary individual, but he didn't believe in himself at all. The driving force behind him mastering something was largely ego. But his deep insecurities had long ago petrified: as resilient as stone, they always won out. So an impressive feat, once achieved, was something ripe to be belittled as a trifle.

My siblings and I thoroughly enjoyed the spoils of Dad's labour. We loved to ride and were pretty game. We'd jump on a horse bareback, kick our heels into its guts, clutch the mane and it was hi-ho Silver. There were Briggs derbies, where Nathan, Donna and I would race around the paddocks and when the horses pulled up sharply the want of saddlery showed — we were either thrown off altogether or found ourselves hanging from their necks like chaff bags. It would always be just the three of us, because Leanne mostly kept to herself. She had that classic eldest child snobbery —

she was aligned with the adult world and regarded her younger sister and brothers as stupid pests who'd spoilt the cosy clique of three she had going. I cared about her attitude at first, then the irritation became mutual, and a bond between us never formed.

The horse I cherished the most was one we could never ride. He was a lunatic black stallion who belonged to Nathan and me, but really had no human master. We got huge enjoyment out of him: he was awesome just to watch — a boisterous, beautiful piece of work with, when nature called, a whopping great donger hanging boldly in the breeze. Eventually, though, he was sold like the others.

Back then Nathan and I were as tight as brothers can be. We got on well and only occasionally fought. It was fantastic as a kid to have a partner in crime always on hand; we never needed anyone else. When we were younger you could quite easily tell us apart because Nathan had lighter hair. By the time we lived in Park Ridge, our personalities provided clear distinction: Nathan was quiet and sensitive while I was bold and outgoing. Okay — I was a cheeky little upstart.

From a very early age Mum began to treat us differently. Since we were born, she'd had this feeling that Nathan wouldn't last long in the world, that he wouldn't live to see twenty-one. Even now she thanks God for every day Nathan remains with us. When we were young she used to mollycoddle and dote on him, while she managed me more at arm's length. Naturally, I was upset. To be clearly short-changed of my mother's affection sucked. She recently told me that she'd thought I was so robust that I didn't need her as much as Nathan did. Still, I have wondered what thought — if any — she gave to how her clear bias affected me. As if being less favoured wasn't going to hurt! Anyway, I never let on. Perhaps I did too good a job of it. But don't get me wrong: Mum was never cold to me. I felt not unloved, only less loved.

Nathan and I went to primary school in Marsden, and school life was punctuated almost as much by fights as the bell. Back then, just about everything was settled with a fight — it was how you made friends, how you resolved disputes, how you established yourself in the pecking order. Nathan and I were well equipped to handle ourselves, because we'd been practising. Mum had confiscated our boxing gloves so we'd just hold pillows up for one another to punch. Every now and then a stray fist would turn play into a proper blue that would be on for young and old. Fighting was commonplace but we enjoyed the whole contest and challenge of fighting more than most.

At school Nathan and I began to be recognised by our peers as two very different individuals. We started making our own friends. At home, though, we still did everything together because most of the time there was no one else to play with. Our parents rarely let us visit other friends' houses and we were infrequent hosts. We were also bonded in support and sympathy, as one would see the other copping a hiding from Dad. And this was when Dad was still at his best, when he was God's little soldier who'd conscript us into going to the Sunday services of the Christian Outreach Centre, a New Age charismatic church. Now that's all good and holy but — and there's always a but — no amount of praying, singing and hallelujahs relieved Dad, and us, of his hands of wrath. And when he took to us, one blow was rarely enough. Sometimes he'd just become unhinged as he belted us. Once Dad was spanking Nathan, who was kicking and screaming, when Nathan accidentally kicked Dad in the face. Dad just lost it and thumped Nathan black and blue. He laid into his boy as he would a hostile drunk who'd touched a raw nerve.

I've always been big enough to say Dad was doing the best he knew how, but sometimes I say it through gritted teeth. I know that at his core Dad is a good person and that he was a captive of his inner torment; when all is said and done, though, you have to take responsibility for your actions. My father has never stood up and said sorry for any of his excesses or mistakes. At the time, he'd feel guilty and bad — that was obvious — but the closest he came to apologising after his drunken rampages or his beating us way beyond the bounds of discipline was, 'Well, that's the way I am. You've got to just cop me for me.' That was always his attitude: accept his terms or fuck off. Not much of a choice for us, really.

Nathan and I would always be happy to let bygones be bygones when peace prevailed in our household. No matter what happened, our love for Dad was indestructible. We were so proud to have such a tough, strong father. And the old man didn't mind feeding our hero worship. As well as breaking horses, he was doing security work, meaning he worked more or less as a bouncer. Some mornings Nathan and I would pester him to tell us about his night's work, especially if we'd seen his shirt was ripped or bloodied. Upon waking Dad would recount his tough-guy stories, detailing standoffs, outnumberings, knockouts and turfings out in his quiet voice. Because when he wasn't yelling, Dad had a very soft, measured way of talking; sometimes you'd have to strain to hear him. He sounded like a native elder speaking over the gentle flapping of a campfire. And his tales were glorious — good guy Dad was taking out the trash. And in all seriousness, there was no better man for such a job.

Soon Dad had his own security company in which he operated as a troubleshooter. He'd go into hard-core problem pubs and clean them up, put his guys on then move on to the next one. And he'd do it single-handed. In my time I've seen some scary men, but few could outdo the menacing vibe my father could project. He's not an imposing man in stature — he's about five feet eight in the old measure — but in his countenance and his eyes you can see the latent ferocity of a wild cat stalking. Fearless, lethal, zoned. The type of presence that stirs up primal fear.

If he confronted you, you'd entertain no doubt as to the lengths he'd go to prevail. You could tell straightaway he would not draw a line. If you went at him with a knife, he'd come back at you with a gun, and all that. You'd have to kill him to conquer him. Once he was hired to bring some order to the Sunnybank Hotel, one of the most uncontrollable pubs in Brisbane. When he came on board, the owners were having a lot of problems with rival bikie gangs. One time, a gang rocked up armed with machetes, axes, shotguns — the lot — to murder a member of the hotel's staff because he'd slept with one of their wives or girlfriends. Dad stood in the doorway and refused to let them in. A shotgun was shoved under his nose. He then proceeded to tell the sergeant of arms that he'd take the weapon off him, shove it up his arse and let both barrels go if he didn't take his boys and fuck off. He said they were not coming in to do their business; they could do it elsewhere. The bikers walked away. This was the respect my father could command.

There was a strange element of secrecy to Dad's work. Every now and then he'd just take off for a couple of weeks on a job. I never knew where he went or what he did, but he'd come home in a weird, pensive mood and would take weeks to right himself. He brought home no stories from these trips. What he did bring home from time to time, though, were guns he'd somehow procured. He set up a firing range out the back of our property and Nathan and I were allowed to dip into his arsenal and blast away. By the age of eight we'd fired every sort of weapon you could imagine, from Ingram submachine guns to crossbows to semi-automatic pistols. We loved it.

There was much about Park Ridge I cherished. But an incident occurred there that changed my life for ever, and for the very worst. In 1983, we shared Christmas with some of our extended family. Amongst them was a guy I'd never met before and would only ever see again in murderous dreams and sick fantasy. He wasn't related to our family by blood but was the stepson or something of my grandfather's second wife. He was eighteen or nineteen and a seasoned guest of boys homes. He was a problem child, you could say. He was the fucked-up piece of shit who raped me.

When they arrived, my grandfather had parked his caravan next to our house and this guy had pitched a tent for himself alongside. He seemed to me to be pretty cool, so I tagged along with him around the place and then he suggested we check out his tent. I made the mistake of going along. I can't count the number of times that I have tried, in my mind's eye, to stop myself entering that tent, but it is of no use. I went in and I was raped. That is as much detail as I will tell you. That is all you need to know.

In the space of a few brutal minutes, my life was destroyed. Between then and now, many, many men paid dearly for what this man did to me. For I did not emerge to suffer alone. My pain was something I felt compelled to share.

Apart from the attack, my memory of that day is sketchy. I returned to the house but I can't remember that bloke being there any more. I don't know if he left soon after or if he was there for two more days. I don't even remember the events of Christmas, like opening the presents. No one noticed anything different about me, if I was in fact any different, but I doubt I was again that brash little show-off; that would have been impossible. I knew that what had been done to me was not right but I also felt it was possibly my fault. There was no way I was going to tell Dad what had happened. How could I? I lived in fear of the man. I wasn't about to divulge to him news of some misadventure for which, I believed, I was most likely to blame. That would be asking for a beating. Any way I looked at it, I was bound to piss him off. So I told no one. I kept it to myself and it stayed with me for more than ten years.

I had no idea at the time that part of me had died — or, rather, had been extinguished: my childhood. From that point on, I would never be the same little boy again and a new course through my adolescence and adulthood was set in train. Without knowing, driven by instinct alone, I set about building iron-clad defences. Forces of war went to work. Older boys and men were the enemy; they'd never again be allowed close to me. I mobilised myself around this notion. Only later in life would I define the vow I was living with pin-sharp clarity: no man was ever going to dominate me again.

No man, that is, but my father.

# IV

## *Disintegrating*

I had become a man in one of the saddest ways imaginable. I say a man — only because I was no longer a boy. I'd been pitched into a state of malformed maturity, lumbered with the hideous task of dealing with the trauma of rape alone. In the wake of the event, the confusion of what was happening to me, and why, would soon drive me to the brink of insanity. The word *rape* meant nothing to me at first and sex had barely existed as the subject of an uninformed curiosity, but I was aware I'd been violated in a profound and lasting way. This was no cut or bruise or scrape or burn or insult — things that can tilt a child's world painfully but temporarily. I could feel something of the indignity of being used and discarded, of my self being of no consequence, my say being of no worth, my power no use. I could not articulate my wholly decrepit state: the weird and horrific response that followed came from forces and places unclear to me. I'd resolved to fortify myself, true, but so much of what happened in my mind came uninvited. In some ways, my rape was far from done.

Two decades on I can tell you I have dealt with my abuse and, as I have said, I won't allow it to stand as an excuse for my worst behaviour, nor allow me to for ever plead victim. But I can't deny that dwelling on it can rouse drifts that sweep me to a miserable and lonely place. I can be stranded there for a day, but will allow myself to remain there no longer. It's a place where I feel powerless to fight my molester's weight and strength, like those dreams where, for all the terror upon you, you can't make yourself move. But mostly it's a place of mourning, where I feel a deep sadness, an immense sense of loss and grief for all the childish things and feelings I smothered in order to steel myself and endure. For that's what I had to do — persist with a process of making myself, yes, impenetrable. So tough I couldn't be hurt. And I succeeded, but sometimes I look at my boy, Isaiah, and see the safe boundaries within which his childishness roams and I feel sharp sorrow for the rightful innocence of which I was robbed.

Almost immediately after the rape I was struck by things I couldn't understand. My mind and body entered a state of shock and things were happening that I could make no sense of, nor could I repel. Only when I was awake did I feel I had a reasonable grip on my world. My nights became ordeals. For a while I had a problem with wetting the bed. Not every night, but when it happened I'd change my clothes and strip the bed so Mum wouldn't find out. I'm not sure if she ever knew or not, but I was too embarrassed to ever raise the subject between us. Thankfully, the problem didn't persist. I wish I could say the same about the nightmares. They stayed with me for almost fifteen years.

My bed became my torture chamber. I fretted over getting to sleep, and sleep itself was a curse. Every night for years I'd fear the onset of the most graphic and violent dreams. My pent-up rage became a powerful, macabre hallucinogen. The central theme to my visions was me as murderer, killing wantonly. One time I dreamt this kid came to our front door saying, 'Our car's broken down. Do you have any jumper leads?' And I invited him in then snuck up from behind and cut his head off. It was so real — the slap of the body on the ground, blood everywhere. I dragged him out the back and was cutting up the body when his dad knocked on the door: 'Have you seen my son?' 'Yeah, come in.' Then I knocked him as well. It would become a chain of murder as the next person came looking for the prior victim. I'd dream I'd killed Mum and buried her in the back yard. Then Dad would come home and I'd kill him and cut him up. Nathan returned from school saying, 'Where's Mum? Where's Dad?' And then the panic that he was going to find out set in, so I had to quickly kill my brother too. I'd wake up rattled and sick with remorse, thinking I'd actually slaughtered my entire family. I can't begin to tell you how disturbed I'd feel and then how relieved I was to realise it was all a dream.

I slept as though hiding. I'd pull the doona over my head, bundle myself into a ball and rest my head against the bedroom wall. I did this year round, even through the hot Brisbane summers. I'd sweat profusely regardless of the season but on hot nights you'd swear I'd wet the bed. A sweat stain developed on the wall from contact with my head and my pillow stank like a gym locker. My saving grace was that Nathan was in the room with me. His mere presence was like my anchor to the real world, to sanity. I couldn't bear the thought of being alone at night. Him sleeping in a bed beside me was more reassuring than he'll ever know. He was my rock. As long as he was all right, I was all right, and that was the last thought in my head before I'd fall asleep every night.

Particularly acute nightmares would set me off balance for a day or two, lingering with me at school. When I got into a confrontation, this side of me would come out and I'd look at my rival and think, *You've got no idea what I could do to you.* I actually felt capable of killing someone at that age. It was not an empowering feeling at all, just unhinged, terrible and frightening.

I did unleash my rage upon other students, but my most disturbing deviances remained secret. By the age of about twelve, for instance, I had a collection of flick-knives that I would use for playing out my morbid dreams with my teddy bears, stabbing them viciously and cutting their throats. I began to think I was doomed to become a murderer, a monster, that I was fucked up and evil to the core. Left to my own devices, I'd veer into the panic of sensing and fearing the onset of my own madness. But as soon as I started thinking I was really crazy I checked myself. It was like, *Whoa, I'm not staying in this room.* Because it would become, *What if I could really do this to someone?*

Mentally, I had some really questionable times. I would feel as though I was literally falling apart — my limbs dropping off — and that I was unable to breathe another breath. To pull myself back together took all the power I possessed, and I really believe that's how I kept myself from breaking down completely: I simply refused to let go. All the same, I was desperately worried and confused: *What is* wrong *with me? Why do I think like this? Am I going to grow up to be a psycho who wants to do this to people?* It was like being condemned despite my innocence. At first I couldn't think what I'd done to warrant such heavy and merciless punishment as the rape and the mental turmoil that followed. I knew I'd been singled out: this could not be some indiscriminate hand of justice. It had to have a cause and that cause, I reasoned, must reside within me. My actions were the crime: I shouldn't have gone into the tent; I was a despicable person who deserved a kind of torture no one could shield me from. Yet within me was also the faint belief that my torment was grossly unfair. *How could this be right? It can't be!* My mind would ache from the pummelling of garbled reasoning.

I don't remember much about Year 3. That period of my schooling is mostly blank to me. I do remember, however, that Nathan and I formed a little gang in which we all wore our jumpers tied around our waist with the flap at the front, like American Indians. Our tough little tribe of twenty overran the school yard. We specialised in targeting Year 7 boys. We'd single one out after school and tackle him — one high, the other low — and get him to the ground, where we'd knock the stuffing out of him. Such incidents prompted the principal to call Nathan, myself and another kid into his office. You could see he found it hard to believe what he was saying, telling eight year olds to quit picking on boys five years their senior. We felt like we were being decorated with medals of honour.

I do remember my Year 3 teacher, Mrs Smith; I was really attached to her. She was so kind and devoted, I believed we had a special connection. But I think many kids thought the same. She made me feel comforted and protected. I was so devastated when I had to go up a grade that I bawled my eyes out to Mum.

Come Year 4, I was back in black. I carried this little dark cloud over my head — not brooding and slow-morphing, but threatening and bristling with furious lightning. I gave lip to everyone — teachers, family and other kids. It was quickly and widely seen that I had developed a chip on my shoulder ... man, a dollar for every time I've heard that. Another buck would be nice, too, for every time Dad threatened, 'Get that chip off your shoulder or I'll knock it off!' And with the attitude I grew a snarl fit for a famished dog guarding its bowl. 'Put that lip down!' Mum would say, appalled.

I don't know what everyone thought. I guess they were confused as to why I'd become so nasty, but they probably figured this is what my brash and cocky nature had bloomed into. These days I'd be put straight on the Ritalin but, with all the awareness campaigns for child abuse, maybe someone would have started asking me some probing questions. I would hope so. Mum had no idea — and by that I don't mean to judge her by today's standards. She simply didn't know what to put my behaviour down to.

I was pretty good at drawing and in my paintings I began using no colour except black. Everything was in black and Mum would say, 'Paul, black is such an unhappy colour. Why are you so unhappy?' I'd just say, 'I'm not.' And that was the end of it. I'd shut her out and she didn't attempt to push through. I guess things were different then. She believed something was troubling me but for her to suspect I'd been sexually abused would have required a quantum leap of logic.

I remember Mrs Smith pulling me aside once. She looked at me puzzled, going, 'What's *happened* to you, Paul? What happened to that sweet little boy I knew? What's with this attitude?' And you know how there's a fine line between love and hate? I was just, 'Fuck you. Fuck you now. You're not on my side any more.' Not that I said it, but that was my reply in kind. I gave her nothing. I was all *Fuck you, world*. I was building my walls and gathering my arsenal. And I was suppressing the rape hard throughout that year, trying to wipe the whole memory of it clean from my mind. All I had left was this feral attitude. By Year 5, if you'd asked me if I'd been abused, I probably would have told you with all conviction that I had no idea what you were on about.

But the bad seed had taken root; the hate had begun to ferment. When I got into fights with other kids, I turned vicious, even over something as trivial as marbles. I remember grabbing this kid by the hair and dragging him round in the dirt and holding him down and smashing his face. I damaged this other kid really badly — I sat on him and punched and punched and punched — and his mum rang my mum absolutely mortified, saying, 'You should see my son's face!' Of course I was punished, but I didn't care. My new credo was *Whatever*. And I began to really *enjoy* fighting — it gave me an opportunity to vent and a mode of expression for all the anger that boiled within me. And when I'd see red, I'd just explode. So to everyone else I'd become a testy little thug and I didn't give a shit. *Whatever*. I took nothing seriously any more. Particularly school. I wasn't learning anything. I didn't want to. I didn't see the point. Getting punished for mucking up or not doing homework was more a nuisance than a wake-up call. Give me your worst, you pricks. *Whatever*.

Nathan and I drifted apart. It wasn't just because of the rape, either. For a while my attitude had been that we were just brothers; we were simply there. Always. My reaction to my abuse ramped up a prevailing trend of detachment. It would be fair to say that if we weren't brothers, we wouldn't have been close mates, if mates at all. As a natural ringleader, I was very popular in the mob drift of primary school loyalties. I had many friends but few close ones. Nathan was more reserved and had one or two select friends. After my rape the contrast grew sharper. The *contrast* — that was always it with us, compare and contrast. Our entwined co-life was a perpetual Pepsi Challenge. And we were becoming rival brands in so many ways: me the model ratbag, him the model student; me the grot, him Mr Clean; me inconsiderate, him caring; me thick-skinned, him sensitive. Nathan cared. I didn't. *What-the-fuck-ever*.

At home, the distance between us was kind of formalised when Nathan and Donna became a team. They'd say to me that they were best friends. It was like a drifting ally nation finally ripping up your treaty and signing with another. Suddenly, there was all manner of confidences and pacts I was not privy to and was suspicious of. They would hang out and play games together and wouldn't include me. *Whatever*. I'd go about doing my own thing; they were welcome to each other. In the fights Nathan and I would have, Nathan would try to whack me good and proper as usual, but I'd be trying to break his arm with my knee. He'd complain to Mum about my excessive intent: 'Paul's seriously trying to hurt me, Mum. It's not like we're just fighting.' And it was true — I really was trying to hurt him. Badly. I'd throw chairs at him and all sorts of things.

My aggression continually worked in Nathan's favour, though, because I was always regarded as the antagonist, even into our early teens. Nathan was sensitive, a quality women tend to see in a man as some rare and precious gift. I don't doubt its worth, believe me, but for all my abrasiveness and hard edges, I had tender feelings too. And let it be said that little Saint Nathan was not above stirring up trouble and fuelling spite between us.

There's a great deal of emotion involved in thinking over my relationship with Nathan. As you'll find out in more detail later, it's not crash hot now, but looking back to those younger days, I know I confused him as much as anybody. I was so clamped up about feelings, I never confided in him, my twin brother. I was going to let no one through my wall; not even him.

Age would introduce pressures upon us where once there were just aspects that distinguished one from the other, familiarities that both bound and irritated us. The older we got, the more we both chafed against the filial rope and those who liked to hold it tight. The bane of both our lives was being compared as though we were a two-horse race and every distinct achievement attained by one showed the other in a poorer light. Nothing could be done without reference to the other. This fuelled competitiveness between us from a very young age and the rivalry intensified as we got older, primarily due to outside expectations. The amazing thing was that, while we were pitted against one another in all manner of benign and acute ways, it was expected that we would always remain tighter than Batman and Robin. We were tight, and I still believe we are, but by this stage it had become a bond primarily of blood, something commanded by fate that we obeyed without thought rather than being willed or cherished above all things. For a long time we were locked in a kind of dance of death, combatants that couldn't escape, or leave, one another. The love between us exists to this day and sometimes that is all I need to acknowledge. It is there, worn in parts to the thickness of a veil and stained elsewhere with bitterness and acrimony, but there nonetheless.

I guess I was the one to pull away. Well, I should say I'm sure Nathan found Donna nicer company than me. I was withdrawing from just about everyone, becoming a loner despite being desperate for company. I don't know how to explain myself then, why I was becoming the outsider by my own choosing. I guess there was some sense of abandonment, of having no one to help me, that instinctively made self-reliance a survival tactic. That almost sounds healthy, but it wasn't. I was shrinking from the world yet remaining engaged with it by way of mutual antipathy. The anger just continued to well inside me — nothing could deplete it. Every time I got into a fight I was just that little bit more excessive — I'd want to hurt someone that little bit more. By the time I became a teenager, I'd have all this hate in me I'd carried for years and have no idea why. For so long I just thought, *This is me. This is how it is. If you don't like it, fuck off. I don't care. I don't need friends. I don't need anyone. I've got myself. That's it. Everyone else can go get stuffed.*

# V

## Fighting Channels

Life did not stop for me and my problems. And life for the Briggs family was wheeling into a new bend ... another calling had beckoned Dave Briggs. Well, he was more answering the call, once again being the horse Leanne led to drink. No sooner had she discovered she enjoyed lifting weights than she wanted to get into bodybuilding. I should have known by then that she was our prophet, that her fancies were the guiding stars of the Briggs family destiny. And, sure enough, before you could pronounce 'Arnold Schwarzenegger', Dad was the leaseholder of a gym, or at least a weights room, that formed part of a large sports complex in Algester called AJ's. As usual it was one in, all in. Dad had found his new religion and our lives began to revolve around dumbbells, tanning oil and anatomy fit to burst.

By this stage we'd left Park Ridge for a smaller property in nearby Waterford West, where I became convinced that Mum and Dad had only had kids so they could legally obtain slaves. No, really, I guess we just lived in a place where there was always plenty of work to be done. While I can say now that the chores taught us to look after ourselves later in life, back then Mum and Dad really had to kick our butts to do them. Not only were there animals to tend to and feed, we were roped into helping Mum do the housework. Laundry, dishes, cleaning — all the good stuff. We even had to make our own lunches, and believe me, I was no Jamie Oliver. I'd get a bit of bread, smudge some Vegemite on it, wrap it in some plastic — just like Mum showed me — get to school and bin it. I'd never eat my sandwiches — I don't know what I ate. We got lunch money only once in a blue moon so I wasn't tucking into a pie and a vanilla slice every day, unless I'd relieved some other kid of theirs. But buying our lunch was such a rare treat that it rubbed in the notion that we were poor. There was this sense of deprivation that we were led to believe was imposed on our family by some external force. Life was a struggle. Money was a worry. I could cope with never having ice blocks or soft drink, and I could live with eating Dad's home-made muesli sweetened not with honey but black molasses, and I'm not saying happiness flows from a box of Fruit Loops, but I think our limited means were unnecessarily overplayed. Dad's outlook was always that of a battler, yet he and Mum never saw themselves as anything but middle class. And to maintain that shackled perspective as though it was an edict of God was a crock. That was how he *chose* to view the world and his life. By association, we all subscribed to his belief and it was a mind-set that proved quite hard to dispel.

The thing about the chores was that they gave us a few *Waltons* moments. On weekends you'd see us all outdoors labouring honestly for the good of the Briggs collective. Throw in a shitty tractor and a sickle and we were poster material for the old Soviet empire. There's a real warmth to such memories; they glow with the affection that prevailed over all the niggles crosshatched between us. Likewise, I recall the simple pleasures of our family outings — to the local swimming pool or out to dinner, where Dad was cheerful king and I court jester, keeping everyone in stitches with my impersonations. Yet such sunny visions often promptly turn dark.

How can I think of doing chores out in the paddock and not recall Dad catching me slacking and angrily telling me to go fetch a particular branch he'd spotted? He laid into me with it, swearing at the top of his lungs while he whipped himself into a frenzy. He then walked away in a rage that cooled slower than lava, shouting, 'Just fucking do as you're fucking told or I'll knock your fucking head off!' This was his language, his tone. And I'll tell you, words like these affected me more than any physical pain he inflicted. That sticks and stones thing is complete and utter crap. What you say harshly, cruelly or vindictively stays with people, especially children. And, to put it mildly, my self-esteem was not fertilised by Dad's rich serves. I was fucking useless or stupid or some blend of the two. I don't know how many times I heard Mum say, aghast, 'How can you talk to the children like that? You can't speak to children like that.' He never got it. He'll never understand the damage his words have done to me and, I presume to add, my siblings. Hearing, as much as seeing, is believing.

Now I feel compelled to inject some balance again, to say he was also a caring and loving father and we children were blessed to see our parents being so openly affectionate. But to be frank, while being true, the balancing act is an exercise, something obeyed dutifully. When it comes to the sum of all the feelings I have for my father, I distil it to this: how a man treated his children. How he acted, what he said, how he handled having consummate power over young beings who loved him unconditionally. And, in a nutshell, Dad has shown me how not to treat children. He tried, I know. There's no manual for perfect parenting. He did everything with the best intentions. And the truth is that he did preach a lot of good things. But that's all well and good; you can sit there and rehearse any sort of speech or saying or verse. What you can't rehearse is *being*, how you react verbally and physically. So many times I'd hear him trying to be a good man but see and feel him not being a good man at all.

These days I'll look at Isaiah and just be absolutely baffled as to how a man could speak to and treat his children like Dad did us. What was so wrong? He always used to blame it on his upbringing and his family, but like my mum used to say, he was in our family for twenty-nine years and with his parents for fourteen. At some point you have to stand up and take responsibility for your actions and your feelings and break the mould. However, I believe that Dad's power to do so, to gain control of his temper, was gone for good once he got into bodybuilding. I'm convinced he began to use steroids to improve his physique, and exactly what can be attributed to 'roid rage or his own violent proclivity is a moot point.

Still, us kids were happy to see bodybuilding events take pride of place on our weekends — they put an end to Sunday church. There was a high price, though. As Dad drifted from the church his grip on the bottle tightened. In the past, whenever he'd gone on a bender and wreaked havoc upon the family, Mum was left to pick up the pieces. And one day, during his most extreme episode, I feared Mum wouldn't live to ever play that role again.

One afternoon Dad had set off to work at the Sunnybank Hotel to meet up with an old war buddy. He didn't make it home that night. Next morning we were all having breakfast and I said to Mum, 'Something's wrong.' I could see she was thinking the same. Our dread heightened when we heard Dad's car pull up. Next thing, the door swung open and Dad staggered in covered in blood with a huge gash in his face that seemed to leave one side hanging. He was freaking out. Utterly crazed. Us kids froze. We were petrified and sick with fear. *What's happened to Dad's face? What's he doing?* I looked out the door and about three or four squad cars were coming down our driveway. I looked at Dad's car. It seemed as though he hadn't missed clipping a single parked car on his way home. Dad then stormed through the house shouting urgently, 'Where are my guns? Where are my guns?' Mum, expecting trouble, must have had the foresight to hide them earlier. So Dad grabbed a knife, opened the front door and walked out to confront the cops. He was screaming, 'I'll fucking kill the fucking lot of you! Come on!' And Mum began yelling out the window for the cops not to shoot, that there were children inside. Meanwhile Leanne, on advice from Mum, gathered all the guns and herded us up, and all four of us fled out the back door down to the bush.

We finally stopped running and found a spot to bury the guns, about one or two rifles. We then sat down in a circle around the weapons, bawling our eyes out. Donna was praying and I was freaking out about Mum, about whether she was going to be all right. Was she going to be alive when we got back to the house? Then we started arguing over who loved Dad the most. God, we were a pitiful sight.

Dad eventually cooled off and was arrested. Turns out he'd got into a blue at the pub and was smashed in the face with a brick.

Two blokes had taken him on and both ended up in dire need of a hospital. He was guilt-ridden for a couple of months afterwards for terrifying us kids like that. But there was no explanation, no apology. The episode raised so many desperate questions about my father: *Why was he so violent? Why is it that when my dad gets drunk they send enough cops to quell a riot? And why were they always so soft on him?* It was like the police had enormous respect for Dad — they were so sympathetic when he went off the Richter. It bugged me that they seemed to know him better than I did. But seeing my bloodied and drunk and enraged father stumble out of the house to face a bunch of tightly sprung cops, the biggest question I had concerning him was one I'd ask many, many times in my life: 'My God, Who *are* you?'

Soon the gym pulled us off the farm and into a suburban home in Algester. I'll not complain, though, for this new phase of our lives was to bring my salvation and my retribution. By this time I'd made fighting such a major part of my life that you could have called it my primary occupation. Now, it was about to become my entire life.

Mum had not yet lifted her boxing embargo. She never did, really, come to think of it. Nathan and I, and Dad, tested her resolve again when we were about eleven. We went to watch Dad spar in a city gym. We'd seen him teach martial arts at home before but this was different — this was boxing training in the snug but hard confines of a proper gym full of contraptions and pads and bags. This was a fighting realm far removed from our unruly school-yard scraps. There was some structure and method to punching that demanded learning. We watched Dad and his mates work on combinations of punches. Their fists exploded into the mitts like gunshots. Nathan and I were captivated. I think we were inspired to do a little sparring because one of us let slip to Mum we had a headache from boxing. She saw the way the world was turning and, rather than try to clamp it by veto, she modified her position and lifted the boom gate a little: the boxing freeze remained but martial arts were given the green light.

This was really where our relationship with Dad began, when he had the go-ahead to teach us how to fight. Our first instruction was in tang soo do, a Korean martial art Dad had become keen on. Our lessons were serious — there'd be no mucking around under Dad's watch. But this was ad hoc tuition given at home. The first martial art we really came to grips with was kung fu. The gym Dad had was strictly for pumping iron: all free weights and mirrors, no fighting equipment. But the sports complex in which it was housed was a second home to Nathan and me. We used to hang out at AJ's every day after school. There was a swimming pool, tennis courts and squash courts, and we had the run of the place. And while Dad was building up memberships as well as his and Leanne's muscles, Nathan and I noticed a man training his son in some kind of martial art out in the car park. We watched them a few times before asking if we could join in. They said yes.

They were Chinese, the first Asians I'd ever met. The father was called Andrew, the son Mark. We became quite close. Andrew was a very humble man and very strong. He was in superb shape for his age — which I guess was mid-fifties. There was a nice, solid bond between these two, a peaceful, mutual respect. I suppose it was my first exposure to a different father–son relationship. Not that I was really thinking this at the time. I just thought they had a nice rapport. I thought my relationship with my father was good, too.

Andrew's English wasn't crash hot and he spoke very quietly, but we managed to catch his drift. A venerable and tough dude, he was really old school — the total kung fu master. This was a holistic art for tempering the mind, body and soul. The ability to defend yourself, and drill someone else, was almost a by-product. Along with combat technique and weapons skills, Andrew taught us about *chi* energy, the force within. He opened my mind to the notion that there's an inner source of strength we can tap, a reserve of amazing power beyond mere muscle.

That was all well and good until I got into a fight at school and tried out my kung fu. It just wasn't working and the fight turned into a scrap. I became a little disillusioned with kung fu and regarded it more as a personal development exercise than a sharpening of combat skills. For me, developing your character and spirit were secondary imperatives. I wanted to get my hands on weapons, not paintbrushes. The timing was right because by then Dad had expanded the business and opened up a second gym called The Muscle Centre in Coopers Plains. It was here that I found a happy medium between martial arts and Mum's martial law: kickboxing. And who better to teach me than Dad?

# VI

## *Anger Finds Its Voice*

From the outset it was clear to Nathan and me that we were going to learn well or not at all. First Dad got us on the punches. Just standing in front of the mirror throwing left jab after left jab, straight right after straight right ... It was all technique, nothing more. A total wowser ploy on Dad's behalf. We were itching to get the gloves on and go nuts, and here we were doing drills. It sucked big time. It was like being taught how to surf without ever hitting the beach. I knew what Dad was doing, though, and I was adamant that I wasn't going to be deterred. There was no way I was going to get the shits and go, 'This is boring', and stop.

After the punches, we were taught the kicks. Front kicks, round kicks, side kicks, spinning kicks. I spent ages practising and got them all down really well. I was the model student. And it was the only study I was doing, full stop. School — at least, the education part of it — was becoming a farce. Exercise books would last me a couple of years — that's how much, or how little, I put pen to paper.

Although we trained together and helped each other develop our techniques, Nathan and I were growing apart in the most literal sense. From the age of twelve, he went through a rapid growth spurt. It was like watching the frigging Hulk. Within a year or so he was almost a foot taller than me and solid as. It did annoy me that he was bigger but what most got on my nerves was other people asking when I was going to catch him up. I was quite happy not to be like Nathan; I actually made a point of it. As a twin, you have to strive for your own identity. Accordingly, I thought sharpening our differences was only reasonable, but I didn't count on nature slipping my brother extra doses of growth hormone. So not only did we not warm to each other's personality, Nathan's size became an unexpected rod for my back.

I wanted to make damn sure we were not in the slightest way alike. In the mornings I'd always check what he was wearing and make sure I wore something completely different. I turned this into a mission and my family thought I was trying a bit too hard. The way they saw it, I was always chipping away at Nathan, snapping at his heels because I was jealous of his size and the fact that things came easier to him than to me. But I didn't care what they thought. The truth was that I didn't need Nathan — who'd become quite a goody-goody — to inspire my errant behaviour. As a twin you live with a constant reference point, but while I certainly laboured against this, my behaviour wasn't entirely about Nathan. I was deviating for my own reasons; I had deep motives for wanting to find my own space.

Nathan never strove for separateness as I did. And while he gave as good as he got, the bottom line was that he was more conciliatory. He tended to value our brotherhood more, while I reacted against it. But any way you look at it, for me to assert my independence, I had to distinguish myself from Nathan, consciously or subconsciously, and often in very immature and spiteful ways. I often came across as an unfeeling little ratbag, I'm sure. Because that's exactly what I was: numb. I had all but killed off my feelings and the dangerous vulnerabilities they presented. So sensitivity was something I was starting to hold in contempt. I never hated Nathan — he was dear to me, my brother — but I did enjoy getting under his skin and showing that I was every bit a boy apart.

Here's a case in point that sums us up ... one Christmas, Nathan diligently saved money from his milk run all year to buy each of us generous presents. He was really thoughtful and wanted to do something special for all of us. Me? I bought a pack of fun-size Mars bars, wrapped up one per family member and tossed them under the tree. And I was a study of indifference when I opened Nathan's gift. Mean or what? Want another? Okay, Mum would always put our presents under the tree a week before Christmas and if anyone snooped, she said, their presents were off to the children's home. Now, Nathan and I always got the same presents for Christmas from Mum and Dad. So to find out what I got, I opened Nathan's, and it looked like he'd snooped. I didn't own up until Mum took our fingerprints on some sticky tape and said when she found the match the culprit was getting nothing. I 'fessed up.

I know I burnt Nathan, but it wasn't a one-way street. With me, though, you could never tell I was hurt.

Nor would you ever guess at any division in our family if you saw us out and about. That's always the way, isn't it? It's quite easy to keep up appearances. It was at Algester that, for the first time in our lives, us kids began to see that our parents' marriage was not ideal and was, in fact, strained. Dad had confessed to cheating on Mum twice, and as usual, although she was utterly devastated, Mum toughed it out. Not just for the sake of the family — she strongly believed in her marriage. Mum was no mouse of a wife. She could handle Dave Briggs better than any man could. And she had long ago learnt to switch herself off to his foul moods, words and negativity and go about her business. Enterprising as ever, she'd set up her own nail salon at home after excelling at her job with Stefan, a guy who built a vast hairdressing empire. She drew in a steady trade, and anyone who came to the house would have believed Dave and Sharon Briggs were a rock-solid couple. But their marriage was becoming something Mum endured, brightened occasionally and temporarily by the flowers Dad would bring her. On the face of it we were such a together family, with Dad leading the charge and Mum the capable lieutenant. More and more that's what we resembled rather than were. So no doubt it would have warmed a heart to see us all out on the weekends, all pitching in at the bodybuilding contests.

The whole weights thing had taken off — it was the new fitness wave following on from fun runs and aerobics. Pumping iron was in. Especially for blokes. Forget the Bullworker — the best comeback for those bullies kicking sand in your face was to hit the gym and return with a physique that could block out the sun. Button-popping muscles were power itself, he-man cannons to put out there as a show of force.

The big thing going for weights was that they worked. Especially when combined with steroids. Dad, I believe, was living proof. He'd shaped himself into such a showpiece, in fact, that he became the Australian Masters champion. See what I mean? The guy was a freak. And with typical zeal, he figured that becoming a champion bodybuilder was a job only half done. So he got himself qualified as a competition judge. As did Mum. Thus, even though Leanne quickly lost interest in competing herself — winding up her and Dad's doubles partnership — our weekends still remained centred on bodybuilding competitions. We'd all head off to some venue in Queensland or New South Wales and watch a bunch of freaks flex their honey-glazed hams for Mum and Dad. By the time Expo 88 came to Brisbane, they had their international judging qualifications and were appraising the world's best in the Mr Universe event held on the Gold Coast.

The bodybuilding scene was okay, but I was interested in one thing and one thing only: kickboxing. Dad had cleared the weights from a small section of The Muscle Centre to make room for a couple of punching bags. They were solely for the benefit of Nathan and I, and I went to war on them as though their mere presence was an offence to me. Standing in front of them, I never had to try and rouse my anger, it would just kick in immediately. I would pound those bags with intent, imagining I was smashing someone. No one in particular, just a man, I guess, who had dared provoke me, who had underestimated me and who would be shocked and crushed by my speed and force. For the first time I began to think that my rage and aggression were things to harness and channel. It was as much about containment as it was release. My anger had found a voice and was acquiring a vocabulary. And I a vocation.

No sooner was I acquainted with the fundamentals of kickboxing than I was dreaming of becoming a professional fighter. I dreamt I'd become world champion. I had a feeling that I wanted to live a unique life and a distinguished career in the kickboxing ring became my ultimate fantasy. I had nothing to base it on, no fighters to emulate and no idea how such a thing could possibly happen. Kickboxing was barely a blip on the sporting landscape, about as big as Greco-Roman wrestling between Olympic Games. My vision had that sense of marvellous possibility common to most fantasies, but mine allowed me to glimpse myself as a being of supreme independence, single-handedly forging a glorious life. I was gladiator, underdog, desperado, hero and destroyer. I was whole in my dream. I felt grand; alone and strong. Physicality had assumed a place above all my qualities as my means not only to survive but also to thrive.

In reverse parallel, my social withdrawal continued by degrees. Friends became acquaintances who became nobodies. I had no urge to hug normality; if anything I felt a degree of scorn for popular approval. I'd been raped and the whole world had continued as if nothing had happened. I'd been plucked from the flow of life and returned damaged and no one had even blinked, no one had seen, said or suspected anything. No one had acted. No one had helped. No one had even fucking asked. I felt cheated. But all I *physically* felt was the rage — I had obliterated all memory of the rape. So this powerful anger was simply there, disassociated from any source. It was just me, or at least a large part of what I was. And, reflecting the way levity had been expunged from my world, my fixation with black extended to my wardrobe — everything but my hair was black, everything lighter of colour was out. I even wanted to paint my room black. Mum wouldn't have it, though, winning out in a huge row we had. She was baffled: *What on earth is wrong with you?*

In many ways I was your run-of-the-mill rebel, toting audacity and disrespect on either hip. By this I mean the rape by no means accounted for every facet of my misbehaviour. As I entered adolescence I struck on a few things a lot of kids found cool, like music guaranteed to freak out your parents. First it was death metal, then the gangsta rap with Ice-T and the hard-arsed Niggaz With Attitude. I got right into rap and dressed up in all the gear — hooded sweatshirts, caps and brands of sneakers that music videos flogged better than any ad could. Rap came armed with outlaw appeal and intoxicating power oldies just couldn't, or didn't want to, fathom. More than that, in the best provocateur tradition of rock 'n' roll, it possessed the threat of kids being time bombs, of lawlessness being one incendiary song away. In 1989 NWA's 'Fuck tha Police' — my generation's 'Anarchy in the UK' — seemed to be the tune to take us over the edge, creating a furore in Australia before being banned from the airwaves. How amusing it was to see adults getting their knickers in such a twist, but how bloody annoying was their invasive power.

I got to feel that power directly, by the hand of the law. I was fully into the hip-hop culture and fancied myself as a real B Boy. I didn't even know at the time that this stood for 'break boy', meaning break dancer. I was a total try-hard. There was a bunch of older guys in Algester who called themselves the B Boy All Stars. Key to this gang were twin brothers Bill and Jamie, who were two of the best break dancers, I swear, in the world. They had also started up their own underground graffiti magazine called *Hype*. These guys were so frigging cool. A couple of my mates had older brothers in this gang and we followed their lead on hip-hop, graffiti and rapping. We had our own little crew and we had the handshakes down, and wore the hats and Adidas tracksuits and shelltop shoes, just like Run DMC.

I'd always loved to draw, so I was right into graffiti art. Of course we'd never buy the spray cans we needed to go 'bombing' — we got the old five-finger discount. One time a mate and I walked out of this store in Sunnybank carrying a stereo and a load of cans — no, not all of them black. The cashier tried to pull us up but we ignored her. So she started up with, 'Hey! Those two boys are stealing!' Very uncool. We did our best to ignore her and kept walking. We made it to the bus stop, where an in-store detective found us. She flashed her badge and said, 'You're going to come back to the store with me now', and we're like, 'Get fucked. What are you going to do? You're a chick.' I said: 'Here. Hold this.' And

I gave her the stereo. Then we made a run for it, only to be nabbed by two security guards who dragged us to a back room in the store where we waited until some cops came and drilled us. Man, did they put the frighteners up us. We were shitting ourselves, but what scared me more was the thought of my old man's reaction. Finally, Mum came and picked us both up. Later, she forbade me to ever hang out with my accomplice again. So *he* was the bad influence? Yeah, right.

That weekend, the two coppers came to my house. They spoke with Mum and Dad about me. It wasn't like they were picking me up all the time. I was a troublemaker and a smartarse — and, yeah, a spray-can thief who'd gotten away with far more booty than anyone knew — but not what you'd call a delinquent. But I guess because of my attitude these guys saw fit to try to strike home a message before it was too late. They sat me down and started talking about a place called Boys' Town, a home for undeterred repeat offenders. They gave me a pamphlet and I stared at it with dread thinking, *Whoa, there's no fucking way I'm going to Boys' Town.*

After they left, Dad came into my room. I was crying, thinking that maybe it might be a good idea to pull my head in. To my surprise, he didn't smash me. He sat down next to me on the bed and said, quietly and sadly, 'Is this where you want your life to go, son? Is this where you want to end up?' He then went on about the old chip on my shoulder again. 'What's the matter with you, Paul?' he asked, not for the first time. I said I didn't know. I just had this feeling that, damn it, no one on the planet could ever understand me. I don't think I realised how much I was hurting, that I had stuff I needed to get out. I knew I had an attitude but I was at a loss as to why. This was how effectively I had suppressed the memory of my rape: the link between event and aftershock had been severed. The reasons for my behaviour weren't something I could begin to articulate. My actions were disassociated from any definable cause. I was so frustrated and confused, thinking, *Maybe I am screwed in the head*. I felt doomed. But I also felt so bad seeing Dad so concerned for my welfare. When he left the room I was amazed he hadn't belted me. Maybe he'd been reminded of his own miserable brushes with boys homes. Regardless, his solemn passivity really got to me. That was the most effective punishment he ever issued. Being grounded was nothing; seeing Dad so disappointed in me hurt and made me want to make amends. I felt ashamed of myself.

No one in my family let me live it down. For months I was ribbed whenever we went to the shops. You know, 'Keep your hands in your pockets', and all that. I felt like everyone wanted to keep me there: the black sheep, the troublemaker, the rascal with a pile of attitude.

At high school it was the same, and I'd succeeded in alienating myself from just about everyone. I stood out at Salisbury High School as being tough, aggressive and mouthy. I took shit from no one and was itching to use my fists. I didn't have to wait long to be tested. The beginning of the year was 'Veggie Bash', a kind of initiation wherein the older boys took free rein to beat up the new students. On one of the first days someone grabbed my head and slammed it into a pole. I turned around to see the culprit, this fat guy, laughing and I proceeded to beat the shit out of him. A lot of the older boys were watching and from then on they had it in for me. I had a reputation as a decent fighter, but rather than giving me distance, they were drawn to pick on me. It was the same with Nathan. It was like they had to bring us into line.

One teacher had a similar attitude. Mr Cooper. What a complete wanker. He took metalwork class and also a bit of physical education. The first day I met him he called me and another guy up to the front and said something I've heard all my life: 'You might think you're tough but you don't know what tough is.' He then grabbed our nipples and twisted them, saying, 'Just try me. I'll show you what tough really is. Now get back to your desks.' He pushed us in the chests to get us on our way. How's that? I'd never met this bloke before in my life. Naturally, I was steaming. *Who the fuck does this guy think he is?*

Halfway through the year someone pelted his car with rocks. So he stood in front of our class swearing at us: 'I'm going to find out which of you little shits did this and you are going to fucking pay.' Later still in the year, he picked on this senior kid — a Pacific

Islander, real quiet bloke. Cooper baited him all the time, calling him Pineapple Head. Finally the kid arced up. After a heated exchange, Cooper suggested they take it outside. He then reported he had been set upon by the student and had him expelled.

Where once I had been a popular kid, most male students now actively disliked me. On the outside that suited me fine — I had no desire to engage in anything at school, it was simply a holding pen. I endured school with indifference. My strongest aversion was towards the senior boys. To me, the football stars and the popular guys with their cool credos and their clumsy, meat-headed chick talk were just stupid wankers. I had no respect for them and I displayed it openly. This prejudice may have been understandable given what had been done to me, but I exercised no such logic.

The only students I really had time for were older girls. They were far more mature, and smarter, and their conversation had more substance. I got on really well with them and began to hang out with them more and more. They embraced me like a little brother. It was odd and was noticed. And, like anything at school, my defiance of what the mob deems to be the norm invited corrective action. But it didn't come for a while yet.

Another reason I looked down on high school boys was that I was spending so much time in the gym with men. By comparison, the guys at school were kids. Also, they were irrelevant to my life. School was irrelevant to my life. My main focus was training myself to become a professional fighter. I openly declared my ambition at school and drew the expected put-downs. *World champion kickboxer, eh? Whatever you say, mate.*

While my dream was surreal to everyone else, in my mind it was becoming more and more tangible. I began to believe that through hard work I could make this happen. I was happy to go about my drills with Nathan, day in, day out. I was a total gym rat. I would come home from school and head straight up to the Muscle Centre. Every day. *Just like a professional*, I would think. When we watched the older guys train, the guys who were serious fighters, I'd think, *To hell with school — I just want to train and apply, train and apply*. That was that. I knew exactly what I wanted to be.

49

My ambition locked into place the day Dad returned from a trip to Thailand. He brought home something that would change my life: Muay Thai, otherwise known as Thai boxing. Muay Thai is actually a form of kickboxing but it makes normal kickboxing look like a pillow fight. Kickboxing is essentially boxing with karate kicks. Muay Thai is far more devastating. You fight with bare shins and feet, no padding whatsoever. You can use your knees and elbows and can strike anywhere on the body but the groin. It's full-on, total fighting. Hardened shins are wielded like crowbars, elbows like rocks. Like I said, I wanted weapons to fight with and Muay Thai offered up a full arsenal. Unlike the martial arts I'd learnt, Muay Thai made me feel immersed in fighting, given to it utterly and desperately and, yes, savagely. The effect was profound. I'd gone from riding a cart on an old road to being slotted onto a smooth and sure rail. Something had grabbed me and was pulling at me and I couldn't, nor did I want to, resist. I had found something to channel all my abundant energy, all my rage and all my hate into. My life had acquired purpose.

# VII

## Caged In A Ring

The core guys of Year 9 had had enough. They were jack of me calling them — the cool dudes everyone else in our year rated — 'cocksuckers' with impunity, telling them they were all homos who screwed one another. Understandably, they threatened to sort me out. But even as a group this lot wasn't game enough to have a crack at me; they had to outsource their dirty work. Their opportunity arrived when an older girl came onto me at the swimming carnival. 'You're gone now,' they said. 'You're fucked. We've got you now.' I was like, 'What are you on about?' 'That's Ivo's girl,' they said. 'Yeah, whatever. She was coming onto me.' 'He's going to fuck you up,' they said. 'Beautiful,' I said. 'Bring it on.'

Bring it on they did. One lunchtime a member of their crew lured me to a spot with the pretence that some kid wanted to fight me. I wasn't buying the story because the kid used as bait was a waste of time. I went more out of curiosity than anything. When I got around to the back of the tuck shop, this big Ivo bloke was standing there. He was about nineteen, more than five years my senior. He was a man to me. He had stubble and acne and had squeezed his big, hairy frame into a school shirt to blend in with the playground crowd. (They'd really put some thought into this, hey? Real *Ocean's Eleven*.) He stood there intense and uneasy. 'Is this him?' he said, looking past me. I looked over my shoulder and half a dozen of those cocksucking buttfuckers were standing there, nodding. I swung back to find the gorilla hyperventilating. He was working himself up and tears were pooling in his eyes. I figured I'd best get the first shot in. Hit first and hit hard, as they say. I went to head butt him but he ducked in towards me, so my face just smashed into the top of his forehead. I then went to punch him but the wankers behind took hold of me. Then, just as Apeman was squaring up to unload on me, his arm froze, his face twisted up with horror and he turned and bolted.

Nathan came flying in out of nowhere and took off after the Missing Link, but he was too late to catch him. I smacked one of the guys holding me and turned on the rest of the gang. They all looked totally freaked out. 'I'm going to get every single one of you pricks,' I shouted, 'if it takes me a year!' And then Nathan came back and looked at me. 'Fuck,' he said. He screamed at the others, 'I'm going to kill you arseholes!' But like them he could not stop looking at me with a blend of distaste and concern. What the hell was wrong with me? I wasn't in pain at all — I was amped to go. But Nathan said he was taking me to sickbay and all the others came along trying to help but they were shitting themselves. 'You'll be right,' they said, as though I was dying. 'You'll be right.' And I'm like, 'Forget about me, dickhead. Youse are fucked. Youse are gone.'

When I got indoors I found a mirror and discovered why they were all so horrified: there was blood all over my face, but the worse bit was that both my cheekbones had been broken, so my nose was hanging between my eyes like a wet dishrag. The police were called in but I refused to take it further. Once I'd seen my face I was worried like everyone else. I needed to get it fixed up pronto — my first proper kickboxing fight was on in three weeks.

The dedication Nathan and I displayed toward kickboxing widened the door between us and our father. Fighting brought us together. In the new guise of trainer, Dad connected with us more fully than we'd ever known. It didn't go unnoticed that this landmark in our relationship came about solely because *we* had moved towards *him*, not him to us. To say he never played with us when we were little isn't a wounded me lashing out, it's just a fact. A photo exists that might have you think otherwise — in it there's Dad playing tackle footy with Nathan and me, but Mum took that photo to capture a rare event, a UFO sighting.

It was only once Dad was convinced of our capacity for graft that he began to nourish our interest in fighting. And once he'd seen our potential, he began to take it very seriously — primarily, I'd suggest, because it plonked him more squarely in the frame of our prospects. Initially, though, he was never pushy about how far we should take kickboxing; we never had the feeling we were vessels for his reprised dreams. He encouraged us to work hard and to have fun. To a point. Fighting was serious business and we had enlisted in Dad's army; we were his two little soldiers. And when he cottoned on to the fact that he had two potential pro fighters on his hands, he couldn't wait to send us into battle.

In those early days, Nathan and I had a beautiful thing going in the gym. We maintained our own regimes but we supported each other, whatever our personal differences, and together we refined our technique and worked on new ideas. That was pretty rare — two young kids having the foresight and drive to practise and learn largely unsupervised. As much as Dad was teaching us to fight, we were teaching him how to teach us. Muay Thai was so new that no knowledge bank existed in Australia. We'd come up with different moves we'd seen on video and Dad was open-minded enough to go with it. We were developing as a team.

I can't overstate the value of having a constant and dedicated training partner. Nathan and I would spar every day. One day I'd get the better of him in the session, the next day he'd be all over me. We both loved kickboxing but it's fair to say I put more into it than he did. He was so naturally talented, although he hated training. Being smaller, I guess, did spur me to go at the weights hard, however, that wasn't the main driving force. I know that's what everyone else thought — that I was trying to compensate for my comparative shortcomings. But I was an extremely determined individual and in my mind I was just doing everything I could to better myself as a fighter. Looking back now, I must have seemed utterly selfish. And no doubt I was — my entire being was an expression of desperate self-determination. Ruthless, you could fairly suggest, and I didn't give a damn how it affected anyone. For as much as Nathan served as an invaluable training partner, I felt he was occupying my turf. Fighting was something I believed was my destiny. Nathan fought for want of alternatives. That his options were limited was not his fault. The way things worked out, he had no choice but to fight.

Even before we were both set on our one-track paths, the difference in our levels of commitment was telling. I'll tell you now we were a case study in what makes, and doesn't make, a fighter. We were perfect lab rats for the scientific study of programming. I have thought so much about Nathan and myself in regards to fighting. What was the difference between us? Well, one of the best things my father had me believe was that nothing beats experience: your own. In your experience lies your truth. And now that I'm armed with almost twenty years' experience in fighting, believe me when I say there are only two types of fighters in this world: those who program themselves for battle and those who program themselves to quit. Even at that young age, my early adolescence, I possessed an inner awareness that I couldn't bullshit myself about taking short cuts. I knew that if I didn't do the work, I wouldn't get the results. What is done in the dark will be seen in the light.

You can practise to fail just as you can practise to succeed — keep doing something and you'll become proficient at it. And from a trainer's point of view it's easy to see what you've got in a fighter. There are those who'll spew their guts up from effort and ask how many more reps need doing, and those who stop. There are those who set limits on themselves, and those who don't. The latter's potential is in so many ways boundless. From the outset, though, Nathan set his own limits. He began to master the art of self-deception. When the going got a bit hard in the gym, Nathan would find a way out, like faking an injury. And Dad would ease up. He'd nurture that growth of falseness. He never did that with me — he'd try to break me, almost, and I'd just go at it silently. Men can talk themselves into anything — you need to be so aware of that, because what you believe ends up defining your reality.

Sometimes, though, our boundaries are set by others. And ultimately Dad never let Nathan devote time to any pursuit other than fighting. We both played a variety of sports at school. All were abandoned, or scratched off our playlists, in favour of fighting. I was a pretty good swimmer and showed promise as a sprinter; what I really wanted to try was ballet. Leanne and Donna were going to dance classes and I wanted to go too, but that idea was swiftly kyboshed. Nathan and I both played rugby league for a couple of years. I wasn't a team player, as you can imagine, and had little affection for the game. Nathan, however, loved it. He played prop, a position in the elite game for big, hard, fit guys; men who have the courage and will to run through walls for their team. Nathan was an exceptional young talent — he'd just storm through the opposition. I have no doubt he could have played professionally. But his runaway body was giving him growing pains that Dad blamed on football. 'You're going to wreck yourself,' Dad would say.

It was my dream to fight. Nathan *made* fighting his dream. Rugby league was what he was passionate about. I've never seen him previously or since be so consumed by something. He knew he was talented and really wanted to keep playing. And Dad just smashed it down like he did everything else: 'You're not playing fucking football.' They went to war over it for a long time. The only reason we played at school was because Mum backed Nathan. 'Let them try,' she said. 'You can't stop them from living.' 'Ah, they're going to get fucking injured,' countered Dad. And don't worry, Nathan's passion got crushed pretty quickly. I feel for him ... I don't know, it's how much you want to live your dream, I suppose. I certainly can't blame him for not pushing harder or trying again later. But when my old man said, 'It ain't happening', it was like God himself saying, 'Forget it, son.' Somewhere along the line Dad had decided that his sons were going to do nothing but fight. I was totally fine with that; Nathan was a different story. I think it would have been so good for both of us to pursue different goals. It would have been awesome. The competitiveness between us would have been diluted. Instead, our rival lives were becoming more entwined than ever. Who knows how things would have turned out if Nathan had followed league? I know when he watches the Brisbane Broncos play or Queensland take on New South Wales in the State of Origin he sometimes thinks, *That could have been me*. Damn right it could have been.

As usual, though, it was all about Dad. And Nathan was shaping up as a really good fighter. We both were. So as soon as he was convinced we were proficient in the gym, Dad wasted no time teeing up our first fight. We were both super keen, itching to test ourselves in a proper bout. My face was still fragile, though, my nose swollen and barely free of bruising. For me to step into a kickboxing ring was madness. But there was no way I was going to miss out. Not in my mind, nor in Dad's. Mum wasn't happy, as you can imagine, but she was no match for us. Besides, it was clear from the beginning that us boys weren't training for fitness's sake. From the word go we had the clear intention of fighting in the ring. I'd waited a long while for that first opportunity, and you'd have had to cripple me to stop me going ahead with the fight. Perhaps Mum hoped a beating might dissuade us.

The venue was a nightclub called Rumours, and to get us bouts on the card Dad lied and said we were seventeen; we were barely fourteen. The place was a complete dive filled with drunken bottom-of-the-barrel types seeping cigarette smoke and screaming 'Fuckin' smash 'im!' over their beers. And that was the women. We fought Muay Thai but weren't allowed to use elbows. I was welterweight, Nathan super middle. I was psyched. I came out and just whaled on this guy, a twenty-one year old, for three rounds and won on points easily. Nathan won too, so the Briggs camp went home riding high. I felt vindicated and believed I had something, that I could really make a go of kickboxing. And I had no fear whatsoever — I wanted to take on anyone.

After the fight the promoter, a mate of Dad's named Malcolm Anderson, came up to me, beaming. He patted me on the back and said, 'Well, done, Paul. You were a little bloody hurricane out there.' I said, 'Hurricane ... That might be a good fight name, don't you reckon?' He said, 'Yeah, either that or Bull Terrier, but Hurricane's probably the go.' Hurricane was definitely the go. Paul 'Hurricane' Briggs — I liked the sound of that from day one.

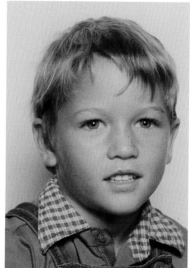

ABOVE: You want a go, mate? Guess which one is me.

TOP RIGHT: Butter wouldn't melt in my mouth.

RIGHT: The Briggs twins lapping it up in my favourite part of Arnhem Land — the beach.

BELOW: Doomed from the start — from left it's Donna, me, Leanne and Nathan.

ABOVE LEFT: Don't you just love the '80s. I had it going on.

ABOVE: The kung-fu master, aged 11, busting some moves taught to me by a real master.

LEFT: Nathan and I, at 14, all spruced up for the kickboxing ball — all set for my first date with Leah.

TOP: My fondest childhood memories stem from our gatherings on the beach in Gove.

ABOVE: The Briggs family clan outside our house in Algester celebrating Donna's twenty-first birthday. The days of this 'happy' family were numbered.

LEFT: Our closest time together — Dad and me in Perth for my second bout with Jason Skinner. The dream of me becoming world champ had just come alive and it was something we shared.

ABOVE: Check the attitude. I hated the world then. And check the difference between me and Nathan both in size and demeanour. Says it all, really. This was before our first amateur fight and we were barely 14, and my nose had been broken a couple of weeks earlier.

LEFT: A rare moment of Dad playing with us. I would have loved there to be more.

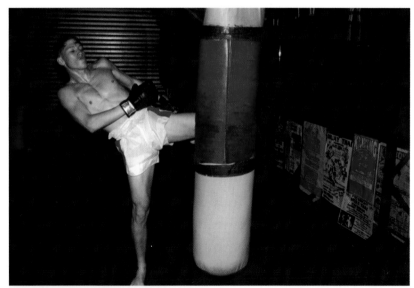

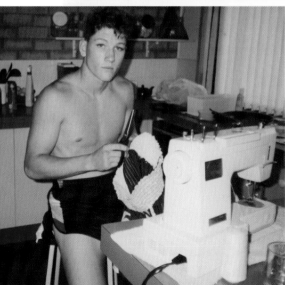

ABOVE: Old faithful. It was like a cement pylon wrapped in cowhide but every day I smashed it. The yellow vinyl gave way so a band of red leather was needed. This was at the Muscle Centre, Coopers Plains. If I'd been allowed to live there I would have.

ABOVE: Making my own shorts and proud of it! I was religious about my sewing — these were my fighting colours, my battle dress. It was the creative and meditative start of my fighting ritual.

RIGHT: Just take the photo ... Nursing a broken nose, again. Life for me wasn't about making friends.

ABOVE: The rise and rise of the Hurricane. The Australian champion had just become South Pacific champion after beating Jacob Ferrani.

ABOVE: Sparring — the most enjoyable times Nathan and I spent together. He was such a good counter-puncher; if I missed, I paid dearly for it.

LEFT: About to learn a big lesson. All set to fight Jomhod, I was in the shape of my life but I was king of the B-graders. Jomhod showed me that in A-grade looking good ain't enough.

ABOVE: With my mate Dumbo on my first trip to Thailand. There was no time for sightseeing on my later visit.

LEFT: Winners are grinners. Me in Tokyo with Thai legend Chamwapet. This guy was a technical genius in the ring.

ABOVE: Paul 'Hurricane' Briggs
— deejay and ex-fighter — rockin'
it with my mate Mr Cameron
Brown, better known today as
MC Sureshock.

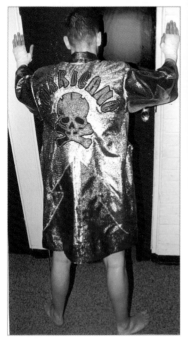

ABOVE: Andre Masseurs, the world
middleweight champion, had never
been stopped. I knocked him out in
the second. Next stop, the world title.

LEFT: Fighting's no game. Getting
set to knock out the New Zealand
champion Shane Dargaville.

My second fight, again at Rumours, only lasted one and a half rounds. I should have earnt frequent flier miles the way I was knocked from one side of the ring to the other. This bloke, a late replacement who was a weight division above me, just fed on the boy thrown to him until the referee stopped the fight. I was livid afterwards. I felt humiliated that the ref had stepped in, as though I believed, eventually, I'd have turned the tide on my opponent.

Nathan won his second fight. And he kept on winning. He would go on to notch up ten straight victories and come to be seen as a great prospect for the pro ranks. My record wasn't so hot. I collected a mixed bag of wins, losses and draws. No one talked about me like they did Nathan: he was cutting a path through the jungle with big, clean swaths; I was hacking away and tripping over branches I'd missed. Playing second fiddle to Nathan as a kickboxer was not in the script. This was my destiny, not his, yet the records were suggesting otherwise.

Without knowing it, though, I handled my losses in a way I would only later articulate as a nugget of fighting wisdom. My losses checked me, but not in a negative way. They steeled me, made me more determined about my training, because I'd been shown that I could not just turn up and expect to win. After a loss I'd work on deficiencies I didn't know I possessed but that had been made glaringly clear in the light of the ring. And I was bloody-minded. A few losses were not going to put me off. Now I know full well that big losses in your life make you sit down and re-evaluate everything. What do your wins teach you? Not a lot. We are inclined to take rewards from wins, not instruction. They are harder to learn from. To learn requires absolute honesty, something typically overlooked in the delirium of victory. Losing helps you win with full mindfulness. The fear of losing is diminished once embraced. When you let go of your fear of losing, you become so accepting of consequence, of reality, of the fact that you are never certain of winning, that you almost welcome losing because you understand what it is. Losing is a gift, not a curse. It's one of the most beautiful gifts imaginable.

Success came too easily for Nathan's own good. He'd admit himself that he cruised. He trained day in, day out, no question.

But his intensity was not the same as mine. I hit the bags ceaselessly. I won't say my comparative lack of success didn't spur me, but the future I'd envisioned for myself had been reduced to the singular ambition of fighting long before Nathan started winning. Yet to everyone else I was still this tiresomely angry boy for whom Nathan's success was just another chip my shoulder strained to bear.

By now Nathan had shed his squeaky-clean streak. I mean, he wasn't quite the miscreant I was, but he was developing his own ego, ideas and values which placed him on a collision course with Dad. Largely on the basis of Nathan's success, I'd say, Dad made the decision to switch career paths yet again. He began pencilling 'trainer of world champion kickboxer' onto his résumé. He became sidetracked and this was reflected in the slow transformation of The Muscle Centre. At first, we had one red leather bag in the corner, an object so familiar that I almost knew the run of its grain. To the sound of clamouring iron, I'd zone into this bag and kick away for hours on end while others zoned in on their reflections. Soon Dad cleared more weights to make room for another bag. Then one day members arrived to find a full-sized boxing ring occupying a sizable acreage previously given to free weights. Their gym was shrinking and they were understandably peeved. Dad didn't care. If they didn't like it, he said, they could piss off.

The boxing ring was ostensibly for us but it was really just as much for Dad. He'd built us a cage from which there was no escape. Fighting permeated the relationship between Dad and us boys to the extent that there would be little else remaining if it were removed. There were plenty of things I wanted to do with my old man that didn't involve punching someone in the face. But kickboxing was all and, unlike everyone else, if we didn't like it we had nowhere to piss off to. For both Nathan and me, Dad's violence became not so much a response to our misbehaviour but a sharp reminder of his absolute control over us. As I grew older, the clip around the back of the head became a punch in the face when I dared to disagree with him. And with the steroids I strongly suspect he was using, his physical vocabulary — the way he related to people — kept being reduced until he was barely ever a breath away from dispensing a fist as easily as a 'please' or a 'thank you'. I crossed the street with him once — he led me straight out onto the road — and a car brushed past with its horn blaring. Dad smacked the back end of the vehicle. The male driver stopped and reversed. They swapped verbal abuse. Dad leant in and bashed the driver's face in while his girl screamed. Another time, a bunch of kids pulled up beside Dad and one of his no-neck bodybuilding mates and fired water pistols at their car. Dad and co. figured they'd have some fun. They forced the boys off the road and went to give them a scare but things got out of hand and they ended up beating them to a pulp. These were grown men.

This is what I learnt from my father: if someone pisses you off, you smack them in the head. You use violence to get your own way. Anyone crosses you, you break them. That's how you live your life. He'll deny that: 'That's not what you learnt from me.' Bullshit. I used to watch Nathan get drilled and wonder why he didn't just work around Dad, because there was clearly no way through him. But Nathan had opinions. If Dad wanted to argue something with me, on the other hand, I'd let him. I'd shut up and get on with it, but Nathan would have his views and want to air them. And fair enough. Even as he was being bashed he would complain aloud that Dad's response wasn't right — he appealed to justice — and that would only incite Dad to strike harder and more furiously. My old man wanted nothing but utter compliance and he had one means of getting it. In a way, he and Nathan were the same: one would insist that the other hear his point. In the end, stubbornness proved to be so costly for Nathan — Dad slowly but surely broke his spirit. Just as his father had done to him.

# VIII

## *Brothers Blooded*

The best day of school was one I wagged. In Year 10, I cut out with a guy called Adrian. He was new to Salisbury High, having been expelled from a private school. He was a cool-looking dude, the kind of guy who gets everyone curious, but he didn't seem to be out to make friends. We clicked straightaway. Soon we were ditching school together to head back to his place to drink beer, smoke ciggies and watch pornos. The choicest day, though, was when we nicked his sister's car and drove down to the Gold Coast. We had to get petrol on the way, and we got a few long looks, but no one questioned us. We did little else but cruise around and hang out at the beach. That was all we could do — our last cent had gone towards petrol. It was the grandest of days. He was cool, Adrian. And he could really drive. His sister found out and busted his balls, but we did it again. That was the best feeling, burning down the freeway in the heat with those suckers behind us in class and nothing but a few cigarettes between us. What a blast it was to feel so free.

School already felt like jail and the joys of wagging only made it even more of a drag. My estrangement had been upped a notch late the previous year when I had been suspended for pissing against a wall. That the toilets were locked didn't seem to matter a damn to anyone but me, and the punishment seemed vindictive.

Other kids began to call me Pisswall after that. Yep, school was a real treat. All day I thought of leaving and shunned just about everyone. I even stopped hanging with Adrian. All I really wanted to do was train. Mum and Dad had said we could leave school when we were fifteen and, come Year 10, my birthday couldn't arrive soon enough.

We didn't have an automatic get-out-of-jail-free card, mind: we had to show due cause. Nathan had it all going on, with a dual career to launch him straight out of the blocks. He was going to be a professional kickboxer and a hairdresser. Both seemed plausible: he was winning all his fights and this hairdresser guy had offered to take him on as an apprentice in his salon. So with his career path approved by Mum and Dad, Nathan bailed. I hadn't come up with anything but fighting, which didn't stack up all that well given my tepid results in the ring. So I was kind of stuck. Only for a short while, though, because my exit route was about to materialise out of the blue.

As part of our physical education class we'd often play tip footy on the oval. For PE I had that wanker Mr Cooper, the guy who nipple-crippled me the first day I met him. There was one kid in our class who wasn't into tip at all and he felt inclined to screw it up for everyone. He got hold of the ball and booted it right across the field. The teacher ordered me to go fetch it. I refused. 'Get the ball!' Cooper shouted. I went and got the ball and when I got back I threw it into this kid's face. He fell to the ground, crying out, and Cooper came over and started stabbing his finger into my chest, telling me he'd had enough of my attitude. I told him to stop poking my chest. 'What are you going to do?' he said, daring me, and pushed me back. I said, 'Don't touch me again.' But he pressed up close again and I've just gone *crack* with a straight right and dropped him on his arse. I just lost it and screamed at him, 'Get up, you fucking dog! I'm going to smash your head in!' From the other side of the field this Scottish teacher, who I had a lot of respect for, bolted over after hearing all the yelling. I made to have a go at him too and he said, 'Don't do anything stupid, Paul.' 'It's a bit late for that,' I said. I turned to Cooper and said, 'You can go get fucked. The lot of youse can get fucked.' All the other kids were stirring, all revved up. They didn't like me but they liked what I'd done. I stormed off. 'That's right, Briggs,' said Cooper, 'you just keep walking straight up to the headmaster's office.' I spun back around and said, 'I'm fucking leaving and if I ever see you outside this school, you're off.'

I was almost at the gate when the vice-principal called out to me. He was another teacher who I rated — that was it, him and the Scot. Anyway, Cooper had bolted up and was standing next to him threatening to press charges. And the vice-principal shut him up and asked me what happened. I'll spare you the language but I told him how Cooper had behaved, that I was leaving, that expelling me wasn't necessary. The vice-principal put his hand out and said, 'Paul, I hope you use your talents and make something of yourself, because you do have a talent.' He said he wouldn't take it any further. I was a bit surprised. I guess they didn't need more drama with Cooper; they didn't even ring my parents. I just went home and said, 'I've left school. I'm not going back.' Mum rang them up but they didn't elaborate on what I had done, merely said that I'd had a falling-out with one of the teachers. Maybe it was a relief for her, me not causing any more grief at school. She no doubt figured I was going to be able to take care of myself one way or another, even though my ambition of becoming a professional fighter was feasible in my mind alone.

Regardless, I was out. I was stoked and immediately threw myself into training full time. Despite my results, I thought I was going from strength to strength. I was having hard fights as an amateur and was relying mostly on good technique — I still had a lot of ground to make up on the strength and strategy fronts. Each fight was an invaluable experience. Nathan was in some respects acting like a champ, like he was a star. I don't mean big-headed, it's just that he would select his opponents carefully. In Nathan, Dad had a potential crowd-puller. He was a natural headline act set to take the professional ranks by storm. Even at fifteen he was impressively tall, solid and good-looking. He was a young Dolph Lundgren, Sly's Russian opponent in *Rocky IV*, and he was on a roll. He was a promoter's dream, and Dad geared the Briggs family fighting program around him. Nathan would watch a videotape of some dude, and if he was convinced he could beat him, he'd call Dad over and say, 'I want to fight this guy next.' Then Dad would set the wheels in motion. There wasn't the same kind of process in finding me an opponent. Dad got whoever was available, so I had no idea who I'd be fighting.

Nathan didn't fully realise what he was doing. From a fifteen-year-old kid's point of view, this was a reasonable way to set up your fights: you check out a guy and fight him if you think you can beat him. That was okay at first, but it continued throughout Nathan's career. As an amateur he'd begun doing exactly what most professional boxers do — hand-pick their opponents. They want bankable fights, they want to know they can win before they step into the ring, to feel assured their record's safe. Nathan wasn't really conscious of it in this way, he just thought that's what you did. As the straggler, though, I had no choice, and I took mine as they came. That they proved hard, tough fights gave me a great foundation for my career. Nathan had some spectacular wins, but my hard grinds made for a much stronger bedrock.

In training, I was a perfectionist. I've always had a natural punch, like you can have a natural golf swing, but I worked very hard on my technique. My day was split between the gym and watching videos of the world's best Muay Thai fighters — mainly Dutchmen and Thais — who I'd try to emulate. They were devastating, these guys: strong, awesome fighters. I'd see something that impressed me — say, a particular type of kick — then head off to the gym, jump on the bag and practise. I wouldn't stop until I had it down exactly like I'd seen on the video. I had excellent visual perception, in that I could see a technique and understand how to replicate it. This had been evident way back in Gove when I'd learnt to do the karate kata just by watching Dad. On these videos I picked up all the little things: the footwork, how they pivoted, how they twisted their hip. Everything. I'd spend all day on the bags. I wasn't getting too sweaty, just practising my technique. Then I'd have my training session with Dad and Nathan. We wouldn't get home until nine most nights.

On one level Nathan and I weren't so directly in competition with one another, because we were in different weight divisions.

And Dad never pitted us against each other. One time we saw a father allow two of his sons to fight each other in a kickboxing tournament. The older boy was vomiting in his corner and Nathan, who was in the corner with him, said, 'I don't know how your father can do this. My Dad would never fight me off against my brother.' But Dad was inclined to bend with the breeze, and the prevailing wind was filling Nathan's sails. Understandably, Dad was excited about having a son who looked capable of making it as a professional. And even though I was a lesser light, the Briggs twins were being seen as an exciting double package. At fifteen we were beating men in their mid-twenties, mainly by outpointing them with better technique. We lacked real power then, but everyone knew that would come with age.

A vital part of our learning was the opportunity to get an authentic taste of Muay Thai. A guy called Bob Jones, who had established one of the biggest karate schools in the country and was recognised as the pioneer of kickboxing in Australia, had cottoned on to Muay Thai and had started organising tours to Thailand to expose Australian devotees to the real deal. Once Dad had told us, Nathan and I were feverish about the prospect of going, but we had to pay our own way. We saved our butts off, banking what we earnt working at The Muscle Centre as well as the modest amounts of cash Dad fed us on the sly for our fights. The trip was intended to be a little finishing school for Nathan and me before we turned pro.

In the weeks prior to us leaving, I'd struck up a friendship with a pretty, dark-haired girl called Leah, who was a regular in the gym. I remembered her from a couple of years back when she used to accompany her mother to our house to have her nails done. I hadn't said much to her then, but now that I was working at the gym and she was there so often, we got to talking more and more. She was a year older than me and very sweet, and eventually I worked up the courage to ask her to a kickboxing ball, where all sorts of awards were to be presented for the year 1990. Not that I was up for any. Leah said she'd love to come, and so we had our first date. Little did we know that this would be the beginning of a relationship that would last, off and on, for nine years. If we could have foreseen the damage we would do to each other, we would not have exchanged another word. But that's life. Things always begin innocently enough.

When the time came to leave for Thailand, I could barely believe I was actually going. Packing bags, driving to the airport. My first trip overseas. And then to arrive in Bangkok ... what an eye-opener. For more than a year I'd been practising Thai boxing, I'd watched a gazillion fight videos, but I had no idea what the country itself would be like. The capital blew me away. I'd never seen such a frenetic bustle of machines and humanity and even Pattaya, where we were based, was infused with an exotic thrill. Very quickly it became apparent that we'd arrived in some kind of playground, a place where you could live like a king. We had rooms in a five-star hotel, and although every day we trained hard under a Thai instructor at a nearby camp, our group did what most Western men do in Thailand — we hung out on the beach and lived large in bars. Nathan and I felt we'd been taken further into the fold of men as we drank beer and met people from all over the world and watched the older guys in our group ride between bar and hotel with one or two hookers on board their motorbikes.

When Bob saw Nathan and me train, he was impressed. He could see we had all the moves, all the skills. He wanted to see us fight, so he arranged bouts for us in one of the Pattaya bars. Up until now we'd been fighting Muay Thai without using our elbows. Here it was all-out Muay Thai.

My fight went really well until the third round, when I got kneed in the guts. Stupidly, I'd filled up on ice cream not long before the fight and as a result I found myself unable to do anything but lie doubled up on the canvas vomiting. I was counted out. I may have learnt a little lesson about diet but it came at the expense of my humiliation. I'd lost. Nathan, on the other hand, stepped in and wiped the floor with his small but handy opponent.

My Thai trainer was unusually kind to me after the loss. He said he thought I had great technique and that I should never have lost. He wanted me to fight the same boy again. So a few days later I did, and I stopped him in the third round. Thank God. I was able to return home with some dignity.

Back in Australia, Bob Jones began talking us up, raving about these two young prodigies. Soon after getting back home, Nathan and I each won Queensland Muay Thai titles, me at welterweight, him at super middle. For me, though, the glory was short-lived. The bright notion that I'd announced myself as a talent as promising as Nathan flickered only momentarily. My next fight, my first title defence, brought me back down to earth with an ignominious thud.

The fight night followed the normal format, with Nathan's bout as the main event and mine the curtain-raiser. The word was out that we were about ready to turn pro and Dad had a beer company interested in sponsoring us. I didn't make it past the first round. I came out blazing with legs and fists but this guy dropped an anchor on my chin and I was out cold before I hit the canvas. Then up stepped Nathan and knocked his guy out with a devastating kick to the head. Nathan never gloated; he never rubbed my nose in my setbacks nor fed on my failure. Yet never was the relief between him and me cast more sharply — him the real deal, me the pretender.

I'd never been knocked out before; I couldn't remember anything about the fight. Afterwards I struggled to retain anything I was told. Several times I asked people what had happened and then I'd forget and repeat my question minutes later. My family grew annoyed at this, thinking I was faking in order to claw for sympathy or cut myself a share of the attention being heaped upon Nathan. Straight after the match, I returned home and the lounge room was aglow with a celebratory vibe. At the sight of me it was like someone just turned the air conditioning on. I stood there and said, 'I know I might have asked this before but where was the guy I fought?' And everyone just sort of looked at me, like, *Stop stacking it on*. Their answer was silence. I said, 'Ah, forget it', and walked out.

Next morning I woke up from a snooze on the lounge and was looking up at the ceiling when Dad's face came into view. Calmly, he counselled me: 'Mate, now that you've left school it's time you had a good, hard think about what you want to do with your life. Because you're not a fighter. That's obvious. You're weak. You didn't even try to get off the deck when you got clobbered yesterday. Now, I don't know what you're going to do, but you'd better start putting your mind to it.' And with that he walked off. I was completely shattered. And pissed. *Fuck you*, I seethed in my mind — I would never have dared say it. *Fuck you, you prick!*

This was the defining moment of my career, my life. Dad says now that he was trying to rev me up. This is probably true. And man, did it work. Over the years, Dad taught me so many valuable things about fighting, he understood so much and was so open to absorbing any ideas he thought could be of help. The fact that, when it came to training us, he was a really hard man caused us a lot of pain. The comforting side we'd seen in our youth had no place here. Yet it saved me, too. It helped me to avoid indulging in delusions. And as much as I hated him being so relentlessly hard-arsed, I realise what a huge factor he has been in my success. As much as there are many qualities of his I have recoiled from, his toughness tempered the steel within me, enabling me to become much that I am today.

Either way, though, my response at the time was to revert to the old fuck-you-all attitude, something I did often in my life. When I felt singled out or really alone, I'd grow as desperately hostile as a cornered animal. This fire would rage inside me — and it proved to be a great resource. I went straight back to the gym that day even though I had a headache to kill a bull. I got onto the bags and trained my guts out. There were comments in the gym — 'Got knocked out, hey? And Nathan had another top win?' — just little remarks that bit into me and stuck. These things never came from my family or from Nathan — so it wasn't their fault, but I was simmering for a month. I was the loser of the family, eh? The no-hoper, huh? We'll see about that.

It was a while before I fought again, but in early 1991 the time came for Nathan to make his professional debut. Oh, and me too. And that's what it was: an afterthought. My first professional appearance had all the fanfare of the arrival of a side order of fries. I'd always thought this would be an auspicious occasion: my career was about to get serious; I was going to get paid. Unlike boxing, there's no difference between the formats of amateur and pro kickboxing bouts. As a kickboxing pro you simply fight for a pay cheque. In boxing you go from three rounds to twelve, from punch-by-punch point scoring to striving to win each round through overall dominance. In boxing, about the only thing that stays the same from the Olympic Games to Caesar's Palace — besides the indisputable authority of the knockout — is the fact that corrupt judges can rob a fighter blind in full view of the public.

So here I was all set to be a pro, a subject for the local press, a hot young talent making an assault on the world rankings and, hopefully, the world title. This momentous step was meant to be my moon landing — or, at least, my strapping into the rocket seat. In reality, however, my giant leap was a non-event.

Nathan signed on to fight this big musclehead in Perth for the heavyweight belt. While Dad was doing the deal with the promoters, he suggested they whack me on the undercard. I was the stocking filler, the steak-knife set. Nathan was getting $2000 for his fight; Dad said I'd fight for $500. At first I was stoked. I couldn't believe it — I was going to fight for the Australian title! Then it was, *Hang on a sec, so's my brother and he's getting two grand and I'm getting halfa*. I was going over as cannon fodder. Man, that cut me to the core, but I was like, *Right, you fuckers, I'll show the lot of you*. I wasn't fazed about my loss in Thailand because I figured it wasn't a catastrophe to get stopped over there. I consigned the defeat to the 'learning experience' department and said to myself, 'Right. I'm turning pro. I've got a clean record, and this is it.' I trained as intensely as ever but there was that extra edge in my effort. I was utterly determined not to simply make up the numbers.

# IX

## The U In Hurricane

My opponent was a guy called Jason Skinner, the 28-year-old super welterweight champion and the hottest name in Australian Muay Thai.

Great.

Skinner not only had an awesome kicking technique, he was superb at grappling, the term given to the work you can do on your opponent in the clinch. It's part wrestling — where you can tire your opponent or throw him off balance — and part fighting, where you can aim to catch him with a knee, a short punch or an elbow. Without a doubt, I'd never faced such a formidable and complete fighter.

Come the bell I got stuck in, although not in my usual dog-in-a-rat-pen manner. I was still fighting more on rabid fury than nous, but this was my smartest fight to date. I didn't just try to bash Skinner; I was more watchful. It ended up being a hard toe-to-toe fight; when the final bell went, though, I was convinced that, because it was so close and we were in his home town, he'd get the decision.

I was standing in the middle of the ring ready to take another loss on the chin when the announcer called my name and the referee lifted up my hand. After a split second of confusion, I realised I'd won. I'd won the goddamn fight! I couldn't believe it.

I, Paul 'Hurricane' Briggs, was the Australian super welterweight champion — the youngest ever Australian kickboxing champion. They came over and put the belt around me and I felt as though I was levitating. The noise of the crowd became fog, the bustle close around me was somehow distant, and I drifted into a beautiful stupor. Nothing mattered but the feeling. Never before had a moment been so sublimely and gloriously mine.

Floating back to the dressing room, someone handed me a mobile phone. It was some dude from *Blitz* kickboxing magazine asking me questions. I was getting interviewed! Then the promoter handed me another phone and it was Bob Jones. So I was holding two cell phones with the belt around me just thinking, *This is awesome. I'm fifteen. I'm the Australian champion. People want to know who I am. People want to know my opinions.* Bob Jones was in my ear saying stuff like, 'I didn't think you'd beat this guy. I thought you were too young. Jason Skinner is a very hard man. You're rising in my estimation more and more, Paul. Now,' he said, 'it's going to be awesome to see how your brother goes.'

Nathan's fight was indeed awesome to watch, but not in a good way. His first ever defeat was horrible to behold. The downside of my unexpected win was that the burden of expectation weighed more heavily on my brother. Like me, his opponent was in another league to fighters Nathan had faced — and destroyed — in the past. The guy was not a particularly gifted fighter but he was a mighty hard unit — you could swing him off a chain to break walls. Nathan had watched a tape of one of his fights at the promoter's house the previous day. That hadn't been a crash-hot idea — doubt set up camp in Nathan's head then and there. This guy was big and fierce; even his face seemed to be heaving with muscle, and it was a six-pack of menace. Welcome to the heavyweights, Nathan Briggs. Off you go.

Never before had the fact that we were boys in a man's world been so stridently clear as when Nathan stepped into the ring. The announcer was talking him up: he was undefeated; he was Australia's next big thing. But I could see that the pressure of it all was weighing heavily on him. His whole persona changed as he moved out of his corner. He came out and hit the guy with everything, all the blows that had dropped everyone else, and the freak just screamed and came after him fit to murder. Nathan's heart fell out of his arse. Then the guy moved in to unload his big guns and Nathan went down of his own accord. I was shocked. The thing that astounded most was the debilitating power of fear. It wasn't, *Oh, my brother gave up. He dogged it.* I never thought like that at all.

I'd witnessed a critical change in Nathan — that fight changed him. He had lost all control, all his will, to fear. From that point on, he had this huge hurdle to jump. The next day he was saying, 'Oh, he hit me with this and he hit me with that', and I was looking at him. We both knew that wasn't the case but we went along with it anyway.

I hadn't learnt about fear yet. Believe me, I would — I'd soon enough find myself in that exact same situation as Nathan. A fighter can experience the sort of fear that is so intense it hurts; it constricts all your organs and you can't breathe and you can't swallow and your bowels slacken to the very point of letting go, and everything — *everything* — feels as though it's going to fall. Gallows fear. The kind of dread that can render you as defenceless as a newborn lamb.

Dad was shattered after Nathan's fight, because the myth that he'd built up had been blown to smithereens. But, you know, all that was happening was that Nathan and I were having normal experiences as fighters. We were *boys* still, as much as we thought we were men. And Nathan was a fifteen year old in the heavyweight division, for crying out loud. Think about it. Now, having said that, Nathan walked into this with — so he thought — his eyes wide open. This experience should have made it abundantly clear he'd been kidding himself.

One of the hardest things for a fighter to do is to adopt a spirit of acceptance. Fights rarely go exactly the way you plan, and you'd be amazed at how many fighters remain wilfully blind to this fact. A lot of men have this romantic view of what it means to be a warrior, and they believe their own delusions. They think they're so strong and skilful that they can win without getting hurt. They dishonour their opponent, reducing him to something of little consequence.

This is an absurd, vain indulgence and an unrealistic view of what it means to be a warrior. If you live by the sword, you will get cut by the sword and you risk death by the sword. A warrior is someone who goes into battle. His destiny is to be hurt, not merely to hurt. You must embrace the fact that in the ring you are going to be hit. If you don't, the reality of being smashed will come as a huge psychological shock. Men who don't prepare for this are men who prepare themselves to be broken, traumatically and stunningly. Dishonour your opponent by underestimating him and you're begging for a rude and painful lesson. That's where Nathan was at. He was getting into the ring, knocking out guys he could bully. They didn't want to come back at him. This guy in Perth inhaled Nathan's barrage, fed off it and then unleashed his fury.

My father expected a lot, and he was contemptuous of failure. True to form, he shunned Nathan as all the attention swung towards me. I was still so angry with him for what he'd said to me before Thailand and I really questioned his knowledge. His subsequent response to Nathan only made me doubt him more. *How can you just turn your back on your son like that because he lost?* Okay, we all knew he'd dogged it, but that's something my father knew a lot about — he'd done it plenty in his time. Nathan needed perspective and support; this certainly wasn't the time for him to quit. But it *was* the time for swift action. He needed to address some home truths, to work on what was not right in his head. All he needed to hear from Dad was that, psychologically, what had happened to him was normal: 'Now, son, you have to pick yourself up and get back on the horse, because if you don't, that horse is just going to get bigger and bigger and soon it will be too big for you to climb back onto.' And in the absence of such support, that's exactly what happened: Nathan's horse got too big. I'm sure he felt that some day he'd conquer his fear, but no one issued him the tools required for the task. As it turned out, he'd never again win his most testing fights, the ones that make you as a fighter.

So, rather than help Nathan deal with fear, Dad compounded it — he went hard on him, thinking he'd toughen him up, and Nathan would resent his mistreatment and buck. And when any battle broke out between these two, there was only going to be one outcome. One time in The Muscle Centre Dad was holding the pads for Nathan and was out to bust his arse. He was doing what many trainers do — trying to spur his charge on by yelling things like, 'Come on, you're kicking like a pussy!' I was able to see Dad as a trainer in those circumstances — he'd piss me off no end, but I'd put my head down and get stuck in. Nathan would take the harsh words to heart and he'd respond by trying to hurt Dad. He'd start to miss the pads deliberately, firing kicks into Dad's kidneys. Now, Nathan had great technique and a lot of power, so he could not have hurt Dad more if he'd swung a baseball bat into him. Kickboxers of our experience rarely miss the pads, so it was patently obvious that Nathan was kicking Dad on purpose. After copping it sporadically for a while, Dad eventually decided enough was enough — he leant in and head-butted his son, breaking his nose.

I hated seeing this; it was just so ludicrous. But they were as stubborn as each other. After the head-butt, Nathan told Dad he was going to get another trainer. Dad's reply was, 'That's fine, Nathan. You can go train with someone else, but I'll be waiting around the corner and will break your fucking legs.' Nathan was like, 'What?!' And Dad goes, 'I train you and that's that. You train with someone else and you'll never fight again.' So right then and there, Nathan and I realised that we were captives. Stuck.

Regardless, Nathan continued to stand up to Dad, to speak his mind when he thought Dad was out of line. If Mum was still worried about Nathan not reaching twenty-one, I reckon this loomed as his fatal flaw: his obstinate sense of fairness. He could appeal to Dad's sense of reason as much as he liked, but he was on a hiding to nothing. He paid dearly for his objections. Dad smashed into Nathan a lesson he'd learnt from his own old man: you *will* back down.

Fortunately, most days passed without such events. There was a new energy to The Muscle Centre. Bodybuilding was still Dad's main interest, but he worked tirelessly on the whole kickboxing side of things. He'd spend twenty rounds on the pads with me every day and then do it again for Nathan, plus he had other guys to train as well. For all his faults, Dad could really put in the hard yards. And after Perth, I was his golden boy. I believed so much more in myself and was eager to push on further. A tacit accord formed between Dad and me: we were going to take this kickboxing thing all the way. The South Pacific champion in my weight division was a Kiwi, so, a couple of months after my Skinner fight, Dad set about putting together a trans-Tasman card. The main event would be me against Jacob Ferrani.

In true Briggs tradition, Dad's kickboxing shows were Briggs Incorporated events. From our very first amateur bouts he'd slipped easily back into the fight game, donning his promoter's hat for the first time since the tent-show fights back in Nhulunbuy. Rounding out Team Briggs was Donna, who handled the take, and Mum, who sewed up our shorts. Mum refused to attend the actual fights: she had no desire to see her boys bleed. Dad was all over it anyway, making sure everything was on track before manning our corner. For this show, however, he'd only have me to assist. Nathan, who was scheduled to fight on the undercard, pulled out the day before.

Ferrani and I went the distance, slogging it out over five very hard rounds. Come the final bell, I'd had the better of it and took the Kiwi's belt. Barely six months out of school, I was South Pacific champion. Paul Briggs. Me — this clean-cut kid any casual bystander would think would be stoked serving up Happy Meals — a champion Muay Thai fighter. Yes, I was a sweet-skinned bundle of rage who'd delight in breaking every bone in your body. Twice.

To keep improving, I needed sparring partners. We put the word out to various gyms that anyone was welcome to come and spar. Heaps of guys came down. The ironmongers didn't mind the increased kickboxing activity so much now — they were kind of excited to know that the kid they'd seen banging away in the corner all this time was some kind of dynamite. The blokes who came to spar me were at all levels. I'd have them lined up and would take them on one round each at a time, giving them tips along the way.

One of the guys who came down was Tony Cockburn, a bullrider from the Sunshine Coast, an hour's drive north of

Brisbane. He'd actually been sparring me before I fought Ferrani. Anyway, Dad got a call one day to say that Cockburn wanted to fight me. There was another fight Dad was trying to set up in Thailand, at Bangkok's Lumpini Stadium — the Mecca of Muay Thai — so we figured that this title defence could serve as a good warm-up.

I trained manically; I overdid it, and my body rebelled. A month before the fight, I developed glandular fever. Two weeks out, I recovered and resumed training, only easier this time. Two weeks later Tony Cockburn was discovering that he'd made a mistake. I'd gone easy on him during sparring, trying to teach him things; he thought I'd been giving it my best. That's why he challenged me: he thought I was ripe for the picking. I destroyed him, dropping him three times. Left hook. Knee to the guts. Shin-kick to the head. Each time I did Ali shuffles, rubbing the crowd's faces in the demise of the local hero. The torrent of abuse they hurled at me was drizzle on a duck's back. *Behold my total command, you dogs.* He was tough, though, Cockburn — a real fighter. He kept coming. Only because I lacked the spinach to knock his lights out.

After the fight I was sick for months; I found myself stuck in a cycle of training and falling ill for what seemed like an eternity. The Lumpini Stadium fight fell through and I was treading water careerwise. For a long while I was just working at the gym, training, taking classes and not fighting. Nathan was doing the same — he'd ditched the hairdressing idea to make kickboxing his core pursuit. So we were more in each other's pockets than ever, which kept the niggle between us simmering, though we'd have probably denied it at the time. For those who knew us it was clear and simple: I, small guy with title belt, was out to prove myself and Nathan, big guy with no title belt, was out to prove that he was better than me. We argued a lot but rarely came to blows. However, girls became a new field in which our rivalry was played out. We'd vie for the same chicks at the gym and go the spoil when the other was making progress.

I'd broken up with Leah a few months before fighting Cockburn. Now my interest had rekindled and I began spending more time with her than ever before. We even began to stay at each other's houses even though we weren't sleeping together. Leah was the best friend I'd had since primary school, the first person in a long, long time who I really trusted and allowed to be close to me. For all my outward aggression and defiance, I had always been in desperate need of company. My nightmares were as disturbing as ever and, now that Nathan and I had our own rooms, I needed someone to clutch onto. So Leah and I began to sleep at each other's houses under strict supervision — separate rooms, of course. She came from a very Christian home and her father, understandably, didn't warm to the idea of us having sleepovers even if it was all quite innocent. Well, I shouldn't sound so holy. Our restraint was the result of Leah's work, not mine.

So Leah began to get to know my family really well. For better or worse. She and Dad warmed to each other; Dad's fondness for her was evident. It was good for Leah to see this side of him, too — it helped balance some of Dad's more out-there moments. Like the time at Leanne's twenty-first birthday party, when he got drunk and scarily weird before disappearing from the party altogether. They cops picked him up hours later after various people in the neighbourhood had reported seeing a prowler lurking in the recesses of their yards. They dropped Dad home like a stray pup. A face smeared with dirt revealed he'd been out on patrol, doing point duty in the jungle that was his mind.

# X

## The Boy Who Breaks Men

My knockout punch — the weapon every fighter thinks he has, even when he doesn't — came to me when I was sixteen. I already knew I could hit: I'd dropped one or two guys in the post-school brawls we used to have against the private school toffs. We'd be punching on and I'd land a beauty and down they'd go. A natural punch is not something acquired in the gym — it's a biomechanical gift, an innate harmonic collaboration of bone and muscle and balance that flows from foot to fist like the cracking of a whip. *Ka-boom*. Your first knockout in the ring is a landmark event — it's like finding your pure and defining voice; it's the perfect answer, the perfect statement, the perfect epitaph. End of story. Mine came at the perfect time: my rematch with Jason Skinner.

It almost never happened. In the first round Skinner caught me with a solid right that rocked me so badly that I forgot to remember the rest of the fight. I found myself the next morning on the lounge in the promoter's house in Perth nursing a shocking headache and an unsettling bout of amnesia. *What the hell happened?* My first thought was that I'd been knocked out again. But Dad looked happy. I said, 'How'd the fight go?' He said, 'What do you mean, "How'd it go?" Fantastic! I'm stoked. You knocked him out.' I had to watch the tape of the fight to refresh my memory. I saw myself drop Skinner to the canvas with a sharp left hook. A one-punch knockout, pure as lightning. I watched myself bolt across the ring and the glorious feeling came back to me and I sat there grinning from ear to ear. *Get a load of me. How awesome am I? I'm frigging Superman.* I sat there for ages, soaking in my little ego jacuzzi, wearing out the rewind button.

I came back down to earth soon enough, though. The promoter walked in and said, 'Mate, you're going to be so primed for Kojima.' I was like, 'What?!' A shot of panic rushed through me. Surely I didn't hear right. 'Yeah,' said Dad, like it was yesterday's news, 'you're fighting him in two weeks.' It was as though someone had thrown a bucket of iced water over me. I was dumbfounded — they had to be kidding. Keizo Kojima was the Japanese Muay Thai champion.

By the time I got back to Brisbane, I was soberly aware that this was no joke: Kojima was coming to Australia to fight me. I didn't like saying that to myself too many times. I headed straight into the gym to do what I do best: train my arse off. As usual, on Saturday mornings there was a line-up of guys leading to The Muscle Centre ring in which I stood, calling them up for their round. I stayed in there for ages. If I needed a break, I'd unload a few body shots and drop my sparring partner. I was very confident by then. Cocky, even. I'd leave guys with something to think about on their way to the back of the queue — a nice liver shot or a good stiff jab to bloody their nose. I kept everyone where I wanted them. And I'm speaking plainly when I say my kicking technique was damn near flawless. None of those guys could come near me.

All except one. Wayne Parr.

Over the previous months, I'd slowly begun to take note of this tough little kid from the Gold Coast. When he'd first arrived I'd paid him little mind — just smashed him and sent him on his way. We were padded up and all but I'd be going at 90 per cent, so I was hurting him. But he kept coming back every Saturday. Next thing he was holding his own.

Then, one time we sparred, he started hurting me with the odd kick. He'd suddenly come into his man strength. I thought the kid could be a really good fighter because he was copping heaps but giving as good as he got. He was like a Mini Me. He disappeared for a while then came back and was hurting me with *everything*. I'm thinking, *You little bugger*. And he was so willing, like, *I'll show you now*. There was no fear about him at all. He didn't care who I was; he wasn't going to back down. Around that time I saw him at a kickboxing show and noticed he'd got himself a tattoo — one of those Celtic armbands. He was obviously proud of it and I kind of laughed and had a go at him about his 'tough sticker'. He was a little wounded and pissed off, like, *Don't you be giving me shit, mate*. I sensed then that he cared a lot about what I thought. But I had no idea how much he really looked up to me. That I saw him as a kid shows how I'd acquired that regal, alpha-male aura of the winning fighter. This nice, humble 'boy', Wayne, was in fact just a year younger than me.

I fought Kojima at Jupiter's Casino on the Gold Coast and Wayne was placed on the undercard. He lost but, watching him, I knew he had huge potential if he learnt proper technique. I came out against Kojima with typical savage intent and mauled him. He hit the canvas twice in the first round. I knocked him out for the count in the second. As I celebrated triumphantly, the din of the crowd swamped me. Everything centred on me, thousands of people hailing me, my fighting might, my strong heart, my warrior spirit. I'd cleaned up Kojima! *Kojima!* I felt like King Kong. Like I had been vindicated. Here I was, living my dream. A three-grand cheque in my pocket. And it was supposed to be Nathan standing up here, not me. He was in my corner, his fighting career stalled. He'd more or less disappeared from my head and the equation of my career completely. I'd attained real independence. Now I was completely on a path all my own.

I was fired up and fearless. The abundant raw aggression within me writhed against the bonds of restraint. I enjoyed owning this destructive power but I enjoyed unleashing it better. When no kickboxing prospects came up over the next few months, Dad and I locked in on an event I'd seen advertised in one of the kickboxing magazines: an American promoter was staging a tough-man contest in Cairns, open to anyone who reckoned they were hard. There were three divisions to contest — lightweight, middleweight

and heavyweight — and the winner of each would take home
$11 000. Huge money in those days.

We got to Cairns and you can imagine the turnout. The sizable
prize money had drawn in all sorts of contenders: bikies, pro
fighters, martial arts experts, bouncers and 'roid heads. The tough,
the mean, the nasty, the stupid. The rules were essentially boxing,
but kicking above the waist was allowed. I walked out to the ring
that stood in the midst of a crowd 8000 strong, passing about
three fights on the way. There was a big Tongan guy waiting for
me. We were both in the middleweight division but at either end of
the spectrum — me around 70 kilograms, him close to 90. The first
two rounds were close, so in the last I began to attack with some
kicks. The first two tries he just smiled at me. The third was aimed
at his head and he raised his hands to block it. The bone of his left
forearm snapped like a carrot, forcing a cry of pain from the guy.
His corner stopped the fight. Next I fought a champion kickboxer
from Queensland who was about a foot taller than me. I spent two
rounds trying to get inside him and then in the third I caught him
with a solid right and then a left hook that sent him halfway across
the ring. He didn't get up.

My third opponent was touted as a Muay Thai expert. *Oh,
really?* I thought. *Well, we'll see who takes who to school, won't
we?* We nearly came to blows on the runway out to the ring — I
was so fired up I was almost beyond control. This guy was in his
mid-twenties and sported what he thought was a tough-looking
goatee, and he was staring me down as though he had a vibe
heavy enough to spook me. This amounted to standing over me,
however remotely, and I reacted with explosive outrage, erupting
into hateful threats — 'I'm going to smash ya! I'm going to
murder ya!' — before lunging at him. Fortunately, Dad took a
good hold of me and pulled me back and tried to settle me for the
fight. When the bell went I practically ran across the ring, kicked
my opponent into the ropes and then knocked him out cold. The
fight lasted fifteen seconds. I was through to the final. In the space
of two hours I'd left one broken arm and two knockouts in my
wake. Naturally, there was a bit of buzz about this animal kid
from Brisbane.

The promoter staged a separate event for the final, two months later, again in Cairns. I'd spent the interim period training, of course, and couldn't wait for the main event. I had relished the chance to destroy these men, these so-called hard nuts I'd crushed. I'd stripped them of their pride, deflated them, outed them as phoneys. I, Paul Briggs, a sixteen-year-old kid, was their master. And I didn't want to stop laying into them. I resented the interference of the ref and the bell. Mercy? That's some foreign word for 'thanks', isn't it?

Standing between the eleven grand and me was a Maori bloke with an outlaw pedigree. He was an ex-con fresh out of jail. He and his mates liked to play on it — the maladjusted time bomb. Check it out and tremble, behold the mean and desperate misfit, a guy with one toehold in society and a cold indifference to losing it. He was in his early thirties and clothed in tatts, including teardrops inked down his face. He looked every inch a hurt figure for whom violence is vengeance. That's just what I was, too, though you'd never tell to look at me. In the press conference it was choirboy versus chain-ganger. He started telling me he was going to eat me alive, that he was going to teach me a lesson, break me up and then fuck me, just like he did with those little boys in jail. And I just stared back at him, going, 'Yeah, right, mate. Carry on all you fucking want but I'm going to smash you. I am going to fucking knock you out cold.' Everyone was hearing this and probably thinking, *Where the hell did this kid pick up that bag of balls?* Then this guy's whole demeanour changed. He could see in my eyes that I was not scared of him, that he could not intimidate me. It was like he could hear me thinking, *I've knocked out everyone else, why should I be worried about you? What you look like doesn't matter a damn to me.* I could see doubt infecting his mind.

The day of the fight I woke with a severe headache. *Just my luck*, I thought. If only that had been all I had to deal with, though. I had a kickboxing mate with me who worked as a chef. He was cooking all our meals and so had brought along his brand new set of knives. Just before we were about to leave for the stadium, I was sitting around the hotel room and he handed me the heavy chopping knife to check out. I took it and was holding it out in front of me when, somehow, I lost my grip, panicked and snatched at it, only to flick the damn thing around so that it fell point-first into my thigh. I froze solid, having caught the handle too late. 'Shit, I've just stabbed myself,' I said, and everyone stopped packing their bags and looked at me. 'Yeah, right. Stop fucking around.' And I went, 'No, look', and I pulled it out of my leg, stood up and dropped my dacks. There was blood seeping out of a neat wound in my thigh. Everyone freaked. And instantly the chef guy and me were sweating ice cubes over what Dad would do when he found out. I was about to fight for eleven grand and I'd just stabbed myself with a bloody kitchen knife. He was going to kill both of us.

However, when Dad was informed, he didn't wig out. The rest of us were all panicked and unable to stop the bleeding. But it's funny — in full-on, hectic situations, Dad was so Zen, so collected. It was the tiniest things that set him right off. 'Just keep changing the bandages,' he said. I wore pants during the pre-fight medical and the doctor passed me. But when I was about to get in the ring the doctor came up and said, 'What's this?' We'd just changed the bandage for about the sixth time, so no blood had soaked through yet. I told him I'd sprained my thigh. I was through.

In the ring before the fight, the Maori bloke and his cornermen began doing a haka. Then right from the bell the guy started with all this talk. He's going on about bending me over and all that rape shit again. My only response to it was that it was weird, misplaced. He could just as well have been mumbling prayers to himself or quoting Shakespeare. No one had ever talked to me during a fight before.

At one point in the second round he was hitting me, going, 'Do you like that, boy?' to which I replied, 'How do you like this?' And I smashed him with a left uppercut. He collapsed to the ground. 'Get up, you fucking piece of shit!' I screamed, standing over him. He got to his feet and rushed me but I hit him with a shin-kick to the head and dropped him again. His seconds shouted at him, 'Get up, Maori! Get up, Maori!' And he raised himself once again and then I've gone in and unloaded on him. When the bell went I didn't stop. His mates jumped into the ring, so did Nathan, and it threatened to get totally out of hand. But we settled back into our corners. The guy had had enough, though, and he refused to come out for the final round.

I'd pocketed $11 000, a mind-boggling fortune. That night we all went out to a nightclub to celebrate. It was one of the few times I'd gotten drunk. I didn't like alcohol much, which I guess isn't surprising given what I'd seen my father do to himself and my family under its influence. But that night was special. In bed, while the other guys were tooling chicks they'd picked up, I began to think of what I'd buy with all that money. There were mag wheels and an Alpine stereo for my Commodore. And then there were turntables. I was going to learn how to deejay. I'd never been to a rave before but loved the new dance music that had been coming out.

I was sourcing these sick tracks to have blaring out of the PA for my fight entrances. Fuck 'Eye of the Tiger' — I wanted this vanguard electro: weighty, thumping and hard-edged. Tunes like 'Everybody In The Place' by The Prodigy and 'Go' by Moby (before he went soft) were the first in my collection, soon followed by 'O Fortuna' by Apotheosis. I wasn't aware that people were dancing to this stuff all night zooming on pills — man, to me ecstasy was still just a sunny kind of mood — but I knew this much: this music was the shit. Nothing besides fighting had stirred me up so much.

When I got back to Brisbane I went out and bought two turntables for about three grand. Mum freaked, saying 'Why do you need two record players?' The cost nearly stopped her clock. She ordered me to take one turntable back. I tried to explain that it wouldn't work; that I needed two decks to mix records. She didn't get it and, since I was living under her roof, I'd have to settle for one record player like most people. It was pretty embarrassing returning the one deck. I bought a bunch of records to console myself.

Life was humming along. I was scooting down the highway and I had everything in the back of the truck: a real career, money, respect and my girl. Leah and I were damn near inseparable. We were spending just about every night at each other's houses. We'd gone from sleeping in different rooms to separate beds in the same room with the door open to sharing the same bed. Mum took the initiative with all this, saying she preferred us to be together in our own houses rather than us running off to do what we wanted. By the time I was seventeen we still hadn't gone all the way. Leah wouldn't have it. She wanted to save her virginity for the guy she was sure she loved, but said that she was too young to know what love was, let alone whether she loved me or not. Did that girl ever have her head screwed on straight. Anyway, old blueballs here sat tight like a gent. Finally, I got the green light. Then, as soon as she left school, she came to live with me.

I was also too young to know what the hell love was, but it couldn't have been much better than what I was feeling. Everything was so damned hunky-dory, I figured we were ready to step up. Armed with a big bunch of flowers, I waltzed into the hairdressing salon where Leah worked doing nails and asked her to marry me. She was thrilled and said she'd love to. Her colleagues swooned. God, it was straight out of *Neighbours*. We were so stoked. Our parents, on the other hand, weren't quite so ready to party. They slapped a reality check on us: they said we were so young that they wouldn't recognise the engagement until we were both eighteen. That was over a year away. If we were still engaged then, they'd be only too happy to throw us an engagement party. We didn't mind at all. We felt so mature, but in fact we were exactly what our parents thought but kindly refrained from saying — two naive kids who hadn't a clue between them about the concept of marriage. For me, being engaged was an ego thing; an adult credential, a status boost. I never really thought about spending the rest of my life with Leah. Such thinking was beyond the range, not to mention the inclination, of my thinking.

Whatever our shortcomings, there was no doubt that we adored each other — we shared a heavy mutual infatuation. We were opposites, Leah so quiet and me so totally out there, but we delighted in those differences as gifts of small wonders. I was very full-on with her, and I liked to make her feel special, but deep down the truth was that I never wanted to be alone and I needed the comfort of her company desperately. If I ever considered such a thing as being not quite right, I'd have regarded it as little more than an unsettling thought I had to set aside. In my mind I was in love and that was that. Whatever stirred deeper within my psyche deserved no contemplation or credence. You could back the fuck off with your analysis — I had neither want nor need of it. Leah was my girl, not my crutch. And anyway, who's going to probe that stuff at that age when the good times are rolling, when life is what every teenager wants it to be: abundant, exciting and fun?

Those good times were about to get a whole lot better, too. Two major influences were set to kick my life up a gear: the rave scene and drugs. They came hand in hand, really. I took to raves like a kid in a candy store. Same with the drugs. Well, kind of. That sounds too playful. I had major fun on drugs, don't get me wrong, but I wasn't your average Saturday night piller. From the outset I had a pretty unique approach. It was combative. I didn't take drugs so much as take them on.

# XI

## *Life, But Not As I Knew It*

The first rave I went to was called Adrenalin, held at The Roxy, a nightclub in Brunswick Street. This was one of the key venues where the dance party scene sprouted in Brisbane's Fortitude Valley in the early 1990s. Across the road from The Roxy was The Site, another usual suspect, and a bit further up was The Beat. I went along with Leah, Nathan, Donna and a guy called Mick. I had no idea what to expect, other than that we were going to a big party that was going to go off. What more is there to know?

From the street I walked into a scene I struggled to process. Wading through a tide of bodies, no end of marvels struck me, one being that I was in the midst of two or three thousand people, straights and gays, all crammed into this club, all going off, and there was not one fight. Not even a scuffle. Security was nowhere to be seen. Guys came up, grabbed me, gave me a hug and moved on. I was on guard as they approached, thinking, *I'm sure I don't know this bastard*, but because they were clearly so harmless and devoid of bad intent, I didn't act on my natural impulse to swing. Girls would do the same. Not in a sexual way — everyone just radiated this rosy attitude and they were so openly tactile. It was plain weird. I was a fish out of water yet these strangers were treating me like I was a long-lost mate. I at least had the manners to keep a smile on my face, however baffled I was. But it didn't compute. I'd just started working security at the Mooloolaba Hotel — one of the pubs Dad had a contract for; he'd put me on underaged — where there was the constant threat and frequent outbreak of booze-fuelled aggro. The vibe in this place was simply beautiful — as peaceful as an ashram but heaving with the frenetic commotion of a loose tribe shaking up some euphoric ritual. The air was incensed with fresh sweat. The vibe of sexuality was overt but muted all at once. There was no awkward urgency about picking up and getting laid. Everything, for the moment, was secondary to having a good time cutting loose to the music. The prospect of sex lurked but for now the mood was all get-to-know-you friendly and refreshingly uncomplicated. Purring smiles oozed satisfaction. Each look exchanged seemed to say, *Isn't this cool? Like, aren't you just stoked to be here?* Yep. Yep, my friends. My face lit up full beam. *This is way, way cool. This absolutely fucking rocks.*

Before my eyes streamed the antithesis of life as I knew it. My fighting, my work, my training, my father — my whole existence was consumed by the capacity to inflict pain. I lived by the imperative of violence and spent every day bettering my faculties to indulge in aggression, to use my rage, to counter hostility. And what was *this*? This was carefree kitty land, a safehouse in which you could go wonderfully nuts without having some shithead come onto your chick or pick you. *So this is what kids my age are into*, I found myself thinking. *Wow. How long's this been going on?* I wandered about with Leah, found the bar, bought us drinks and soaked it all up.

What struck me more than anything, though, was the music. You felt it as much as heard it. A fast cannonade of bass thumped through your body like a second pulse, so insistent it jogged your bones. If you weren't moving, the music moved you. And what filled your ears over the beat was a kaleidoscopic wall of electronica — a surround-sound, textured, driving flood. And, up there, through the sweeping, cutting rays of coloured laser light, was the deejay, the man with his finger literally on the pulse of a cast of thousands. Leah and I entered the vast crowd to dance —

or, rather, we were swept up and consumed by it. We did not stop smiling. *How awesome is this?*

The others came and went, and I noticed that they were all acting a bit odd. Leah and I were tired and hungry by about two, so we went home and grabbed a burger on the way. The others didn't want to leave. Turned out Nathan was speeding, Donna was stoned and Mick was tripping. None of them had told me. They thought I'd spew at them because I was so staunchly anti-drugs. I probably would have spewed too. At that time I was firmly of the belief — something I'd adopted from my parents — that drugs were insidious things that ruined young lives. I had the whole escalation pattern fixed in my brain, the old pot-to-pills-and-powder-to-smack horror story. Of course, alcohol was never depicted as such an evil sinkhole but that was one thing I didn't need to be warned against. I was never going to be a drunk, nothing could be more certain. I was a very light drinker — two beers and I was Aunt Mary's. And as a health fiend I savoured my vitality. Illicit substances were, at the very least, vile pollutants.

Over the next few weeks, though, I got to thinking. I'd been told that some ravers would party all night and day, then night and day again. Forty-eight hours on the go. How the hell did they do that? By taking speed and ecstasy, I learnt. Not just one pill or line but several. Then I went to another rave, this time at The Beat, where I met Bill and Jamie, the twins who'd formed the B Boy All Stars back when I was at school. I still rated those guys highly. They were minor celebrities around Brisbane, and by that stage so was I. When we met I was surprised to find we had a little mutual admiration society going on. We talked a lot of shit and then I queried them about the club culture and drugs. They pointed to people who looked to be in their right mind, having an ace time, and said, 'They're on ecstasy.' Drugs weren't as bad as I thought, they said. Then Jamie came up to me later, telling me he had dropped an E. And he looked more than fine — he looked sublime. And he wasn't flipping out — he could still hold a conversation with me. Good for him, but I wasn't over the line yet.

I went back to my training and did my shifts at the Mooloolaba Hotel. Man, what a horrible place that was. It doesn't exist any more, which is no great loss. I had my first experience working doors here. This was a beach-front pub on the Sunshine Coast and the order of the day and night was binge drinking. *Get as much piss into you as you can.* It was always full of football players and surfies, and every now and then there'd be a rodeo in the car park out back, bringing in the cowboys.

The cowboys were always really well behaved. They just wanted to drink. Never had a problem with them. But, man, they could fight. All the problems were with the football players. They seemed retarded in every way but physically, getting through life with an eight-year-old bully's view of the world. Even the elite players were knobs. I had to deal with a few Queensland State of Origin players — you know, throw one or two out for being imbeciles. One time when I asked one to leave the dance floor, he sneered back, 'Don't fucking patronise me.' And after I'd led him off, he and his team-mates stood around giving me the evil eye, snarling. I was a kid, seventeen, but I was thinking, 'Don't stand there and look, fellas. If you're going to have a go, come and have a go.'

I learnt a lot about male ego and front at that pub, I suppose. I also learnt a lot about what slimewisers men could be. I'd pull guys up dragging some girl out who was rag-doll drunk and I'd go, 'What are you doing?' 'Oh, just, just giving my girlfriend a ride home.' 'That's not your girlfriend. We'll get her a cab.' The shit-heel would slink off.

Some bouncers were as bad as the patrons. Guys would start off with a really good head on their shoulders, but then they'd want to get bigger and start on the gear and become a problem. It was all about ego. A bunch of peacocks walking around with their feathers up. The head of security got on the steroids to beef up and started beating up every guy he threw out. I had to pull him up outside and tell him, 'All you've got to do is get the pricks out of the premises. You don't need to punch their heads in; you don't need to prove anything to them. Just get them out.' Although I was young, they respected what I had to say — one, because I was the boss's son, and two, because they knew I could kick their arses.

Of the clientele, though, the front-rowers were the worst. They always caused the biggest trouble, and none of them could fight.

One night there was this cowboy drinking at the bar and these two props were falling back into him deliberately. I'd gone over and told them to pull their heads in or I'd have to ask them to leave. They kept doing it, so I went over again, but the cowboy was on his feet by the time I arrived. 'It's all right,' he said to me. Then he addressed one of the front-rowers: 'Let's take it outside.' And I'm like, 'Yes, this will be good.' If they wanted to go outside and kill themselves, I didn't give a damn.

I watched as the cowboy walked across the road and onto to the traffic island, rolling up his sleeves. The footballer was following, mouthing off all sorts of meat-head trash. A herd of his mates were mooing the same. As the footy player stepped onto the island, the cowboy hit him with a left–right and then a left hook — one, two, three — and knocked the guy out cold. He then picked up his hat, put it on and came walking back over the road rolling his sleeves down. All the security guys were out the front, clapping. He said to us, 'Listen, fellas, I just want to finish my beer and I'll be on my way.' We said, 'Come in, mate. We'll shout you one.'

Now *there* was a natural knockout punch. He might have been the size of a jockey, that bullrider, but he had the kick of a horse in those hands.

This was how I earnt a crust between kickboxing bouts: teaching kickboxing classes at the gym by day, and dealing with drunks and 'roid heads by night. The raves I'd witnessed seemed part of some Utopian bizarro world. I was enamoured with the whole scene but the drugs issue gave me pause to think. Everything I'd seen and had been told recently made drugs seem so much tamer than what I'd been led to believe. Compared to alcohol, drugs looked harmless. Actually, they looked fantastic. All the evidence pointed to one fact: drugs got you more out of life.

God, did I struggle between curiosity and caution. One night, finally, my wall of resistance collapsed. Not piece by piece. It came crashing down.

The night of my eighteenth birthday we were all going to a rave called Black Out, which was being held at The Roxy. I guess I used the date as an excuse to make an occasion of the night. My mate

Mick had said we'd be able to get some speed for the party. I was nervous but excited as well. At a friend's house for a pre-party barbecue, Nathan and I were having a beer when he suggested we smoke a joint: it would prime us for the party. So he started mulling up, cutting up a bud and rolling it up with some tobacco. It amazed me that he knew what he was doing. He'd been smoking pot for six months by then, it turned out. After we smoked the spliff, I felt nothing. It was like waiting for a train to arrive but none did. I felt completely normal. Nathan was saying, 'You're stoned, man. You're stoned.' I said, 'Sorry, I don't feel anything.' I thought grass was a complete waste of time and money.

We drank all afternoon. Well, I didn't — I only had a couple — but Leah and Donna got smashed on wine coolers. They were both so sick that they had to stay in the car when we got to the party. As soon as we were in, Mick went off to find his mate with the speed. Next thing I was in this car outside the club sitting beside the driver, who was pouring some white powder onto his street directory. He then pulled out a credit card and started marshalling the powder into lines. Then he said, 'Here you go', and he handed me the street directory and a rolled-up note. And I was like, 'What do I do with this?' 'You snort it,' he said, not sure if I was joking. I cracked up laughing. 'No way,' I said. I was sure that would make me sneeze.

Then I thought it over for a while, just staring at the four lines of powder in my lap. I said, 'Nah, sniffing that stuff just doesn't compute with me.' 'Well, just eat it, then,' he said. 'Will it work the same?' He said, 'Hell, yeah. You can eat it, bang it or snort it.' 'What's bang it?' I said. 'Shoot it up. Inject it.' I was like, 'Whoa, don't even talk about that shit, man. Druggies do that.' He just looked at me funny, like, *Yeah, okay, mate.* He must have been thinking, *Druggies? What are we, you idiot?*

Suddenly I stopped myself from thinking, bent down, licked up the speed and fought the bitter powder down my throat.

'Got any water?' I gagged, handing the directory back.

'Fucking hell, mate,' the guy said. 'You ate the lot!'

Mick leant over from the back. 'What the fuck are you doing, Paul? That was for both of us.'

Panic shot through me. *Fuck! I'm going to overdose!* The guys reassured me I wouldn't. 'You're just not going to sleep for two days,' they said. The guy sorted Mick out with some more and the three of us went back to the party.

Inside the club I started to get annoyed that, again, there was nothing happening. I'd forked out eighty bucks and had all that speed and for what? Bugger all. I went up to the guy we scored it from and demanded my money back. He said, 'How come?' I said, 'This shit doesn't work.' 'Stand still,' he said. 'What?' 'Stand still.' I tried. Then I was like, 'Oh, shit. I can't stand still.' I was shifting from one foot to the other, looking all about me, moving around. 'Stop moving,' he said. And as much as I tried, I couldn't. So I was like, 'Oh, so is this it?' 'Are you getting rushes?' he said. 'Rushes? Ah, nah.' 'Well, you're going to be like this for two days.' 'Two days? I'm going to get bored.' And he's like, 'No. No. Go and dance, man. You're going to be able to dance for ever.' So off I went and danced for about two hours. It felt like five minutes.

Later I bumped into the twins and Jamie told me they had a birthday present for me. He said it was over in their shop across the road. So I was thinking nervously that it had to be drugs and followed them and their girlfriends out of the club. The mall was packed and we crossed over and took the back entrance into the shop. Jamie pulled out a bag of pills and spread a few on the desk. He took one and set it in front of me. My life hit pause. I swear, I have been in some situations that have filled me with fear, where I have absolutely shat myself, but I don't think I've ever felt such dread as I did staring at that pill. *Now*, I was thinking, *I've really seen drugs*. The speed didn't seem to count. The joint definitely didn't. But this pill looked serious — it had that pharmaceutical clout of something made to have an effect. It was a portent of change. *This will definitely affect you.* It was a one-way ticket. Swallow it and there was no turning back.

Jamie cut it in half. His girlfriend, who was pilling, was like, 'It's okay. I've already had one and I'm fine.' And, indeed, she looked like she was having a good time. The girl said, 'This is what it does to you. It's why they call it ecstasy, because you just feel love and it's just amazing.' Jamie was going, 'Trust me. A half is all you'll need.'

It's hard to describe what I was feeling, but it was something akin to a sad and heavy wisdom. In my young stupidity there was something solemn and cautionary, as though I was fully aware of where I'd end up. I knew my personality. This was not just taking a pill: this was crossing over. Deep down I sensed that my life was about to be transformed, but not in a good way at all.

I put the pill in my mouth and swallowed. Within half an hour my trepidation was so forgotten. An orgasmic feeling surged through me. Those people in the room became my bosom buddies for the rest of the night — from that point on we were a family, and we would fret if one member strayed from our company for too long. We danced for hours and hours. At one point I noticed Donna watching us with this perturbed look on her face. *Look at you guys.* I tried to talk to her but she was too normal. I had half a pill and the party changed. I had half a pill and my life changed. In an instant the drug changed me. Changed my perspective on life. That half a pill was an earthquake that shook me completely.

Life wasn't just about fighting any more.

# XII

## *Crushed*

I'd rounded a bend, not left the road completely. I wasn't about to let anything derail my dream of becoming world champion. The rave scene had opened up a new world to me and I had no doubt I would be going back for more. I felt it had given my life a new dimension. After years of a strict regimen and singular focus, a more exciting, rounded existence beckoned. And why not? As long as it didn't impede my career, getting out and enjoying myself every now and then seemed perfectly apt for a guy my age. But raves were trivia nights that dotted the industry of my life. Breathers. I had one fight looming before 1993 was out and I set myself to preparing for the challenge.

I was to face a new Kiwi champ named Shane Dargaville and I was wary. I'd seen tapes of the guy fight. Against some very tough units, he'd weathered a hailstorm of blows before unloading a thunderbolt right that knocked his assailants flat out cold and all but snoring. I had to be very sharp and very focused or Dargaville would smash me into slumberland too. I hit the gym with typical vigour. Training was always a proudly masochistic challenge for me. I never went easy. I would punch and kick myself way past the point where my muscles were screaming, reduced to feeding on lactic acid, their own scalding waste. As ever, they were slaves to my mind. As it should be. *Shut up and take it.*

My work paid off. I destroyed the Kiwi. Dropped him with a left jab in the first round before applying a clinical onslaught over the next two. He was too hammered to come out for the fourth. This was my seventh stoppage in as many fights and my most accomplished display so far. I finished my year on a high and I was keen to go out and get myself in a similar state by synthetic means. It was Christmas and I wanted a break. There were a few raves coming up I intended to get fully amongst. I wasn't planning anything too radical — just to cut loose and, yes, neck another half a pill here and there. Maybe try a whole. And party time began straight after the Dargaville fight.

The next day, though, I received the news that my holiday was cancelled: Dad had other plans for me. A guy from All Japan Kickboxing, Japan's leading kickboxing promoters, was putting on a big event in Melbourne and one of his fighters had pulled out injured. After seeing my latest performance, he contacted Dad to sound me out as a late replacement. The show was two weeks away. When Dad told me, I was furious and indignant. I refused. The last thing I wanted to do was hit the gym again. Of course we had a massive row that I had no hope of winning. It was at times such as this that Dad would lay it all on the table to let his sons know who was boss. That wasn't so bad in itself — for, in hindsight, he was right on this occasion. The promoter had said that he was so impressed with me that if I won this fight by knockout, he'd offer me a contract to fight in Japan, paying US$5000 per bout. This was a career landmark; too good an opportunity to pass up. I didn't push my argument too far, because I could see what was on offer here.

On top of that, I was only too aware of what lengths Dad was willing to go to in order to win out. While my successes had warmed his heart, I'm sure, they'd also tripped an alarm inside him. Seeing his sons beat grown men seeded in his mind the notion that we'd one day rise up and overthrow him, just as he'd done to his old man. So he began raising the stakes. When he perceived his ego to be under threat from us, he felt compelled to attack and enforce submission. To wait and defend if necessary wasn't his style. To me this revealed his deep insecurity as a father. He lived constantly prepared to attack us.

Both Nathan and I had come to realise that we were never really out of the ring with Dad, that we could never escape it. I guess the only way he knew how to care about us was to hold us with a white-knuckle grip — compelling us to need him. So if a confrontation with either Nathan or me gained heat, he'd end up saying, 'Any day you think you're good enough, you just have a go.' It was absurd brinkmanship. I'd think, *That day will never come, you idiot.* I'd never say such a thing, of course. That would have been suicide. But I just never understood his thinking. Why would you want to fight your son? To punch, hurt, bloody and break him. Your son! And why would I want to fight my father? One time I just said to him: 'I'll never fight you. Not because I fear you, because I don't fear you', which was a complete lie. 'I'd just stand here and let you go for it, just out of respect for you,' I told him.

That respect steadily diminished over the years until barely a shred remained. But at that time I still loved my father, despite everything. I couldn't think of anything worse than fighting him. The thought made me feel sick. I didn't hate him that much. In time I would. For now, though, I backed down and the matter was settled — I was going to Melbourne to fight Taiei Kin, the latest Japanese champion. Nathan was coming too, having been slotted into the bout before mine.

I had two weeks to prepare for this nuggetty little brick. I'd seen him demolish Rick Kulu, an Australia kickboxer for whom I had huge respect. Taiei Kin had kicked Kulu into curry paste. Going on the brutal damage I saw, those stocky legs of his landed with all the clout of fence posts spat twirling from a hellwind. To say Taiei Kin was highly rated is an understatement. In kickboxing circles, the prevailing view was that he had one hand, and a chunky thigh, around the world title. And to add insult to my indignation, my fee for taking on this hotshot was only a grand. Over the year, I'd worked up from 500 bucks a fight to 3000 or 4000. But I came to realise that this was a huge opportunity, regardless of the money. I hauled myself back to the gym, although not in the breeziest of spirits.

When I reveal the outcome of the fight, you'll think I'm so up myself. All this build-up about the formidable opponent, and what did I do? I cleaned up the bastard in the first round. At the weigh-in I said to the promoter that I was going to knock Taiei Kin out in the first round with a knee to the head. 'You're only paying me for one round,' I said, 'and that's all you're getting.' They laughed. *Ain't this kid a piece of work? Cocky little son of a bitch*, these fat burghers no doubt thought. *That'll soon be knocked out of him.*

I was so fired up when I arrived at the ring, partly because Nathan had lost when he shouldn't have — I was getting so jack of him not putting in. I was, therefore, of a mind to show everyone just what Paul 'Hurricane' Briggs was about. I started with Taiei Kin. Before Muay Thai fights, the combatants perform a ceremonial dance called the Ram Muay. The dance is choreographed to reach all corners of the ring to invoke the power of the four elements of which everything is made: fire, water, wind and earth. Parents and mentors are also given thanks during the dance. When I got near Taiei Kin during the Ram Muay, he eyeballed me, trying hard to look tough, but I could sense he was scared. After the dance comes an improvised element of mime that the fighters carry out to assert themselves and intimidate their opponent. Its purpose is similar to that of the All Blacks' haka. Fighters make up their own signature schtick. Sometimes, I'd pretend to dig a grave in which I'd bury my opponent. On this occasion, though, I fired make-believe arrows at Taiei Kin. They were not make believe to us. He pretended to catch them and break them. But I saw them do their work — they sank deep. I saw that the guy feared me. For all his front, my opponent was impaired before we began.

This is one of the amazing things about fighting: you can plan the way you want to fight, but when all's said and done, what takes place in the ring is often a product of chance. You can watch tapes and deconstruct your opponent in your head but in the ring you face a being, a warrior, and everything ceases to become predictable. Sure, there are sad mismatches staged for made-to-order outcomes, but in genuine contests, as long as your opponent has two feet and a heartbeat, he can win. In the initial engagements of the first round, you take quick stock of his physicality and will, and you get a measure of his worth that no videotape can provide. And in this case, no sooner had we squared off than I knew I'd win.

In the grapple I threw Taiei Kin around like a dog on a stick and fired a few solid knees into him. I manhandled the guy and it shocked him. I was harder, stronger, fiercer — and he knew it. This was not what he had been expecting. I rocked him with a left hook. Then his body surrendered. You can sense defeat in your opponent as surely as you can smell his breath. Bodies go through chemical transformations in the ring: a winning fighter is energised and buoyed by endorphins; a losing fighter, a fighter suffering hurt, has to contend with a body intent on slowing down, cowering, to preserve itself. That instinctive recession is felt as oppressive fatigue and pain, and it stirs up potent fear and overwhelming hopelessness. In essence, the losing fighter has two opponents.

To turn that around, to overcome a body and mind so desperate to quit, takes an indomitable spirit. Taiei Kin had conceded before I knocked him out with a knee to the head, just as I had predicted. He was totally unprepared to meet the likes of me. I was a fearsome piece of work to behold. By the sheer scary force of my presence, I'd broken this guy before we even began trading blows. I was unaware of the intimidating power of my presence then. When I went into his dressing rooms to thank him, he was slumped in a chair with his gown over his head, bawling his eyes out.

First round knockout. Annihilation. This was rather big — me, this eighteen-year-old kid, had swatted Taiei Kin like a bug. Really, this was a sensational performance. I was immediately perceived by the Japanese kickboxing contingent as being some kind of bad-arse Boy Wonder. And something to behold, too — a fire-breathing dynamo possessing a savage heart, hard fists and brutal textbook kicks. There was more than a little static about me; immediately I was being hailed as a potential superstar in the sport. Paul Briggs had arrived on the world kickboxing stage on the tip of a lightning bolt.

No time was wasted signing my contract with All Japan Kickboxing. I was set. At the time, US$5000 was like $10 000 Australian. If I fought nine fights the next year, that would be ninety grand. Enough to buy a house. And I was going to go fight in Tokyo. I'd just destroyed the supposed heir to the world crown. All of a sudden, becoming world champion did not seem too far away.

When I got back to Brisbane, we hit a rave at The Site. I tried acid for the first time. I had two tabs and nothing happened. I went back to the guy I got them from and told him to give me more. He said, 'You've got to give them time. They take a while to come on.' I said, 'Give me some more.' He handed over two more and I swallowed them. As in the ring, I had no idea how scary I was to other people. Only years later did I realise that guys cringed in my presence, that friends chose their words carefully, trying to say what they believed I wanted to hear. Everyone was on edge around me, even as they wanted to befriend me. I had no idea. It's only now that I look back and see how I carried myself: tough and fearless and demanding. I exuded the threat of violence unconsciously, as though it were aftershave. I had become my father in fundamental and lamentable ways, but I was entirely oblivious to the fact. The thought would have horrified me. But I didn't give it any thought — I just got what I wanted.

Speaking of my father ... he was on a roll. He and Bob Jones had set in motion plans to bring out Thailand's Jomhod Sor Chitlata, the reigning world champion, for me to fight. Huge promotion with whizkid Paul 'Hurricane' Briggs out to seize the world title. 'You're killing everyone,' Dad told me. 'You're the man.' Dad had gotten hold of tapes of Jomhod's fights and I sat down and watched. I could not believe it — this guy was a freak. For the first time in my life, I was scared of an opponent. The record showed that this guy was undefeated, but the footage brought that record shockingly to life. Watching Jomhod wreak havoc, I felt my heart sink. Oh my God.

I considered myself a realist and I knew I was not in this guy's league. I told Dad as much, that I wasn't ready for this guy. Dad was having none of such talk. My reluctance to fight didn't have the same motivation as when I resisted taking on Taiei Kin. That was petulance, this was stone cold fear. But I got back into the gym — I was still doing as my master told me. It was business as usual: he picked my fights and I fought them. I figured the least I could do was train hard. And then I got into the ring at Brisbane's Festival Hall and this bloke crushed me.

For the first time in my life the roles were reversed — I was the one running scared, at least figuratively, as my whole being shrank before this man. The fight began and ended with him smashing my legs, and somewhere near the start he broke me mentally. What I'd seen happen to Nathan and what I'd seen happen to my opponents was now happening to me: I was breaking down. And what a lonely, frightening and godless experience it is to die in the ring. A fighter learns of his fragility like the abrupt receipt of mortifying news: inner faultlines quickly widen to reveal chasms of gut-wrenching depth. Everything about yourself that you held as faith is rendered a falsehood. That mirror reflecting your boundless strength and courage shatters to reveal the whole lot of nothing that lies behind. As it had happened for Taiei Kin, my entire being began to desert me. Struggling to stem my abandoning of ship, I hit Jomhod with a shin-kick to the head, the blow that had turned other men to water. He glowered at me, banged his gloves together, grunted like a bull and pressed forward. This reaction, dreadfully, was a shocking revelation: I could not win. Now I was the last man on deck, the captain clutching the sinking wheel. I lashed out with a big front kick and that pushed him across the ring. He bounced off the ropes and came flying back to land an elbow on the top of my head. This was my first major bout in which elbows were allowed, and what a caustic introduction. It felt as though someone had belted me fiercely with a hammer. For a few seconds I was aware of nothing but the most excruciating pain I'd ever experienced. Then the voices started — appeals from the men in the lifeboats for me to join them. *This guy is a machine. He's stronger than you. You cannot hurt him. You cannot beat him. You just kicked him in the face and he's laughing at you.* And all the while Jomhod was kicking my legs with shocking effect. Emotionally and spiritually, I followed my body in retreat. After three rounds I couldn't go on any more. I was a mess. I was rubble. To my boundless shame, I too abandoned ship.

I went back to the showers and just sat under the spray of water and cried my eyes out. Just like Taiei Kin. If anyone came in I turned on them with wounded ferocity, swearing torrents at them to leave me the fuck alone. My Dad responded in his typical stupefied way: he lost all his belief in me. As I had. For the first time ever, I thought, *Maybe I'm not what I think I am*. I started questioning myself, triggering a downward spiral into the wilderness of my identity.

That night I went out and partied and tried a new drug, crank — a.k.a. crystal meth or ice. It was just what the doctor ordered, so to speak. I was peaking most of the night rather than dwelling morbidly on my humiliating loss to Jomhod. The high was a comfort to me, leading me to realise that drugs weren't just fun: they could ease my pain. I arrived home from the club the next morning to find Dad and Bob Jones in the lounge room. They told me I was going off to Thailand. Alone. They said the Thai millionaire who brought Jomhod out thought I was an awesome talent and reckoned I'd do well to go train in Thailand and learn Muay Thai for real.

I strained to comprehend this — it was as though they were speaking another language. I'd walked in after an all-nighter, my brain not quite back from Jupiter, my body sore, my legs fucked, my spirit broken. I hadn't even stopped to process the feelings I'd had in the shower after the fight. I'd just gone out straightaway and numbed them with drugs. The seed of self-doubt had been planted in my head. I had no idea any more if I had what it took to be a fighter. I'd been found out as a phoney. And I get home to these two saying, 'We've talked to the Thai trainers and we are sending you over there for three months. It'll do your fighting the world of good.' Of course I arced up, but as if what I thought mattered.

One thing was clear: the loss had stained my shiny new contract. If I went over to Japan and lost, that could well be the end of it. According to Dad's rationale, I needed to step up, to rise to world champion grade quickly. And who better to help teach than Jomhod's trainers? *What?!* I reeled. 'Tell me this is a sick joke.' 'It's not. You're going to train with Jomhod.' My brain snapped quickly into the here and now, Earth time. 'You cannot be serious. I never want to see that bastard again in my entire life.' I could not have been more appalled if they'd told me they were sending me off to live with the bloke who raped me. I felt coldly cheated; sold to slave traders. This bloke has just ruined me and you're going to send me off to live with him?

I hated these two men before me — all they seemed interested in was Paul Briggs Inc., their potential superstar and money-spinner. God, did I protest. But, in the faintest of ways, I knew I should go. If I was still to fulfil my dream, I had to go and face my fear, even though the thought of it reduced me to tears.

Two weeks later I was on a plane to Bangkok. In the space of a month I'd reached spectacular heights, only to come crashing down. And at a time when I thought I'd be at home preparing to make a spectacular debut in Japan, I was on my way to a boxing camp in Thailand, unsure if I wanted to be a fighter at all. And waiting for me there was my nemesis.

Three months I was meant to be there. What further torture and humiliation awaited me? After that, if I lasted, it was straight to Tokyo. It was funny how things had changed. I'd never lived out of home before and here I was going to live in some Third World country. A few weeks ago I was young and fearless and unbreakable. Now I was young and wracked with doubt. What the fucking hell was I doing?

# XIII

## Exile In Thailand

I was greeted at the airport by steambath heat and an old man who had the wisdom of several lives. He also had a thirst for several beers. 'Let's wet our whistle, eh?' he said as we left the airport. Who was I to argue? We took a stool at some bar where he set about downing one beer after another. *Great*, I thought, *my welcoming party, and my driver, is a piss-head*. It was hard not to warm to the guy, though. As the beer went down, sage words spilled out. He was a Muay Thai aficionado and I enjoyed listening to him. Turns out he was one of the trainers at the camp — the full Muay Thai master. In time I'd learn much from this old timer about true Thai warrior spirit. He was priceless, may his soul rest in peace.

But the old bastard did what Thais do to all *farangs* — foreigners — who come to learn Thai boxing: he threw me a test, the first of many. The Thais have an immense sense of pride and ownership over Muay Thai, to the point of snobbery. They believe the *farangs* are, more often than not, mere browsers happy to commit little for shallow reward. On face value, they're seen as impostors — white guys wailing Delta blues. This scepticism becomes prejudice in the ring. When a *farang* fights at Lumpini Stadium or Rajadamnern Stadium, the Wembleys of Muay Thai, he'd best knock the other bloke out, because that's just about the only way he'll win. The bias of Thai judges against foreigners is a cultural fixture, so the doors to Muay Thai are not exactly wide open. For non-Thais to really make ground, they have to pay their full dues. And that means suffering.

The old man left me at a hotel in Bangkok. I thought this was weird — no one had said I'd be based in a hotel. From what I'd been told, my home for the next three months was half a star up from the Bangkok Hilton, the city's notorious Bangkwang prison. The next morning I was taken to this crappy little gym where I was supposed to train. It was a joke. The place was empty and was about as state-of-the-art as the steam engine. I'd come all this way to train here? Get real. The next day I said, 'This is not good enough. Where are the rest of the fighters? This is supposed to be training camp.' And with that I passed my first test. I was told to check out of the hotel and was then taken to the proper camp, which lay on the outskirts of the city where slum strips divided suburban blocks like mould between white tiles.

My reception there was very cool. The owner of the camp told me that he'd only ever had one *farang*. A Frenchman. He had lasted three days. 'We'll see if you can last two,' he scoffed. *I've got one plane ticket on me*, I thought in reply, *and it goes from Bangkok to Tokyo. I'm not going anywhere, you fat prick.* Pretty soon, though, I would sure as hell be wanting out. I had no idea what I was in for.

Every morning we set off at about half past five on an 8-kilometre run. I'd never run that far in my life — I never did road work. Then we'd train intensely for two hours on the bags and pads and doing sparring and grappling. We'd finish at about nine-thirty and have breakfast. After that we'd all wash together, standing around tipping water over our heads, drawing ladlefuls from a common basin. The toilet was a reeking hole in the concrete floor. Speaking of concrete floors — that's where we slept, collapsing to gain some precious rest before the afternoon session. Having been woken again, we'd go out on the road again for a 5-kilometre run, and then the real work started: three to four hours of hard-driven training that would go beyond six, seven and sometimes eight o'clock at night. The food was our only indulgence — awesome, authentic Thai; plenty of it and all freshly prepared on stoves behind the house. The first couple of nights I was so exhausted I nodded off into my meal.

We didn't have to go far to reach bed — once all the dishes were cleared, we just claimed a spot on the bare cement floor and lay down. We had pillows but no mattresses. The greatest comfort at night was the fan; it was just so hot and clammy, we'd fight over which way it blew. If you went to sleep with it on you, you'd certainly wake up to find someone else had turned it their way. Ultimately, I was too tired to care. And it would seem as though I'd just drifted off when I'd feel the trainer kicking my feet and telling me to get up for my run. I'd try to move but my body would be all stiff and sore. But out I went. We did this seven days a week, which came as a particularly rude shock.

The first Sunday I was there, I figured it would be a rest day. But I awoke to my feet being kicked. I was like, 'No, no, my God will be angry if I train on Sunday. I cannot train Sunday — it is against my religion. I have to rest.' They said, 'Okay, no problem. Just run.' 'No, can't train Sunday.' 'Just run.' 'Fuck, all right. I'll just run then.' I come back. 'Okay, now jump on the bags.' 'No, you don't understand — my religion ...' 'No, listen: you train seven days a week or go home.' So the days, the weeks, just melted into one another. It was like, 'What day is it today?' What did it matter? Just another day of pain.

There is a high churn rate in Thai boxing — there are about 50 000 guys trying to make a buck — or should I say baht — in the ring. For every fighter who succeeds, there are plenty left broken and broke. The glut of raw material makes everyone dispensable. And when it comes to training methods, sports science just doesn't come into the frame. Tradition is the dominant textbook; every great Thai boxer is a product of brutality and training overkill. Don't change what ain't broke. Old school — can't beat it. They have no concept of the benefits of rest; if a fighter goes stale under this relentless system, they think he's bludging and push him harder. I'd come to see guys totally clapped out by twenty-five.

But no one had said this was charm school. There were around twenty boxers in the camp, aged from seven to late twenties. Boys were deposited by their parents in the hope they would grow up to support the family — you know, send their brothers and sisters to school, buy Dad a water buffalo. It's the same way girls are delivered into whorehouses. All of a sudden this seven-year-old kid has an almighty responsibility: he must fight and he must win. One morning I woke up to go for a run and this little boy was sitting in the corner crying. I went over and said, 'Hey man, you right? What's wrong?' You know, trying to be big brother. And he quickly rubbed out his tears, pretended there were none and walked off to put on his running shoes. I thought I had it tough leaving my home, my family and my girlfriend in Brisbane at eighteen to come to this place; this kid was just a baby.

I began to gain a keener sense of the hardships people in Third World countries endure. They were fighting for their next breath — these guys weren't fighting because it was a dream they had when they were a kid. Most of them were compelled to be here. They were press-ganged crewmen on a ship at sea for life.

The major reservation I'd had about coming to the camp — facing Jomhod — disappeared pretty quickly. We were paired up as grappling partners and he flung me around the ring like a dishcloth for two months. The last month, after I'd gained a lot more strength, I began to hold my own. Once I even dropped him with a body shot. In sparring sessions I came to realise I had it in me to beat this machine who'd terrorised me. Spending time with him, I learnt fighting is not about the physical. *I had the tools to beat you*, I thought, *but you beat me mentally*. His mind was so strong that he oozed destruction; he was simply terrifying to stand in front of. But he was one of the nicest guys I've ever met in my whole life. I have him to thank for so much of what I learnt in Thailand about training hard — and I learnt plenty, I can tell you. We ended up very good friends. Well, as good as you could be with Jomhod — he was so aloof, a real loner. After I'd decked him, he said to me, 'You and me are friends. We will never fight again.'

Friends we may have been, but during training we were arch rivals. It was the case with every fighter there. There was no slacking off in our training sessions. We had two or three world champions in the group and every single session was do or die. Every boy was trying to show he was the man, to show the trainer that he had it. The spirit was, *I'm going to outdo you today, tomorrow and the next day, and if you are still here the day after I'm going to outdo you then too.* This was from the seven year olds up.

I think the most torturous aspect of the camp, though, was the boredom. The middle part of the day was the worst. All the young boys would be at school, the trainers and the owner would leave the camp to do whatever they had to do, and all the older boys enjoyed some chill-out time. It was pretty cool to start with, but it got to the point where I'd sit and stare at the calendar like it was a clock. It's the fourteenth. I'd leave, come back, look at the date again and think, *Fuck, it's still the fourteenth.* A couple of hours later: still the fourteenth. *Can't wait for it to be the fifteenth . . .* I did that for about a week, which drove me mental, so I stopped.

In the second month the homesickness kicked in badly. I was desperate to go home. I was jack of sleeping on a concrete floor and I was jack of Thailand and its people. It was fairly tolerable, I guess, until I saw a guy get shot. That kind of did my head in.

I was out on a dawn run with Jomhod and Lu Lum, another champion who was younger and lighter than me. Early in our run we passed a couple of guys who looked like they'd been on the piss all night. As we approached they were arguing, and from what little Thai I'd picked up I gathered that the squabble was over cigarettes. Each was claiming he owned the one pack between them. We'd just passed them when I heard this almighty *crack*, like a huge firecracker going off. I turned around to see this guy's head hitting the ground. Then I saw the gun in the other guy's hand, a little .38 revolver. He laughed, saying, 'Whose cigarettes are they now?' I must have stopped, because Jomhod grabbed me and said, 'Run. Come on, just run.' I said, 'I am running.' He said, 'You're not running! Keep running! Look straight ahead. Let's go!' I can't remember the rest of the run; I was totally numb. When we got back to camp, no one said anything. Not a thing. I was like, 'What the fuck's going on here? What is wrong with you people? Aren't you guys going to talk about what we just saw?' Jomhod ignored me and went out to get some fish for lunch, and we were sitting around eating and still no one had anything to say. I had to talk to someone. I was not okay with seeing a murder. Shot dead. I didn't feel okay at all. I tried calling just about every person I knew in Australia and I couldn't get hold of anyone. I ended up speaking anyway, leaving a trail of voicemails. Back in camp I put my Walkman on, playing a tape of this deejay I was into. I couldn't stand it; I couldn't listen. I turned it off and kept seeing the murder over and over again. Then the anger started rising and found its target in everything Thai. I was like, *You guys suck. This country sucks. This is just fucked. I hate the lot of you.*

At the afternoon session I went absolutely berserk. Parts of my past — everything I was angry about — started coming up without me realising exactly what was going on. It was the fuck-you-all attitude. *You think you're going to break me? Bring it on, you fuckwits.* I was doing pads and I was kicking the shit out of them. We'd do it by rounds — go hard for three minutes then rest for one. The trainer holding the pads could sense the rage in me and was pushing me on. I was yelling and kicking — *whack, whack, whack, whack, whack* — and for the last thirty seconds the boys started shouting out, 'La! La! La! La! La! La! La!' — like, 'Pick it up! Pick it up! Pick it up!' — and the bell went and I kept kicking and growling and the bell sounded again and a new round had started — I've kicked through the fucking break. Smart one, Briggsy. To spur me on the trainer tried to hit me with the pad, but he missed and punched me with his closed fist. My lip blew up and bled but I just kept going.

At the end of the second round I was utterly wrecked. No other fighter in the gym had done anything for that round. They were all just standing around watching me kicking like a man possessed. They thought I'd flipped out. I gained instant respect. They were convinced that I was a force to be reckoned with. As of the next day, instead of trying to break me physically, the trainer began teaching me things technique-wise. The boys started talking to me. Until then I hadn't been accepted. But now that they'd all done this about-face, I was like, *You know what? You can all get fucked. I don't care any more. Fuck this place.*

The next day Lu Lum invited me to lunch. He was cashed up because he'd just won a championship. Down the end of our dirt road was this little makeshift restaurant where they set up a table and chairs in the gutter and cook your order on a portable stove parked in the street. Lu Lum ordered up big and we pigged out. When we were done I thought, *This guy's okay.* But then he got up and walked off, and the restaurant dude came over and handed me the bill. I said, 'Whoa, hang on a sec. I'm not paying for all this.' I called Lu Lum back and when he came up he started getting angry. I said, 'Man, don't you try to fucking screw me.' I was jack of these guys thinking that because they lived in a Third World country it was okay to rip me off. I was livid. I said I was paying half and nothing more. Then the restaurant guy started at me and I told him to get fucked. Then Lu Lum picked up a knife off the table — it was just crazy — so I lifted up my shirt and said, 'Come on. Stick it right here and I'll snap your fucking neck.' He shat himself and put the knife down and became all appeasing. 'Oh we're friends, we friends,' he was saying. I pushed him away and said, 'Fuck you. You can pay for this.' I then gave the restaurant guy another spray and walked back to camp. Lu Lum paid and chased after me and put his arm around me. I shrugged him off me — 'Fuck off. I'm fucking over you monkeys.'

I got back to the camp, found a spot to sit down and began stewing over all the things I hated in my life. Jomhod saw me and came over. He had such a peaceful presence about him and was such a wise young man. He came from northern Thailand and had quite dark skin. He was not like most Thais I'd met — he respected me and wanted nothing from me. And without speaking a word of English, he consoled me. He let me know that he understood what I was going through, that he knew things were hard, and that I'd be okay, that I should just soldier on. It was one of those moments when language is superfluous and two people from two different worlds connect for the basic values they share — things that don't need to be spoken about, like dignity, compassion, humour and respect.

It was never the same between Lu Lum and me after that, though; I just had this bitter taste in my mouth. And it made me just harden up more. I thought, *Right, I'm here to do a job, and that's to train and turn into a machine.* And I knew who I was going to fight in Tokyo — a Thai called Samart, who was renowned to be an awesome kicker — and I just told myself that I was going to smash him. I was going to take it all out on him. So I trained harder and harder, and next thing I knew the fight was a week away and Mum and Leah had come to Bangkok to see me. Dad came in from Zurich the next day and almost immediately he and Mum proceeded to have some humdinger rows.

Over the previous few months, the gyms had been bleeding cash. They were viable, I reckon, it was just that Dad essentially had stopped running them. He'd added a third Muscle Centre in Fortitude Valley, but as modern as this gym was, it was still performing badly. Dad hadn't moved with the times. Gyms were becoming fitness centres that had an exclusive feel and offered a wide variety of classes. They were becoming what Dad called A Load of Bullshit. He'd say to prospective members, 'Do you want to go to one of those yuppie gyms, put your tights on and pretend to train, or do you want to come down here and do it for real?' And people would go, 'Yeah, actually, I'll go put my tights on and pretend, thanks.' The financial problems placed untold strain on my parents' marriage. And in the middle of all this, Dad got Nathan to run the Coopers Plains gym and Donna the Fortitude Valley gym, and he took a job as a bodyguard for these commodities brokers who were off to make their fortunes in Zurich. Dad made promises to Mum of earning big bucks on the back of these guys' deals, so she had let the mortgage run on his assurances. When Dad arrived in Bangkok with no money to sort out the bruising finances back home, Mum lost it. I reckon that was the beginning of the end for her.

It was a very strange time when I left the camp to see my family. It was like I'd been released from prison. What had been normal before seemed so alien now. I'd been locked up for three months, and then to meet Leah and spend the night with her was just weird. I was almost glad to get back to the comfort of camp life's regimen. The trainers thrashed me on the pads — thinking I'd been screwing all night — but I just flew through it. A couple of days later it was time to go. There wasn't much ceremony or emotion. I just did the rounds and walked out, but not before offering particular thanks to the guy who had destroyed me and then helped make me even stronger: Jomhod. I will always be proud, never again ashamed, to say I lost to that man. He was a giant in so many ways.

I had expected a fight in Japan. What I got was a revelation of stunning clarity. While the bout prior to mine was in progress I got gloved, donned my robe and walked out into the hallway to wait. Samart was already there, ready to go. Our eyes met and he gave me a wink. This guy seemed to have a lot in common with Jomhod, who'd destroyed me with kicks in my last fight — he was a big-kicking, tough Thai. Fear and panic started to hit me as they did against Jomhod. But I moved to check them. And this thought process started to unravel. *What is it that I fear? All these things that might happen. I'm fearing products of my imagination, not aspects of reality. My fear is based on speculation. My fear is not real. So what the fuck am I scared of? What is real is that I've done all this training, I've busted my arse and I feel like I've been to hell and back to be ready for this fight. And here I am sitting here, building up this guy to be some kind of monster. I am acting like a little boy who's scared of the dark, who's convinced a bogeyman lurks in the closet.*

And this revelation just clicked: *There is nothing to be afraid of.*

But then another thought struck me: *If I'm creating my fear and it's so full-on that it can actually stop me from performing — it can stop me from doing* anything *— then how can I make it work for me rather than against me? How can I turn that into fuel? How can I make fear my friend? Okay, so what is this thing that happens to me when I'm scared? My heart starts pumping; I get this adrenaline rush. So that means my body is starting to prepare itself for war. It's producing endorphins, natural painkillers, so I don't feel pain and can't be distracted by it during battle. I know it's only after the fight, when I will no longer have such feelings, that the pain starts. So this fear is actually a good thing, it's my friend; it's preparing me to go to war. So I don't fear this bloke, because he can't hurt me, because my fear is going to protect me.*

So I got in the ring and I looked at Samart with this massive smile on my face and he came out and hit me with three of the hardest chopping kicks to my leg I've ever felt in my life. And I just smiled at him again. We ended up going the distance, but I thought

I'd had the better of him — I dropped him in the third round, for starters. The judges, however, ruled it a draw. I was pissed off, sure, but the fight was not the point. The point was what had happened before I stepped into the ring. At that moment I jumped a massive psychological hurdle many fighters never clear: I'd discovered that fear was a resource to be harnessed. To try to attain fearlessness, I realised, was the misguided pursuit of a myth.

# XIV

## The Need For Speed

Gaining insight doesn't mean getting wise. The difference is application: what you do with what you've gleaned. Wisdom is about having the will to live by what you know to be true. For me, at that stage, wisdom was about as here and now as Confucius himself. I was a young man charging, picking up new weapons and tools on the run. I was in a hurry to prove myself, not improve myself. And if I ever gave the matter thought, I would have concluded that they were one and the same thing.

I thrived on what elevated me. Everything I acquired on my first lone venture into the world I fed to my ego like red meat. All that I'd experienced and endured, all my triumphs of mind and body, served to inflate and bolster me. And my epiphany regarding fear ended up being just another gizmo for my utility belt. The Superhero-me was back, new and improved.

Despite the Samart fight being judged a draw, I felt I was the undisputed victor. This was a huge psychological boost: I'd obliterated my fear that I was inferior to Thais; I'd slain the monster that, in the form of Jomhod, had crippled me. I was the master again, no longer the mastered. I returned to Australia not humble and enlightened but ten feet tall and bulletproof. I had cash and the promise of more from the Japanese promoters who thought I was red hot. I was going to buy a house, a car; I was going to get loaded and get into my music; I was going to train hard and win myself the world title. Everything was on track and mine to seize. I came home swinging from vines. Lord of the jungle, I was. The ego had landed.

I couldn't wait to get out of home and into my own place. Leah and I bought a small townhouse in Calamvale, a southern suburb of Brisbane, and revelled in our new-found independence. We'd been living under Mum and Dad's thumb — I mean, roof — for a couple of years and were glad to be free at last of their control. We'd copped it on two fronts. Dad had always been so strict about me, and hence us, going out. The source of his concern arose out of him being part-father, part-trainer. He would freak if he found out I'd been to a rave in the lead-up to a fight. And because he knew most of the bouncers in Brisbane, there was no hiding from the guy.

One time close to a fight, Leah and I went to the Madonna concert saying we'd be home straight afterwards, but we left halfway through to go to a rave. Dad was all over it and gave me a bollocking the next day. He had the city wired. Mum, on the other hand, was simply overprotective. When we were young we were rarely allowed to visit friends, let alone stay over, and in my late teens she'd bar me from going here or there or else demand to know exactly where we'd be at any tick of the clock. She'd say, 'It's not you I'm worried about, it's other people.'

Bit late for that, I'm afraid, Mum.

From the moment we moved into our house, Leah and I began to really think about what it meant to be engaged. There had been nothing auspicious to date about the whole deal. Even the party her parents eventually threw seemed to lack real significance — we were simply a young couple, boyfriend and girlfriend, yet the ring gave the relationship weight and a vague momentum. Out by ourselves now, we both felt a dawning sense of commitment to which we responded differently. Leah, God bless her, took up her role of future wife with all the good, unblinking will of a young girl in love. She quickly shouldered responsibilities as light but necessary loads. She had a job working full time doing nails with Mum; she kept tabs on the mortgage and the bills. She stood up to be counted. This was it for her: we were, for all money, a married couple. I wouldn't have ever had her think otherwise but, truthfully, I had no idea about our future. Although I needed her more than ever, my predominant feeling after leaving home was that I'd escaped prison and I simply wanted to enjoy the luxury of my liberty. Above all else, I wanted to indulge in nothing deeper nor more responsible than doing whatever the hell I liked.

We had a great thing going for a while. We'd be out at clubs every weekend, and soon a new circle of friends formed. Sounds pretty neat, but the truth is that I recall the person I was then with a mix of shame and embarrassment. I was a complete wanker. As I've said, I came back from overseas with head and shoulders squarely lodged up my own sunrise. I couldn't throw enough of me out there. In closer circles, I was fun but loud — I had to be seen and heard. If any onlooker had a problem with that then they had me as their problem. In a crowd I'd radiate a vibe of latent ferocity. Maybe, 'radiate' is not the word. I didn't swagger about like some chesty ape — I was civil and chilled. But I was a double act. Sit down and have a drink with me in a bar and you'd barely meet my eyes. I would be scanning the room constantly to catch any guy who so much as glanced at me. I'd fire my gaze specifically at men who were overtly proud of their physicality. Any guy who looked like he thought he was half hard copped my glare with both barrels. I'd just keep looking his way until he noticed. Then I'd lock on, and it was as though I had him by the throat.

I wanted these blokes to tacitly acknowledge me and my superiority. I liked to see them cower, yet I itched for them to cross me. And if they did, my response was swift and violent: I'd smash them without breaking stride. No big scene, just some wannabe tough guy hitting the ground, his ego gelded. I'd actually walk into a venue and make a point of scanning all the bouncers. A couple of bourbons would get my juices going and I'd do the rounds, staring them down like some surly hood in a subway carriage. *You looking at me?* That kind of shit. My friends would usually be none the wiser. I mean, I was discreet. But sometimes I'd work myself into such a state that I'd be absolutely beside myself with bridled rage and wreck everyone's night. One time about fifty of us went to a steakhouse for someone's birthday. I walked down the stairs to the lower section holding a drink and this bouncer, a really nice bloke, said to me, 'Paul, you can't take your drink through, mate.' That was all. Knew me by name and was as polite and reasonable as can be. I glared at him, seething. Who did he think he was talking to? *Right*, I thought, *you're going to wear this fucking glass in your face.* But I checked myself and, after giving him the evil eye, I turned and walked back upstairs.

'What's wrong?' asked Leah with knowing concern when I joined her — she could so easily tell when I was on the brink of exploding and she'd make every effort to defuse me. But it was rarely of any use. After we got home that night I told her I had to go to the 7-Eleven. I drove down, hung around, picked some guys and smashed their heads in. Then I drove home, satiated, and Leah was none the wiser. I'd gotten my twisted little fix of brutality.

As surprising as it may seem now, I did have friends. And they were good people. I wasn't a complete tosser to everyone, otherwise I'd have been no more welcome among the ravers than a belligerent skinhead. I was a better person for being in the mellowed confines of the rave scene. In the absence of common boozy bravado, my aggro was mostly holstered. I got on fine with a lot of people, and among them was where I felt safest and most relaxed, as opposed to being in bed alone. I was not without humour and, dare I say, charisma. When I was out, everyone knew who I was. Promoters of parties came up and introduced themselves. Leah and I never had to wait in line or pay for tickets. It was all very cool. Everyone wanted to give me stuff, by which I mean drugs. I was in with the innest crowd. I had my Colgate ring of confidence, I could dress with style and I didn't come across as some dipstick pug — I didn't spit my words out in noxious gobs, nor sound like someone had lodged a Q-tip up my nose and another in my brain. I could get down with these people. I could relate to them, no problemo.

I met a heap of deejays and loved talking music with them. I really wanted to spin records, and learning how became a real mission. I'd set up my two decks in my house and was stuffing around on them any chance I could get, but I began to really improve after I became friends with one of the best deejays on the scene at the time — DJ Angus. This guy was an awesome scratcher and he taught me a lot about the basics of mixing and also how to use three decks instead of two. I promptly went out and bought myself a third deck.

Leah and I had our days mapped out: she got up and went to work with Mum, and I'd get up and go to the gym. Then I'd come home and spend all day in my room spinning records. Leah didn't really embrace the deejaying at all. She didn't get it. 'What's this you're getting into?' she'd say, as though I'd taken to building little ships in bottles. But I loved it. For the first time in my life I felt I had balance. I could train, really throw everything into that, then go home and immerse myself in my music. It was awesome fun, a real escape, and so relaxing. Once a week I'd head down to Central Station Records to check out new stock. There weren't a whole lot of genres. These days you've got deep house, handbag house, Goa trance, Euro trance and so on. Back then you could split dance music into house and hardcore. Then trance started to come on. The vinyl I liked best came from Dutch labels like Rotterdam Records. These were really hard-driving tracks — kind of like the *doof, doof, doof, doof, doof* beats you hear pounding out of hotted-up cars laden with monobrowed try-hards.

Three months after coming home I was back in Japan. I fought a Belgian called Petsetas Spiridon in a good fight. I knocked him down in the last round and won by decision. The result pushed me close to the top of the world rankings. The world title shot was now just one fight away and everything was going sweet. I was doing things my way. I had fashioned a lifestyle to my liking and I was still fit, hard and strong enough to beat the best kickboxers in the world. I had a couple of fights in Australia but these just kept me active, sharp and hungry.

I can't say when, exactly, but somewhere along the line I began to take speed on a daily basis. It kind of crept up on me. For the most part drugs were still peripheral to my lifestyle. It was use, as they say, not abuse. I'd do the odd E at parties plus a bit of speed here and there, and I'd smoke a bit of weed when I got home. All quite innocent and unremarkable. But the goey was becoming part of my routine. When I came home from training I'd neck some speed and head into my room, and I'd be rushing off my tits while I spun away on the decks. I'd pour the powder into a cup of coffee or else swallow speed bombs, where you wrap the speed up in a small piece of tissue or toilet paper. I liked the way this drug just accentuated real time, turned the present into an intense moment. I became so alert. There was such urgent clarity to the high it was perfect for deejaying: I could stay in control of the records while enjoying ramped-up pleasure from the music.

Leah had no idea I was doing goey every day. This was one of the first things I concealed from her. She tried to be the voice of reason in our relationship, making valiant but unsuccessful attempts to keep our partying in check. She'd say from time to time, 'Let's not go out tonight', and I'd be like, 'What? You've got to be kidding! I'm not about to stay at home and watch a video.' I wasn't giving up fighting or clubbing — I could keep doing both. No worries. It was all totally under control. My self-deception had begun.

Getting into dealing was a practical move: it kept my supply of speed steady and free. I quickly went from scoring grams to quarter-ounces because I could divvy up quarters into grams, on-sell a few and recoup my outlay. As my consumption increased I stepped up to half-ounces. This was the kind of liberty I was talking about enjoying — having drugs around the house without worring about Mum or Dad stumbling across them. Not that Leah knew quite how much I was going through. As far as she was concerned, I had only a modest little habit and trade. Which was true ... for a little while.

I still trained with Dad but I was glad for the distance between us in more ways than one. My parents' relationship was breaking down and, together, they were hell to be around. Since Dad's failed treasure hunt in Zurich Mum had begun standing up to him, which didn't go down too well. I was so glad to be out of their house — I had a little static-free zone all of my own. Once training was done and I could escape Dad going on about Mum, I'd head back to my cave, get some goey into me and start playing my music. Everything else, the outside world, just ceased to exist. There was some real purpose to this — these stints were practice. I knew I wanted to get good, and from my years of training as a fighter I knew that the only way to do that was to put in a lot of time and effort. I'd hole myself up and spin records for eight or nine hours straight. Day in, day out. I'd attempt to figure out the mixes of deejays I liked and, just like my work on the bags, I wouldn't stop until I got them right. I knew how to get good, all right. I had to program myself — and before that could happen, I had to believe I could be programmed.

I played my first gig on New Year's Eve 1993. Angus got me an early slot at a party and I played for nobody — barely a soul had arrived. I didn't care; I was into it. A week later I was scheduled to fight in Japan again. This was the world title eliminator — the winner earnt a shot against the world champion. I was one step closer to that dream I'd had so many years earlier.

I almost never got there.

My speed dealing had, well, expanded; I kind of went pro. I was buying ounces or multiples thereof. The driving demand was purely my own, the profit entirely for my own consumption. It got to the stage where I had two sources and I'd play one against the other. The key was that I was always able to get the speed on tick, meaning, take delivery of the drugs now, pay later. The way grams were priced, I'd have to sell 60 per cent of an ounce (28 grams) to cover the full purchase cost. That left me with 40 per cent to eat myself and zero cash profit, which was fine. Problem was, I began to eat more than that 40 per cent, so I'd be left with less to sell and end up short to pay my source. So I'd go to my other source, get more gear on tick, and try to sell more than 60 per cent to make good my outstanding debt. It was very leaky accounting. In theory it was a workable system; in reality it became a mess of thinning trust that kept me in speed but always owing, and my sources financially exposed and agitated.

Two days before my flight to Tokyo, I figured I'd make some easy spending money. I planned a deal that would be a simple, quick and clean exchange. Basically, I was just playing driver. I had sourced 4 ounces of pure speed on tick and I had a buyer waiting.

He'd pay me, I'd pay my source and I'd walk away five grand richer. Five thousand for fifteen minutes' work — not bad, huh? How did I do it? The source was my contact. Back then there were a few about, because speed was such easy money. If you had the lab gear and chemical know-how you could produce — or cook — pounds of the stuff. At up to ten grand an ounce, that's a fat little earner. Offloading the gear was often the hard part if you didn't have all your contacts in place.

I met cooks by word of mouth. There were all sorts: truck drivers, bikies, even opportunistic propeller-heads fresh out of our fine university chemistry labs. On this occasion, I knew a cook ready to sell and I had an eager buyer, a dealer I knew. This dealer could buy my ounces for five grand more than I had paid because he was looking to sell street ounces. He'd cut the pure with glucose, increase the volume and sell his street ounces for a tidy profit. The guy who bought the street ounce would do the same — cut it and so turn an ounce into an ounce and a half, and flog it by the gram. But I wasn't getting involved in all that trickle-down shit; all I had to do was play pizza boy. Too easy. I thought I'd get the deal done before lunch, head home and no one — meaning, Leah — would be any the wiser.

Once I'd picked up the gear, I stuffed it down my pants and drove off. No sooner had I left, though, than this unmarked police car came flying up and drew alongside me. I was so stunned that all I could do was look straight ahead as if they would just go away if I wished hard enough. Only my eyes moved, flashing down to the dash as I tried to think how the hell I'd caught their eye — speed wise, as in kilometres per hour, I was sure I'd been a model citizen. What the fuck was going on?! I'd been set up! *I'm fucked! I'm fucked!* I had to try so hard to keep it together. I attempted to relax my face as I stared oh-so-attentively at the road ahead that I hadn't noticed the souped-up V8 that had vroomed up beside me to hover there inquisitively. Nor could my admirable focus on the road be broken by a dude in a suit leaning so far out of his car that he almost had his head through my window, screaming 'Pull over, driver! Now! Hey! I said, pull over!' I snapped a glance at him. 'Stop the car!' he said. I squeezed a little puzzlement into my face before turning back. I could hear him scream, 'Hey! Pull over! Right now!'

*Sure, whatever you say, officer. I'll pull over. Just after we're off this bridge … Because my concern — apart from the icy torrents of dread and panic gushing through me, not to mention my frantic nerves or the visions of me being arrested and thrown in jail, of me throwing my whole career and life away for a bunch of stupid fucking powder, of my father coming at me in five different moods to kill — is that there is no side lane to pull into. We were on a bridge. So best I keep on driving.*

I made feeble attempts to communicate this in sign language — you know, shrugs and what-can-I-do? gestures. Like, 'It's best if I stop up ahead where it would be safer for all concerned, officer.'

The cop wigged out totally, as though I was blatantly defying him. Funny that. 'Hey!' he shouted. 'Didn't you hear what I said? Stop the car! Now!' And with that the driver surged ahead and jagged in front of me to cut me off. I hit the anchors hard and sat there not knowing what the hell to do. I was gutted. My flesh was stone cold. I was gone. Busted. Four ounces of pure speed — a six-figure street value the newspaper hacks would crow about under my mugshot. No first-timer let-offs in court for that, my friend. I was as good as in jail.

The cop jumped out of the car, still screaming at me. I went to get out and he slammed my door shut. I was thinking, *He's a bit full-on, isn't he? That's a bit over the top.* I began to think of my career: I was about to fight for a shot at the world title and here I was with enough speed to keep Brisbane up all night in my pants, facing an irate cop with what seemed to be heavy retribution on his mind. I figured the only thing I could do was to clamber out the passenger door, whack him and jump off the bridge. It didn't matter if the fall broke my legs — I was as good as dead anyway. Dad would see to that.

But the cop started yelling about the fact that he'd followed me for 2 kilometres, which was right about where I picked up the gear. How the fuck did he know? Then he's like, 'Do you know why we've pulled you over?' 'Well, yeah,' I said, 'it's pretty obvious.' 'Well, if it's so obvious, why don't you do something about it?' I looked at him. He had me stumped. 'Why don't you put the fucking thing on?' he screamed. 'What are you talking about?' I said. 'Are you patronising me, kid?' I'm thinking, *Kid? He's barely a year older than me.* Then he spelt it out: 'Put your bloody seat belt on!' I just looked at him, unconvinced he was for real, that any of this was for real. However, to my amazement, it was. I slowly reached for the seat belt and buckled up. Seeing me strapped in seemed to calm him down, and he backed away righteously like he'd saved me from all manner of sin. That had to be the guy's first day on the job in plain clothes, I'd bet all the drugs I had in my shorts on it.

I flew off to Tokyo cashed up and eager to fight a Dutch guy called Andre Masseurs. He'd never been stopped before, let alone knocked out, and I let him know in no uncertain terms what it felt like. He barely survived the first round after I dropped him twice — first with a right uppercut–left hook combination and then with an elbow. At the start of the second he came flying out of his corner and had me on the ropes. I unloaded a left hook so sweet it felt like a light tap but it struck Masseurs so hard that his brain switched off and he collapsed to the canvas. The last obstacle to my world title shot lay in a heap at my feet, waking up lost.

# XV

## Champion In Name Only

Be careful what you wish for. Damn lame, smug cliché, if you ask me — you only ever really get it in hindsight, after you've been slapped by the unforeseen consequences of your ambition. I get it, though — it's about having a really honest assessment of your motives; about being humble and aware. Well, I'd spent the past six years driven by one desire: to win a world title. What inherent folly in that should I have seen and been wary of?

The idea that there could be a downside to becoming world champion was absurd. That belt was going to be the crowning glory of my life, my springboard to greatness. It would make me the happiest man on the planet. The fitting reward for all my toil would be profound satisfaction, pride and self-respect, not to mention enough money to set me up for life. My dream was soaked in the vain mist of a fresh and great conquest — it fairly zinged with the dizzy prosperity of a massive lottery win and there was also something else in there that was important and soothing, some reassurance that everything from that point on would be better. I felt painless in that dream. I felt different. Validated. Fulfilled. In that dream, the world title brought the gift of change, the beginning of my new life. In reality, it proved to be the beginning of my end. Tell me how I could have seen that fucking truck coming.

I was back in Tokyo, the host of my rising star. My office, if you like. I was not what you'd call famous there, but I was somebody. One time I was bailed up by ten or so people because some guy recognised me from the fight magazine he was reading at a newsstand. He dashed off and returned with a few mates, then other people joined the queue, not knowing who on earth I was but thinking they'd better get my signature anyway. But that was a rare event. I never claimed to be 'big in Japan'.

However, kickboxing was a big enough deal in Japan to make the fuss — TV cameras, press conferences, interviews, promotional appearances — contrast sharply against the below-the-radar profile I had in Australia. Previously I'd fought in Korakuen Hall as the main event in front of about 10 000 people. For the world title I was part of a bigger card, and a few belts were on the line, so it would be televised across Japan. Winston Walker's super middleweight title was the one I was after. I'd never ranked him among the greats like Jomhod but he'd beaten a very well-respected Thai to win his title and he hadn't lost in three years. He was a worthy champion. That was about the best I could say.

I didn't arrive in Japan alone, of course. Dad and Nathan came to man my corner. Dad, though, had a few things on his mind — like a failing marriage and business — and he was busying himself more and more with these spurious bodyguard missions with his commodities cowboys. Also, like many trainers whose fighter has had sustained success, he'd begun to get complacent, resting on our laurels and thinking his boy was invincible. I'd taken to running my own race, overseeing my own training. I'd never really needed anyone to push me as I'd always had a very strong work ethic. And after my experience in Thailand, I knew how to train very hard and never went easy on myself.

I was majorly pissed off with Dad because, no matter what negatives there were, we'd worked together to get to this point. And now here I was about to fight for the world title and he's gone mentally AWOL. I was, like, *What's going on here? You're losing the plot. You're just not here. Get a fucking grip!* Not that I said any such thing. The time for that would come a few years down the track.

Let me be clear: I did not get to that point alone. Despite his recent lack of focus, my father deserves a lot of the credit for me reaching it. Yes, he had doubted me along the way, and more than once. But he also put so much time into teaching me, training me and managing my career, I'll never deny that he made me a worthy contender for a world title. He inspired me and helped me and encouraged me and believed in me. Sometimes when he conveyed advice, speaking in that soft voice bearing good, firm knowledge, I could almost forget he possessed such destructive and hurtful capabilities.

My fondest memories of him are all in the context of fighting. They're not exactly warm and fuzzy. The frosted slow-mo montage of our Mentos moments, our 'Love You, son/Love you, Dad' exchanges, our shared belly laughs and our tender tears would barely last a sip of Sprite. No, the memories are more to do with the appreciation of sharing something of real value with him. We had an amazing time. I travelled the world with Dad and there were times when we got along as mates more than as father and son. I had a dream and we set about achieving it together. That's pretty rare and it will remain special to me until the day I die. But it was rough along the way as well, as I've already pointed out. Our relationship was always polluted by hate and resentment. I'm done trying to describe it. It was just real. It was what it was. My father, his son.

Nathan, meanwhile, wasn't kickboxing any more. He was partying hard and barely training, just running the gym. He looked in okay shape, but he wasn't. I'm not exactly sure what he was into; I do know that it was leading nowhere fast. He was doing some stupid stuff, much of it illegal. He wasn't blessed with a whole lot of common sense, I have to say. I know, I know — as if I can talk. Truth is, though, I definitely thought things through more. Nathan wouldn't think anything through. The stubborn kid became a bull-headed young man, a repeat offender of bad moves. He seemed to think he could push his luck for ever. Like his ongoing refusal when we were younger to keep his mouth shut, work his way around Dad and save himself a hiding, Nathan never took stock of signposts, even if they were dead ahead and brightly lit — he just ran right over them.

Nathan wielded a big stick around Brisbane as much as I did, because he was a Briggs and a kickboxer, and he was huge. That not only bought him a lot of kudos — it cut him a lot of slack for some of the daft shit he got up to. But Nathan's life was Nathan's life. He kind of dwelled on the edge of mine, never too far away yet never close. That kind of sums us up. I don't think he was ever living any dream through me — he has always been respectful of what I achieve. While he was getting sidetracked, though, I was making progress. He was always a kickboxer to other people and they compared us as though his career was still active. Three years before, he had seemed destined to go all the way. And now, in Tokyo, I had a shot at a belt and he wasn't following in my footsteps; he wasn't even on the same path. He was teaching at the gym, and I'd flown him over to be in my corner. It was enough for him being a professional kickboxer in name only. All the same, Nathan, my brother, was always in my corner, and that meant many things, both sad and valued.

I was in excellent shape for this fight. I'd put aside every distraction — meaning clubbing and drugs — to train, keeping music as a healthy outlet. By the time I hit Japan I was taut on the chain, busting to rip this Winston Walker to pieces. I met him a few days before the bout in the offices of All Japan Kickboxing. They'd just brought him off the plane and were waiting to take him to his hotel. We got to talking and he was surprised to learn I'd knocked out Taiei Kin, who was a very big name. I was surprised Walker hadn't done his homework. 'Yeah,' I said, 'I knocked him out in the first round.' Walker's eyes widened. I said that there was a tape of the fight floating around the office if he wanted to check it out. 'Sure,' he said.

That was the worst thing he could have done. He sat down and watched me smash Taiei Kin cold. And I watched Walker sink into his chair. The tape didn't take long, and when it was done, Walker stood up, looked at me and said, 'Yeah, good fight.' I said, 'Yeah it was, wasn't it?' I was looking right through him. I was so onto him. It was like, *I can smell your fear*. He was scared. Now, being scared is one thing, but having your opponent know you're scared and making you aware that he knows is a whole new world of fear. You are naked before God — or the devil. Walker was beaten then and there. To make matters worse, he came to watch me train before the fight and, like I said, I was in devastating form. That was all he needed: he knew he didn't stand a chance.

And that's the way he fought. Or, should I say, didn't fight. In the Tokyo Dome, before a crowd of around 20 000, he made it one of the lamest fights I'd ever taken part in. I got the better of him for five lacklustre rounds — but that's like saying I got the better of a mannequin. Walker's mission from the start was only survival, to avoid getting knocked out. He went straight on the defensive and remained there. Not once did he take the fight to me. Not once did he push me or offer stern resistance to draw out my strengths. Not once did he test me and force me to rise. He covered up and I simply amassed points to win a world title. It was like raking up leaves.

I won't say I wasn't happy to win, because I was. The joy did not strike very deeply, though. In the change rooms afterwards, my greatest achievement began to feel hollow. I didn't feel I'd earnt the belt. I'd been passed the parcel. I'd made no definitive statement in that ring. There was no bloody coup, no storming of the palace, no seizing of the throne. The fucker had just turned belly up without firing a decent shot.

I was furious with him.

He was supposed to be a world champion, a warrior, and he didn't even fight. I'd built up all these expectations for years, dreaming about being world champion. What was meant to be heroic turned out to be prosaic. I didn't feel like the best fighter on the planet. To be denied even a whiff of that was humiliating.

Why did it matter so much? Because I'd put such great store in what I'd demonstrate in winning. The deep issues I couldn't define were supposed to be dispelled in one fell swoop. And the truth was, I still didn't fully believe in myself. For all my front. For me, what mattered was what others believed and saw — that's what made me. I wanted them to be in awe of how good I was. I'd expected to show the world my might. This was supposed to be my biggest ever fuck-you moment. *Fuck you, Dad, for telling me I wasn't a fighter. Fuck you, all you wankers who scoffed at my dream. Fuck you, Thailand, if you think only your boys rule. And fuck you, Winston Walker, if you think you can keep that title from me.* But the bastard never even tried. He told me at the bar that night that he had just wanted to last the distance, that he had been determined, above everything else, not to become another KO on the record of a nineteen-year-old kid. I was stunned. *What about defending your title?* Did I say this guy was a worthy champion? Seems I oversold him.

Now I was world champion and I felt no different. All these disturbing feelings deep inside of me remained; there was no wondrous transformation. I felt so disillusioned. I celebrated my victory with everyone but, deep down, the rot I thought I would be cleansed of only began to fester more. After the press conference and all the palaver that went on, I got back to my room and sat down with the world title belt in my lap. I felt like a hoax. I mean, my dream had materialised — and it had turned out to be some cheap counterfeit. If my greatest achievement felt like nothing to me, what did that say about my life spent pursuing it? Was my existence pointless? I felt lost, and cursed the whole fucking pathetic outcome.

Despite the strength of my reaction, I was never going to let anyone in on my doubt and confusion. I put on a convincing act — I was a picture of self-satisfaction. I soaked up the glory again and allowed my ego to gorge. Since I'd been fighting in Japan, I'd been getting bigger and bolder, rougher and tougher. Even before the world title, my ego needed its own postcode. But when I became world champion and something more substantial failed to appear, I looked into myself and found that my ego was just about all I had. It struck me as a bad joke: *So, this is it, huh? Well, in that case, fuck it. If that's my reward, if that's how skin deep it all is, then so be it — let's rock 'n' roll. I'll dwell in the shallows and ignore the depths.*

I began acting like I was invincible all over again, and pretty soon I felt that way. I was back to that rabid, angry, fuck-you-all kid in the tough-man contests, but now I had a huge ego to go with it. I strutted my stuff. I, Paul 'Hurricane' Briggs, was the champion of the world. I lapped up and fanned the praise.

And you know what? The ego trip worked. It helped me feel good. Sure, at some level I was aware I'd made a choice of mind and ignored my heart. But my decision had been made: this was how I was going to cope, to shield my emptiness. I didn't choose to face anything, and I didn't care. I chose to sidestep whatever was eating at me and revel in a falsehood — the cult of me. I guess I shouldn't be too harsh on myself, because back then I simply didn't have the tools, the map, the awareness to address, or even try to identify, my darker forces. I didn't know what I was dealing with. I figured that the bleak shadow across my soul was bound to be my lifelong companion. The best I could do — the only thing I knew to do — was to shun it. So I left my grim little cave and walked onto a bright stage, where everyone, including myself, thought I was really something. Real shit hot.

Brisbane was always a good place to land for a pistol like me. The rave scene was set to go ballistic, courtesy of this guy called Ben who I'd met about six months earlier in a club. Nathan came up with Ben, who's no lightweight, tucked under one arm and introduced us. We were the same age and got on okay, but didn't really get to know each other. When I returned after my title win, though, Ben was preparing to shake things up. He'd come to Australia from Holland and knew exactly what was going down in Europe. He was, like, 'You guys reckon this is the rave scene? You're kidding me. I'll show you the rave scene.' And he began organising a rave of unprecedented scale. Before he came along, a crowd of 2000 was considered huge. This Dutchie went way supersized. He based his party out of one of the Brunswick Street clubs, closed off the surrounding streets to gain more leg room and set up decks inside and out. In the lead-up he printed fliers saying that these wicked Dutch deejays were coming to Brisbane and he did heaps of merchandising. He made sure the stores were carrying the records these guys were putting out so we all got a taste of this awesome music and then — *bang* — the party's on, the deejays are here and my friends and I all have butterflies in our stomachs in anticipation of the scale of the rave, the light show, these Dutchies playing live, the drugs, the whole box and dice. And we got there and 5000 people have turned up, these dudes from Holland are playing this unbelievable hardcore and everyone's wide-eyed and pilling, going, 'Faaaark, how awesome is this?' I think the first rave was called Thunderdome, then came Thunderdome II, then Hellraiser. All in Fortitude Valley. Single-handedly, Ben took Brisbane raves to a whole new level.

I quickly resumed my former lifestyle. The only difference was that I firmly believed I was invincible: I figured I could indulge in the partying more without it impacting on my fighting. I mean, the fact was I'd become a world champion while being a recreational drug user. So drugs had lost all their menace — from my experience, they were part of having fun. I no longer had any notion that they were the portals to hell posing as the gates of heaven. The idea that you could take one pill and become an addict was laughable. Absolute crock of shit. I had it sussed; everything was under control. There was nothing wrong with what I was doing. I was strong enough to train hard and party hard. And that's exactly what I did. I opened the throttle on my drug intake. I'd be out a couple of times a week necking a few pills each time.

As if that wasn't enough, the world title took my celebrity to a new level: I had prestige. My rave scene friends loved it — I mean, I'd been a welcome character among them before, but now even they shone a little awe on me. I'd always been superfit and dedicated to my fighting — they'd seen that. They'd seen me rock up to recovery parties having not attended the previous night's rave. I'd be fresh from a good night's sleep after a hard day's training, and I'd just hang out and listen to the postmortems of their sleepless, E-fuelled night. It was nice, and then I'd get up and leave them. They knew how committed I was and respected me for it. But as the world champion, I was a made guy. *World champion*. It's amazing what doors those words open, and what faults are eclipsed by their gleam.

It was a rare bouncer who didn't know me now, who didn't speak to me politely and respectfully, just as they did to my old man. My achievement as a fighter was so pleasing to everyone because I was so young, clean-cut and with it, so unlike the misshapen, hard-faced men with harder luck who seemed doomed to populate the ring like convicts in a hulk. I could mop the floor with such men — me, this rising star, barely of legal drinking age yet a kickboxing world champion. Exactly what lay ahead was, I began to realise, something far less definitive than what I'd just achieved. Sure, the idea now was for me to defend my title, draw the crowds, keep winning and keep making money.

But that next fight didn't come up. Well, it was a long time coming, and a while before it materialised I began to sense the finality in reaching my lifelong goal at nineteen. *Is that it?* I asked myself. I'd climbed my Everest. I'd got my tattoo to mark the occasion — an 'H' for 'Hurricane' on my right shoulder. I considered myself a man now. I was the champ; my fight name was now my prime identity. All these things had come to be but suddenly purpose and direction were seriously lacking.

As it turned out, I wouldn't fight again for many months, which left plenty of time to practise getting off my face. But if, after much time had slid by uneventfully, someone had said to me knowingly, 'Be careful what you wish for, eh, Paul?' I would have known exactly what they meant. And I probably would have smashed them — for all my new understanding, the bearer of such irritating wisdom would have pissed me off no end. I wanted the hollowness and treachery of my victory known only to myself. That was my miserable little secret.

# XVI

## *High Roller*

When I'd signed with All Japan Promotions, the sums had looked pretty sweet. My payment per fight, at US$5000, was about A$10 000 at the time. And by the rate I was going through my opponents, I figured I was looking at 80 to 90 grand a year. Not bad for a lad just shy of his twenties. After my world title win, though, those expectations turned out to be the stuff of fantasy. Instead of the door of opportunity being flung open, it slowly swung shut on me. I never defended my title in Japan, nor earnt another cent from those guys. Over the following year and beyond, they failed to put together a single bout for me. Couldn't find anyone in Japan who'd fight me, they said. Then when a fight in Tokyo did begin to take shape, it fell through at the last minute. The same thing happened twice with fights in Holland. It was absurd: the world title was supposed to be a breakthrough, and here I was shelved and fading, becoming as vital as old flour. I couldn't free myself from the contract and sign with another promoter, either. I was theirs to do with me what they pleased, which was two-fifths of fuck-all.

So, whether I liked it or not, fighting assumed a lesser role in my life. I never stopped going to the gym and kicking pads — my work ethic remained strong, even though I was training for fights than never materialised. But, given that I'd started off disappointed with my great success, a long period of inactivity could only make things worse. It wasn't entirely bad, though, because I was free to make up the party time I'd missed for the sake of my fighting career. And, slowly but surely, the drugs began to erode my motivation and inspiration.

For a good while I could dine out on my world champion status but that was a steadily fading sidebar of yesterday's news. One of the first fights I could get after the world title was an eight-man tough-man elimination tournament in Melbourne. It loomed as an easy ten grand for me; I threw myself into training anyway. The partying stopped completely. This was my thing now: I could switch from one track to the other and resume with equal intensity. But I lost my fight and was eliminated. I know it's easy to say now that I shouldn't have, but the result was at best an upset, at worst a rip-off.

When looking for answers for my poor performance, Dad didn't reach for a jar of perspective — he tore shreds off me, scalding me with his new-found belief in my complete ineptitude. It was chastening stuff, all the more because deep down I knew he was right. Where my head was at was not good at all; I had no business being in the ring.

Focus is the essence of fighting. Not heart. Not strength or stamina. Everything follows the mind. What matters most is how successfully you can de-clutter your head space — clear the attic — to leave only the imperatives of battle. Over the previous eighteen months or so I'd been going to Japan to fight the world's best kickboxers, and I'd demolished them. Since Samart — my first fight after Thailand — the only guy who'd gone the distance with me was Walker, and he'd only managed that by locking himself in a cab and paying the driver to do laps of the ring. Those results were not fortuitous; they were acts of mindful annihilation.

At home in Australia, with my personal funk deepening, my drug intake rising and my ring time shrinking, I was in the throes of an unhealthy flux. Part of the problem was that, in my misguided way, I was enjoying myself. I had the freedom to do what I wanted, and getting off my chops was a key part of that liberty. Still, I was always training, getting myself into superb physical shape. But that's not enough for the ring. I was always out doing drugs so, no matter how fit I was, I was not all there.

And a fighter is never at 100 per cent without clarity of mind. When the going gets hard, you can't just go *grrrr!*, switch on and pocket yourself in the zone. The zone? Where's the zone? The zone's in some club at three in the morning zooming off your dial amid a sea of fit chicks going 'Woo-hoo'. The body is the vehicle; the mind is the control tower. I had to learn what controls what.

I used to be able to get into the ring and unleash my anger like a pack of hounds, and I'd be fit enough to last the manic chase. But you can't sustain a fighting career on anger or aggression, on emotion. When Kostya Tszyu has called to wish me luck before a fight, the only thing he has said by way of advice is, 'Keep your emotions in check.' Your mind determines the state of your body and emotions determine the state of your mind. Emotions can rule your life in any way they see fit, if you let them — but the choice is yours, not theirs. You can be their slave or their master. Who or what is in control?

A mind given wholly to the very essence of your being is the right mind for battle. For all intents and purposes, fighting is a matter of life and death. Fighting is not a game; it's not something you play at. It samples our primitive struggle for existence. What does a man do, what can he do, when he is cornered and attacked? And how can a man prevail over another desperate, intelligent creature he craves as a meal? Wits. Strategy. Patience. Focus. All mental things. That's what fighting comes down to: the mind. Everything else is secondary. In some fighs I was so not there mentally, I'd find myself jolted by a brutal reality check. It was like I'd been dragged from the table at a formal dinner party, thrown into a pool and ordered to swim laps in record time. *Huh? What?* In the ring, if some guy's coming at you with your destruction in mind and you're not ready for it, you're in for a major psychological shock. The traumatic effects can impair a man permanently. Take George Foreman after Muhammad Ali, Mike Tyson after James 'Buster' Douglas. Head cases. They were shot. Mental laxity in the ring invites utter ruin. A fighter knows he should quit when his head goes, not his body. But that's why so many true fighters quit too late or end their careers as losers — their minds just won't give up.

I needed to stay active to convince myself I was still a fighter. To simply train and train is fine for a while but eventually it becomes like pacing a cell: you might be keeping everything in working order, but it's no substitute for stretching your legs in daylight. As one fight after another fell through, I was climbing the walls. So when I got the opportunity to have my first boxing match, I seized it. My opponent was a thirty-year-old southpaw named Ronnie Doo. He'd had fifty-seven fights for forty-three wins and was handy enough to have once claimed the Australian junior middleweight title. But that was four years earlier. When I met him he was two wins into a comeback. We went ten rounds, twice the distance I'd ever spent in any kickboxing bout. I won the decision. It was quite an unusual pro boxing debut. Normally, boxers starting out are nursed, their opponents hand-picked specifically for their inferiority. For my first opponent, I hadn't wheeled in a stiff from the morgue to make sure my record got off to a flying start. Doo was expected to keep his comeback on a roll. Instead, his boxing career ended that night.

As much as I enjoyed the boxing, I was a kickboxer first and foremost. Truthfully, though, I was that in name only and it was becoming a drag. My career — my life — was going nowhere. *Thank God for the drugs*, I thought. I craved not the high but the numbness: they deadened me to that nauseating sense of falling. Outwardly, I was having a blast. And, really, I was. And sometimes I wasn't.

I was on my way to becoming a deejay. I scored a gig on Wednesdays playing a hard-core night called Overdrive at Tube nightclub in Brunswick Street. I was on the three-to-five shift — the dreggy hours of a moderately popular night. No matter to me — I gained some good experience and was even gaining a little following. It's hard for me to say whether I was any good or not, but I did a lot of practice and I had pretty good taste in vinyl, which was a damn sight more than some deejays had going for them. I enjoyed going there, doing some goey and sipping on a couple of beers while I played. The pay wasn't too bad, 50 bucks an hour. And from there I landed other gigs playing parties. I was working a couple nights a week tops so I was earning little more than pocket money. Which was fine, because there was very good money in drugs and my little speed racket was humming.

My drugs story was the same as many: a tale of gradual escalation. Some call it a descent into drugs; that's the last thing it felt like. I wasn't caught in a whirlpool, I was blasting off, hooting and waving out the window. Down was not on my route. Due to my enthusiasm and appetite for drugs, I found myself as the go-to guy for my circle of friends. And, if I do say so myself, I performed a tiptop job of keeping everyone pilled and chilled. We had moved beyond the stage of leaving drugs to chance; no more getting to a club and seeing what might be available. We wanted surety, so our nights started earlier as we went on the hunt for drugs.

Similarly, the scene was beginning to change. As it got more mainstream via the huge raves, and the parties got more regular, the sense of occasion diminished, and the festive karma the gay crowd provided faded as their numbers shrank. That was a shame, because the gay guys were a cack, the frigging life of the party. Now they were an endangered species at the large raves, having retreated to the sanctity of their own clubs. Eventually, we'd even start to talk about the 'old days' as the glory days. We weren't taking up knitting just yet — the big raves were ace — but we kind of went pro with the drugs. We got better systems in place to reduce inefficiencies. That's where I came in, helping to remove that awful hit-and-miss element of getting high. That I never paid for drugs just happened to be a perk of the job. I already had my speed chain established. Now a new line opened up: ecstasy. I began filling orders for my friends and, in due course, I was offered bigger and bigger amounts to off-load. Opportunity was knocking.

Meanwhile, the speed was getting serious: I'd upsized from ounces to pounds. Two-point-two kilos of pure. About 100 grand's worth, triple for street. This was a step up the food chain. Now I was dealing directly with cooks who were stayers in the market, steady revenue arms for the big players like bikie gangs and underworld mobs. The vibe was much heavier, which was understandable given the amounts of cash involved. In that industry, more money means heavy people, and heavy people employ violent PR — from occasional messages to whole campaigns. I was edging closer to the heart of the criminal bonfire. But I wasn't one to step back. It took only a matter of months for me to be able to get however much I wanted, when I wanted.

Business came to me. No need for fliers. Grass and cocaine were added to my books, albeit as irregular items — out of the blue I'd get someone enquiring whether I'd be interested in a pound of hash. How did these people find me? Well, I hadn't exactly spent these past few years performing for the opera crowd. And while I'll wager that there's no shortage of corporate crooks sighing their way through *Madame Butterfly*, the fight game draws all manner of men who operate outside the law. I didn't open up shop, so to speak, as a new kid on the block; I'd had years in the ring, and a whole bunch of what society would deem to be unsavoury types as fans. They liked to know a man who could prevail through violence, who championed a lone man's right for respect, who claimed single-handedly irrefutable command. There's nothing too cryptic or veiled about it — they dug warrior mojo. They wanted to brush shoulders with it, bask a little and catch a few rays for themselves.

My father had it going on. Through his self-defence classes, his gyms, his security business and whatever else he got up to, he had an amazing network of contacts on both sides of the law. All of them kowtowed to Dad. And me? To start with, I was a Briggs; I was a world champion kickboxer; I was game, uncompromising, a force to be reckoned with and, for all they knew, mad — that's worthy of four gold stars in the shady realms we're talking about. Problem was, I knew it. I was accustomed to men submitting to me. Bouncers, muscle heads, bikers, fighters, hard men twice my age, men with dark pasts and men with menacing reputations ... they all submitted. Not always overtly — often just in the exchange of a look, and when they'd see in the cool resolve of my eyes my capacity for total devastation, their expression would soften. It was the deference the centurion shows the general. *Me, Maximus!* I came to expect it. And I found the respect shown to me in the street extended into the drug world. So, on my ego steed, I advanced into extremely dangerous territory as though it was a public park. So utterly sure was I of my power, I figured I could do whatever I wanted. I became a law unto myself.

It all started with the dealing side of things, when business began to boom. At no time was that more the case than when one of Ben's raves loomed. Suddenly, there were 5000 people in Brisbane planning how — in what way, shape or form — they were going to get off their heads on the night. Under such demand things could get a little hectic, a tad stressful, even. Times like these, I was rolling into high-volume traffic. It was peak hour, all right.

I had ready access to speed, so that was on hand. It was the other drugs that posed problems. The demand for ecstasy had spiked because of the party, obviously, but it jacked up even more when everyone discovered that supply had dried up in the wake of a huge bust. I had a source in Sydney, so I did my rounds, getting orders — first up my friends, then some ravers who wanted forty or fifty pills each, then a couple of guys wanting one or two hundred to divvy up into their deals of twenties and thirties. So I called my contact in Sydney and placed an order for 500 pills. On top of that, the Dutch deejays who had flown in for the party were after an ounce of coke. On the night before the party, I figured I needed help. So I hooked up with a dealer mate of mine to pull the whole thing off. Let's call him Dave.

We went into action the morning of the party. I started off with a couple of big hits of speed. I dropped Dave at the airport and he took a plane to Sydney to collect the pills. At twenty-eight bucks a tab, this was a fourteen grand deal. But it wasn't like he had to fly down cash in hand; I had an understanding with these people — the gear was on tick. Anyway, Dave was due back at midday and my plan was to get all the pills out, then drive two hours south to Byron Bay for the coke. He got back and everything was sweet — I picked him up, he handed me the pills and I started getting them out. In a couple of hours they were gone. That's when I started getting the phone calls: the pills were duds. Absolute crap. Good friends of mine were ringing me having necked two pills, and 'ecstatic' is the last word you'd use to describe their condition. Then Dave called: 'Get them all back. They've just rung me from Sydney saying they're no fucking good. They've been stiffed; they'll sort us out. I've got to go back to Sydney.'

Nightmare. Right at that very moment, people all over Brisbane who were too amped to wait for the party to start were dipping into their supplies. These pills are spreading, deal by deal, and being gobbled up with glee only to deliver the worst effect: no effect at all. Whatever, they were pills I needed back. Now. I jumped on the phone and called everyone I'd offloaded to and told them to retrieve all the gear. The drugs were defective — a product recall was now in place. I had to visit a few people and convince them to play ball, because I was not about to start handing money back. I needed buyers to stick with me, no backing out or looking elsewhere. They didn't warm to my no-refund policy.

'What are you trying to do — rip me off?'

*Whack!*

Down goes a kid a year younger than me but a world apart.

'Gimme back the shit. We're replacing it.'

He hands back the shit. I go to my next call.

'I want my money back!'

*Whack!*

The prick's jelly at my feet, pissing-pants scared.

'You're not getting your fucking money back. We're getting new pills this afternoon. Now go get me the gear.'

He gets me the gear. And so on. I work my way around, slapping and thumping until we're all on the same page.

When Dave got back to Sydney he called to say they were having dramas getting the real pills. I was driving around like a madman, keeping everyone in check, and growing more and more ropable as I realised I had run out of time to drive to Byron for the coke. So I cancelled the order and called a contact I had in Sydney. He was good for an ounce, so I rang Dave — who by this stage had the new pills — and told him he had to go pick up the coke. When Dave finally got back to Brisbane it was getting dark. I'd organised for some guys to meet us at the airport and take the Es and get them out. By this stage the ravers were just about frantic, thinking their money had gone and the drugs weren't coming. But the cavalry arrived. And behold, the gear was good.

Dave and I drove down to his apartment on the Gold Coast to cut up the coke. We needed to turn one ounce into one and a half. We'd give an ounce to the Dutch deejays and split the rest into 14 grams. In theory. In practice, a couple of grams of the uncut went straight up our noses — well, it had been a pretty stressful day. After cutting the coke we jumped in the car and raced up to Brisbane to the party. Now, I don't normally get neurotic on coke, but I swear an unmarked car was tailing us. If they want to really check you out they never sit behind you — they overtake and slow down. After they went past us the second time, we turned off the freeway and looped back on again. We did this twice more, for good measure. Maybe we *were* paranoid.

When we arrived at Brisbane, Dave dropped me at the Crest Hotel and did blocks while I took the ounce up to the deejays and collected six grand. Finally we arrived at the party and off-loaded whatever coke and pills we had left. And that was it: done deal. I can't even tell you how much money we made, but it was heaps. You could say it was worth the effort.

The next morning, Dave suggested we head to Sydney. We felt as though we'd spent the previous night fart-arsing about rather than really enjoying ourselves. So it was like, 'Let's go and party in Sydney.' All the way down we were doing hits of coke from our bump bottles, little containers that had snorting spoons attached to the lid. We took a hotel room in Kings Cross, got a heap of people over and then went out clubbing. I woke up the next morning to a room filled with transvestites, bikers, tough guys, poofs and ravers. They'd all come straight from the club after I'd left when word went out that the recovery was back at ours. Dave and I didn't return to Brisbane until Tuesday. I had a fight coming up the following weekend and had to train. He drove me to the gym from the airport; I did bumps of coke all the way. I spent four rounds on the bags and went, 'Fuck it, I'm wrecked', and headed home. Needless to say, I lost the fight.

Which fight? Who knows? Who cared? I didn't. Actually, I did.

I did and I didn't.

It was my second boxing match. I trained for Larl Zada on the bong and took a knockout hit in the third. In a split second, my cavalier attitude was shattered. A sore truth was humiliatingly exposed: I *did* care, more than anyone knew. I was no one without my fighting. And in the wake of this loss I felt I amounted to nothing. I was a hoax. I was all ego, no substance. My self-loathing really kicked in. And it was just warming up.

# XVII

## Going Nowhere Fast

For my twenty-first birthday I was awake for four nights and five days and consumed about twenty-five ecstasy tablets, at least 6 grams of coke, two or three bottles of ethyl nitrate, a few lines of ketamine, a pile of speed, tokes from joint after joint and drinks from bottle after bottle of vodka. Nothing was planned. I was just taking it as it comes — 'it' being every drug my friends and I could lay our hands on.

A pattern had emerged: big nights out were becoming mere preludes to binges lasting several days. It was incredible. Incredibly good, mostly. I had some phenomenal experiences and some stratospheric highs. But in the process I came to learn something very important about myself: no matter what I took and no matter how much I took, I could never entirely lose myself. For a good while this strength of mind was the bane of my life. In time, it would prove to be my salvation.

I had my low moods but I was never a downcast figure, however much I fretted inwardly over the increasing irrelevance that was my fighting career. Like all the party animals I was hanging out with, I wanted to get ripped and have fun. But it's also true that I badly wanted to escape my reality, because waiting for me whenever I chose to step out of rave wonderland was a drab world wriggling with dismal problems. My parents were going through the hellish throes of a disintegrating marriage, which affected me far more than I ever would have imagined; my relationship with Leah had bottomed out; and Nathan, whom I'd had very little to do with of late, was pushing his cursed luck way too far. The seedy, reckless route he'd taken meant he had one of two things coming: death or prison.

From what I knew of my raver friends, drugs didn't do me the same service they did others. I'd listen to people I knew go on about how they were so out of it they didn't know what they were doing — like screwing a mate's girlfriend, or screwing a mate. I thought that was a total cop-out. I could eat twenty pills and still know what I was doing; I could still make the decision about whether or not I was going to touch another girl besides Leah. Forget this 'Oh, I was so out of it' bullshit. No, your inhibitions dropped. That's all. You knew what flesh you were touching. As much as I was cynical about such excuses, I envied and craved that abandon. But the more I took, the more contemplative I became, and the more into my head I went. No matter how off my face I got, I always knew exactly what I was doing. And I hated that; I hated the fact that I could never obliterate my conscience. To be denied that relief was another curse I'd for some reason attracted. Why me, for fuck's sake?

As much as Mum and Dad's marriage breakdown may have been inevitable, it was hard to watch. At the heart of it all was the fact that the gyms were going under and Dad seemed unable or unwilling to stem the decline. Mum was working her butt off to keep money coming in and the banks at bay. Even I helped out with the mortgage until Mum twigged that I was slipping her drug money and backed me off. She redlined her nails business, with Leah and Donna pitching in for the cause. In her downtime — well, Mum never really had downtime — she'd get on her sewing machine and work on her new business, lingerie. She'd launched her own label and was selling it Tupperware-style by way of home gatherings. She had a few ladies enlisted as reps and it was moving along nicely. Beyond that, Mum didn't have the time, money, expertise or inclination to step in and save the gyms. Someone needed to, though, because Nathan and I weren't up for it and Dad had decided to head off to South Africa on another treasure hunt. He left for six weeks and was away four months. Before leaving, he'd convinced the entire family that a fortune was coming our way as sure as sunrise; we'd all never have to worry about money again. 'It's already happened. Believe it. Start looking at cars and where you want to live, where you want to go on holiday.' But when he returned it was like, 'It's not going to happen.' End of story, no explanation. So we had to close the gyms.

We owed lots of money to people — they'd paid up their memberships and we didn't have the money to honour refunds. Lawsuits started coming. My parents were under huge pressure that Mum felt deeply and gravely. Dad did a good job of not seeming to give a shit. His attitude was, 'Fuck everyone. We're doing the best we can and that's that.' But I think the truth was that he was again feeling crippled by his self-fulfilling prophecies of failure. The other thing was that Mum and Dad had planned a European holiday to celebrate their twenty-eighth wedding anniversary. When Dad got back from South Africa, he said the trip was off. Not according to Mum. She went anyway, with some girlfriends. The night she left Dad went out, got drunk and wrote off the car. He got his copper mates to help sort it all out so that insurance would come through and he wouldn't see the light of court. Mum came home to more mess. Her perseverance was just about shot. Yet still she stayed. For the time being.

Not that I was the relationship master. When it came to Leah, I did what I wanted and said what suited. She followed me into this crazy lifestyle centred on clubs and drugs, but she was only there because I was. She partied with the best of them but she had no idea of the extent of my drug excesses — the volume of my intake, the scale of my dealing. The idea that buying a house was the first step towards settling down together evaporated pretty damn quickly. I was off the chain — first from my parents, and more and more from my fighting — and I had some miles to run yet. Our home was my playhouse, where I was free to play my music, free to stash my drugs, free to have everyone back for pre-dawn recovery parties, free to grow dope out back and free to do whatever I pleased. Leah's mind was for ever cast forward to some ideal, to days beyond, when my young madness would be spent and I'd regain focus to find her there, and us being a couple in a real and conventional sense.

In real time, she was a passive participant in my hedonistic lifestyle. Tied to me, she trailed in my wake — sometimes it was like she wasn't there, other times I felt her pull as an anchor. As someone I could clearly never lose, I began to throw her away. I'd cheat on her, break her heart and then wheedle my way back. One night I'd say to friends at dinner that I wanted us to get married and the next morning I'd behave like all I wanted was out. Other times it was the reverse, we'd be out some place and I'd carry on like she wasn't there, like I was a single guy, a real player, then when we were home I would turn all attentive, tender and caring. 'You only love me when we're alone,' Leah said. And she was right. I couldn't live without her — she kept me safe from my deep-rooted childhood fears of loneliness and abandonment — but I was not in real love with her. Neither of us knew what love meant, what love asks of us in relation to ourselves as much as others.

But one day, convinced of my detachment, I announced I was leaving. I said I didn't want to be with her any more. She was absolutely devastated; I was her world. She raised the things we had together — the engagement ring, the house, good times shared — as reasons to stay. To me they were reasons to go, to put it all behind me. I didn't want marriage and a mortgage. I just wanted to deejay, dance, deal and get loaded. I was on the run. Desperation and panic were in the air but I latched on to that sense of promise you feel when escaping. At some level I might have known I was running away, not just from Leah but also from deeper concerns, but what really mattered was that I was moving. Any direction would do.

Leah turned to Donna for help. As usual, Donna was a rock. Oh man, she had no time for me then — and with good reason. While everyone else thought I was the man, she thought I was an A-grade tosser. She and Leah were close friends, and Donna hated the way I treated Leah. She would try to make Leah see she was better off without me. So when she was faced with losing the house, Leah asked

Donna to buy me out. This came at a bad time for Donna. She was about to head off to see the world. Typically organised, she'd saved all her money, had work lined up in London and so on, but then she changed her plans. She refinanced, took out a loan and bought me out. Suddenly, instead of being somewhere in Europe with nothing but a backpack weighing her down, Donna was away on a short-term break in London, tied to a bloody terrace house in Calamvale, Brisbane. Not long after she arrived in London, though, she learnt that Leah and I were back together. If she'd known voodoo and had had a doll at hand, I would have dropped dead then and there. And Leah would have expired soon afterwards, I've no doubt.

It wasn't like Leah and I moved in together again, though; we remained separated for the first time in five years. I moved in with my deejay mate Angus and partied hard on the money from the sale of the house, which supplemented my now sizable drug income. About the only drug I wasn't dealing was smack. Other than that, I was a regular 7-Eleven of illegal substances, plying my wicked trade on the high street. Day in, day out, I was good for speed, coke, ecstasy and marijuana. For the party crowd I wasn't just somebody to know — that world champion kickboxer guy — I was somebody good to know. I got to meet a lot of people, and to know a few as well.

To celebrate my twenty-first birthday, I wanted to keep things pretty simple: *let's just get absolutely loaded and party for days.* Drug-wise I had a mind to scoff every chocolate in the box and it was nice to have like-minded friends. My birthday always coincided with the Ekka, which is an annual ten-day event staged at the Royal National Association showgrounds in Brisbane. It's part fun park, part agriculture and livestock event — you know, the type of event where kids pester their oldies for overpriced showbags. For some people the only bags worth having were those containing drugs, and to cater to such party fiends, my friend Ben stepped up to stage one of his humungous raves. My crew and I didn't go too hard at the party because we were pacing ourselves. It was a Wednesday and the extent of our plan was that we were going to party through to Monday. So I just had a few Es and kept a bump bottle containing about a gram and a half of coke handy.

From the rave we headed down to my mate Dave's apartment in the Gold Coast, the recovery party pad from hell. It was a penthouse suite twenty-two floors up overlooking the beach. It was spacious and pimped out with all sorts of cool shit, including a big spa in his bedroom. Gather a few bods, crank up the stereo, rack up some lines, eat some E and away you go. People you've never met but who seemed cool would be all walking through the place, stopping to have a toke on a scoob — 'Oh, g'day mate. Who are you? Oh, yeah? How's it going?' — before moving on. The place was party central.

We hung there for days. What did we do? Well, we partied. Once we'd gotten started, this buzz just kind of prevailed. People were going off, drinking and taking pills and smoking joints. Everyone was hanging out, getting into how out of it they were, talking funny shit, talking nonsense, talking philosophy, talking God. Every now and then some mission would arise — more drugs or more booze, usually — for which we'd spring to action. Every new drug was a new ride, every new mission an expedition. They all meant the world and nothing at once. All that really mattered was the company and the highs, and that the fun kept on keeping on.

We'd go on drives with guys in drag hanging out the windows. We trashed this guy's car taking it bush-bashing through the scrub near the Sheraton Mirage hotel, smashing it into trees. It was all harmless fun ... to a bunch of twisted freaks.

Not everything was light entertainment, though. I got into a blue with a couple of guys when I went out to fetch more vodka. A few words from the car turned into a fight on the street. I swear I didn't start it — but I ended it. I left one of them missing half a cheek and the other lying in a heap. I had to spit the guy's blood from my mouth before I stepped into the bottle shop. I returned to the apartment noticably flustered. Nothing a few lines wouldn't fix.

Our drug intake was like mixing cocktails. Different drugs countered each other in different ways. Drop two Es and they'd take about half an hour to come on. So in the meantime you'd snort two or three big lines of cocaine. Now, cocaine will overpower ecstasy but it doesn't last long. So after you snort the lines you're coking off your head, then an hour later, after the coke's tailed off, you're absolutely peaking on ecstasy. The transition is so sudden — you just smash into the peak of your E. We were doing this all the time: going up, down, left, right, round and around, have this now, now this.

One morning I was lying on the lounge with this very cool girl massaging my hands. The music was pumping and the sun was pouring in from over the ocean and people were starting to file into Dave's pad after clubbing all night. All up, I was feeling pretty sweet. Then Dave came up holding a plate of lines. 'Here, birthday boy,' he said, 'try this.' Wicked, more coke. So I've snorted it then gone, 'What the fuck is that?' He said, 'It's special K.' 'What the fuck is special K?' 'Ketamine,' he reassured me, like some doctor who'd just shot me up with vitamins. 'Give yourself about five minutes, mate,' he said. And in no time at all everything went *whoosh* sideways. This amazing power surge ran through me. I stood up and tried to walk. It was all very trippy but up like coke at the same time. I felt invincibly good and all the pills and coke and everything else in my system seemed to reactivate all at once. *Fuck, this is full on.* Don't know if I said that, but that's what I was thinking, repeatedly, and I'd wager that was all I was capable of saying. So now I'd tried ketamine. The last pill of my binge went down at about six o'clock on Sunday night. When it finally petered out I fell asleep until lunchtime Monday. It had been some birthday party.

I didn't know how Nathan celebrated his twenty-first. I didn't really care. He played only a cameo role in my life at that point and with each appearance he looked more worse for wear. I barely cared. The years of incessant competitiveness, acrimony and suffocating proximity had eroded even the pretence of affection between us. Once we had been very supportive of each other. Once we had been each other's backbone, the staunchest of allies. We had grown up watching Dad smash our twin and had formed a protective shell of disdain against him. The closeness between Nathan and me had for too long had something corrosive about it. Certain things we did to each other — not worth mentioning here — served to keep old wounds open, and any time we shared would result in some aggravation, slight or significant. Being together just seemed to have no value, even under the most benign circumstances. He got on with his life; I got on with mine.

And what was my life? It was turmoil and mayhem. And vacancy. But I'd be telling myself, *I've got my shit together, I've got stuff going on.* I was so in denial about where I was at. Did I say I was on the run? I must have been on drugs when I said that. Because I wasn't on the run at all; I wasn't moving. My life was effectively on hold. And drugs, for all the fun and exuberant fury they generated, were the pause button. Because when I was off my head, nothing else was happening. The only thing going on was that I was off my head; that was the total sum of what I was doing. I did little else but be twisted for days. But I had nothing else to do with those days. I had time to waste. And what better waste of time than taking shitloads of drugs?

# XVIII

## Taking Care Of Business

Our lives are the sum of our choices. We are the living history of both our actions and our inaction. True, there always exists an element of chance — those things that come your way without rhyme or reason — but how you decide to react to what's in front of you not only determines your future; it affects the tides of chance. I have no doubt: your choices influence, even court, your fate. In ramping up my drug trade, I'd walked into some pretty shady territory without blinking. I didn't stop at the first danger sign and turn back; I marched on. I knew that in the realm I'd entered I was hardly going to find better things for myself. Sure, I found more drugs and money, but also more risk, more danger and more pain. I hadn't chosen to traverse meadows and mountains — I'd chosen seedy alleyways of menace and decay. I chose to become a drug dealer. I chose to become a rather big drug dealer. And although I could see that this path was leading me deep into no place good, my pace didn't slacken. A good place — a state of emotional wellness — was not what I was seeking; it was not even on the map. To me, a good place was my next high, not some positive life objective. I mean, I chose to start robbing drug dealers. Such a choice was not exactly going to invite peace, love and mung beans into my life, was it? I knew the opposite was true. I *knew* that. And yet in I waded, chin up and chest out.

I'm not exactly sure at what point I started blatantly ripping people off, but once I started I didn't discriminate: friends, acquaintances and strangers alike were all fair game. If it didn't suit me to pay for my drugs then I simply stiffed whoever was dumb enough to supply me. Soon enough, no one wanted to supply me but they were too scared not to. I didn't so much throw my weight around as be around — calmly getting in people's faces, knocking on their doors. I wasn't shy about making demands of anyone. And my gift of the gab and civility were never so persuasive as the disturbing vibe I projected — no one doubted that I was ever ready to resort to extreme violence. Yet I never had to when it came to drugs. No one was prepared to check me, to deny me, to challenge me. I came to have free rein.

A typical case was when this deejay called Paul van Dyke was coming out from Berlin and I was supporting. Naturally, the music was going to be very nice for E. On short notice I went to see a bloke I knew who had ready access to pills. I rocked up with no money and told him I wanted a hundred tabs — three and a half grand's worth. He was cool with that — well, lukewarm to tell you the truth. 'No worries,' he said, sensing he was on the cusp of a bad mistake. 'You're good for them, aren't you, mate?' 'Of course, mate,' I said. *Good for eating them*, I thought. I was getting used to speaking empty words.

I went along to the party with my hundred pills. Immediately I faced the twin hazards familiar to all drug-pig dealers: scoffing, where you get high on your own supply, and spillage, where you completely lose track of money and gear. This is always how it would end up — I needed to recoup money to pay for the pills, but the pills were primarily for me to get loaded on. I needed to sell seventy pills at fifty bucks a pop to cover what I owed. That left thirty for me to eat and give to my friends. But this was not science. People were rocking up saying, 'These are wicked. Give me three more and I'll sort you out at the recovery.' 'Sure. Sweet.' But I never saw the money in the morning. 'What? No, I didn't have four — I only got one off you.' And as if I knew exactly who had what. Drugs may not have enabled me to lose my mind, but they didn't exactly sharpen it. And I didn't want to argue with every single person. It would not have been cool for me to go around slapping people down at a recovery party. The money was gone.

A couple of days later the supplier rang me, asking after the cash. I told him I needed a week to collect off people. 'All right,' he said. I only had forty pills left, so I sold them and gave him the proceeds plus the few hundred I'd made from party sales. I was still about $1500 short. Where was I going to get that kind of money? I had no product. So I decided, *Fuck it, I'm not paying*. I said, 'Mate, sorry but I've got no more money for you. That's all you're getting. Thanks for the party. It was fun.' And he wasn't quite sure what to say but started going on about the dosh he owed for the pills. 'That's your problem,' I said. 'You deal with it.' And he was like, 'I got 'em off bikies and they're going to come and break my fucking legs.' 'Well, just tell 'em that I got 'em off you. Tell 'em to come and see me.' I didn't give a fuck, which was just stupid — you can't win against bikies. He was saying they were really hard-core. Well, everyone's hard-core in the drugs game, aren't they? For a while afterwards, though, I lived with the creepy feeling that I was a breath away from some kind of savage reprisal.

That guy was one of the many dealers I burnt. And nothing happened. Not a thing. I don't know how many times I was warned that some bad-arse was going to bring a world of shit down upon my head. 'Well,' I'd always say, like I was handing out my business card, 'tell 'em to come see me.' No one came knocking. Pretty quickly I got a feel for where I stood in this weird underworld, and I wasn't some smacked-out chancer scunging away his luck — I was an audacious force that made those who had reason to punish me hesitate. Even so, a bullet in the head would have sorted me out the same as any junkie.

Sometimes I'd work my way up the food chain to make my point — I didn't care who I was dealing with. I once got fifty Es on tick, had a couple and found they were tripstasy. This was bad. Like the name suggests, the effect of tripstasy is a cross between an acid trip and an ecstasy high. It packs far more mind-fuck potential than ecstasy and carries greater risks of overdose and psychosis, particularly in unsuspecting users. It's been said the psychotic shock can 'scare' people to death. I didn't like the picture: some kid drops one of my Es that turns out to be tripstasy, he wigs out completely, winds up in hospital barely alive if he's lucky, and all sorts of bad karma comes my way. So I went and saw the guy who sold me the pills. He was a mate of mine. I told him I'd flushed them because they were shit; I told him I wasn't paying for them. Suddenly he owed a sizable debt that needed repaying *pronto*. He piped up with his little despair moment: 'Oh God, I knew you were going to do this — I *knew* it. What am I going to tell my guy?'

'Well, as it happens, mate, I want to know who your guy is.'

'I can't do that. You know I can't do that. That's not how it works.'

I insisted. He gave me a name. Some big guy who was supposed to be really heavy. And I don't mean by way of KFC.

So I went to see him. I took my mate Pete as back-up. Pete was one scary piece of work. He stood about five ten and over two or three years had shot huge doses of testosterone to bulk his 80 kilos up to 125. The extra beef wasn't for show — it was pure aggro for hire. You'd have been hard pressed to get more fright or wilful damage for your money. It may have taken nothing to spur my latent rage to violence, but I was Mr Congeniality next to Pete. A bad man you want to have on side, and, given his blitzkrieg temper, one I had to be constantly mindful of keeping on side.

We dropped by this guy's house a few times but he was never in. So we made a few calls and found out he spent most of his time at his girlfriend's place. So we went around. I knocked on the door and the girl answered. I introduced Pete and myself as friends of her man. I was all smiles, as sweet as a vicar. She said our mutual friend was due back from the gym any tick of the clock. I said, 'Of course. We're a bit early, now that I think of it.' I said we could wait in the car till he arrived. She said, 'Don't be silly', and asked us in. I thanked her very much. Taking seats in the lounge, Pete and I exchanged smiles. *Isn't this nice?*

Next thing, in walks this big steroid head. He could barely swing his arms for all his tit muscle. Our cordial chat with the missus stopped. The guy looked familiar — I knew him from somewhere. He knew exactly who we were. My mate would have warned him.

Still, he was more than a little surprised to see us, and less than a little pleased. 'What are you two doing here?' he said, dropping his gym bag. We weren't there to fire up the PlayStation. I greeted him like it was my place. 'Hey, man, come in and sit down,' I said, motioning to the spot beside Pete. He didn't move. 'Sit down,' I said again, nice and easy. He lowered himself next to Pete but didn't sink back, opting to perch himself on the edge. 'Now, you,' I said to the girlfriend. 'Get the fuck out of here.' 'What?' 'I said fuck off. Now.' And she looked at her bloke, who goes, 'Listen — just go and let us talk, all right.' She upped and left, steaming.

As soon as she was gone this bloke went on the front foot: 'You're going to pay for those pills.' He was trying hard to take charge. Pete leant forward and said quietly in his ear, 'Lower your voice.' The guy felt a chill — Pete was as warm as an old tombstone. He grinned at me from behind the guy before sitting back again. I said, 'We're not paying for shit. Understand? We —' 'You are going to pay for those pills. You don't know who you're fucking with.' 'Oh, really?' 'Paul,' he said, trying to hammer his point home, 'you don't realise . . .' Then Pete grabbed his shoulder and pulled him back. 'You raise your voice again, dickhead, and I'll knock you the fuck out.'

The 'roid head shat himself. He was gone. Pete was amused. I motioned for him to continue. His front obliterated, the waterworks started. He was blubbering away, saying he didn't want to play this game any more. He didn't want to sell drugs. He was getting out. The guy totally went to pieces. I was thinking, *Jesus, just pretend, man. Just pretend you're not scared*. He was pathetic. He said he got the drugs off some mercenaries. (The story gets better with every guy, doesn't it? Everyone's so, so hard.) 'They're bringing them in. You go front these guys and they'll shoot you.'

'Really?' I said. Pete and I were just about pissing ourselves. We got a name and left.

The mercenary story turned out to be bullshit. The guy was just some big Tongan. But you don't march in and fuck with a brother, or else you end up at war with the lot of them. You kind of sound them out. Same with the Lebanese. You don't go treading on other people's toes. I, myself, had taken calls from Lebos telling me to tell Nathan to pull his head in. This was the way we all went about business, usually.

Pete put a courtesy call through to a Tongan mate of his. Asked if he knew the guy. He said he did, but he was a bit of an outcast and a lot of a fuckwit. He told Pete to go for it. We did a bit of homework on the Tongan and he had a few runs on the board — he was a fit and mean 120 kilos, could fight and had plenty of go in him. Paying him a visit didn't loom as a tea party.

When the time came to move on him, I was out of town, heading down to Byron Bay to pick up 2 ounces of coke that had just come in from South America. A smaller shipment had been used as a decoy — while the cops were back-slapping over their seizure, the main drop went down. My guys couldn't just hold the gear for me, because the stuff would walk off the shelves — unbelievably pure, stamps still on the blocks. I could cut my 2 ounces into 4 and get nothing but raves from my buyers. I was on the road when Pete called asking where I was; I said I was gone for the day. He said he'd teed up a meeting with the Tongan. Pete had asked his friend to invite the Tongan over. He said he was outside the house and had just seen the Tongan go in. He was pissed off at me not being there. 'What the fuck am I supposed to do?' he said. I told him there was no way I could make it, I was halfway to Byron. He said, 'Fuck you. I'll do it myself.' So in he went.

About an hour later, Pete called again. He sounded pleased. He said everything was sweet. He'd walked in and taken a seat. The Tongan had had no idea who he was. Pete had said, 'So I hear that Paul and Pete ripped you off, eh?' 'Yeah, I'm going to fucking shoot the pricks,' said the Tongan. 'Really?' said Pete. And he got up walked over to the guy. 'Well, as it happens, cocksucker, I'm Pete. Take your fucking shot.' With that, Pete cracked him hard in the face. The guy got a few words out before Pete smacked his mouth shut. Eventually he got it and kept quiet. 'He was pissing his pants,' Pete said, laughing. It was sorted. The only thing the Tongan was likely to come after us with was a Christmas card.

I felt I had it over these shit-heels. These supposed rock-hard dealers who had all their underlings running scared were soft-cocks. So I pushed my luck further. If they rang asking for money,

I'd tell them straight out that I wasn't paying. If they threatened to visit me to collect, I'd put the welcome mat out — 'Come and get your money, mate. Come over and try.' Not once did they come. Not one single scary outlaw went, 'Fuck this for a joke. I'm going to sort you right out.'

So how did I still get gear? If I had money I paid, if not I'd tell them I was coming over and that they'd better have something for me. And they'd have it. Sometimes I'd set up a deal, take hold of the gear, tell them I wasn't paying and that anyone who objected was welcome back at my place. It was madness. I just began thinking, *Fuck 'em, fuck 'em all*. These scumbags were all full of shit. But my perception was so warped by the drugs I was taking that my grip on reality was tenuous at best. I acted like I had immunity, but I knew no such thing existed. Everyone could be got. There are some very heavy people out there, trust me. I just didn't quite get to them, thank God. I wouldn't be here if I did. And the fact is that I really had no idea how close I was to getting knocked. I would imagine I was in the crosshairs of more than one scope. For one reason or another, though, no one pulled the trigger. Did my father exert some influence? He knew everything and he knew all the people at the top end of the operations I was upsetting. And each one to a man liked to have Dave Briggs on side. Maybe he did some talking to save my arse; maybe not.

This was about all the action I was seeing. My priorities had drifted further and further away from kickboxing. Actually, it was more that the distinction between the lives I'd once kept separate — the rave scene and my fighting — had become blurred. No longer would I switch from one to the other completely. I lost three fights, and in two of them I let myself — not to mention other people — down. I don't want to take anything away from the guys who beat me but there was only one fight that was taken out of my hands: a Frenchman named Stefan Nakima knocked me out cold. Hats off to him — I trained hard for that fight and was good to go, but he caught me with a beautiful shot.

When I trained to fight Anthony Vella in late 1997, everything was mixed up. I mean, I put in at the gym and I entered the ring with pin-sharp focus — there was no way I was going to lose. Yet as much as I considered my body and mind to be pristine, I was kidding myself. I trained on speed. If I was a bit flat, I'd neck a speedbomb to boost me into gym mode. When I say I stopped smoking pot, I mean I'd only have a few cones here and there. When I say I didn't do coke, I mean I took it line by line rather than gram by gram. And yet I destroyed Vella, the Australian champion. Not just that: I ended his career. I broke him. He was reduced to a writhing clutch of agony on the canvas, a crippled animal fearing its wound is mortal. I don't say this to gloat over his misfortune, because I respect him for his courage. I state it merely to illustrate a more acute aspect of fighting. Sometimes a man loses everything in the ring — I'm talking things way deeper than pride. Essential matter, like hope and faith, is stripped from his soul. It's a gaping wound left by truth, and its pain is holistic, real and clear. Their lives don't stop — that's not what I'm saying — but they must restart, as they know they have died in the ring. And as though I'd drunk from his soul, the horrible ruin of Vella's loss tinselled the grandeur of my victory. What remarkable powers I possessed. My Superman suit was back on, quick as a flash. Do I rule, or do I rule?

Yeah, but the new reign was brief. Such a consummate win was probably the worst thing that could have happened to me at that time. My ego flourished again in a riot of triumph; I was convinced I could do it all. I could party *and* train. I could down drugs like they were vitamins and still forge my body into armour and my mind into steel. I was that fucking good. Like Vella, though, my kickboxing career ended with that fight. Not straightaway, but the end was as surely nigh as my delusions of invincibility were false.

# XIX

## Force Of Darkness

**M**uch of my life was a cheap act. Everything I had to offer was reduced in value. I'd say what people wanted to hear or whatever suited me — just lie without a moment's stalling. I'd lie to make my stories better, myself larger, taking needy grabs at being the entertainer like some B-grade actor suffering attention deficit. I used to have integrity; now even my closest friends took everything I said with a grain of salt. They knew I was either telling half the story or one and a half.

Something I talked less and less about was fighting. I was such the former world champ it wasn't funny. I never let on how bitter and loathsome and disillusioned that made me feel, how it ate at me that I'd been stiffed on my golden dream deal; how I seethed at such hollowness within me being my reward, my curse; that common contempt festered where the seed of greatness was supposed to have sprung and thrived and empowered and healed. I never let on how intensely I brooded on my hatred of many things — targets I blamed. And I never held my experience of rape as being the headwaters from which so much of my rage might have sprung. I was never in a mind for such historical cause and effect. Oh, I hadn't completely forgotten about it — that's not how suppression works. It was more that the memory of what happened to me back then was simply not something I could dwell

158

on. Doing so risked being trapped in a vile and hopeless state that loomed as the prelude to insanity, suicide or murder. I'd learnt to kill any sickening reminder of that event swiftly, as I quelled whatever feelings were roused. I coped by way of denial.

Another matter of which I spoke little was the new line of work I'd found for myself: the pain business. Standover jobs. It paid very well, but it wasn't all about the money. I *liked* hurting people. And I never much cared about how or why that was.

The jobs began fairly innocuously. A friend complained about some junkie who owed him $400; he'd pretty much kissed the money goodbye. 'I'll get it back for you,' I said. 'Really? If you do, half the money's yours.' Sweet. So I visited the junkie, escorted him to the ATM and got the money. Too easy. 'Wouldn't mind the guy getting knuckled,' my friend might say. 'No worries,' I'd say. 'For a little extra, consider him knuckled.' One thing led to another, word got around, and soon I found I was on a nice little earner.

Heavier work came through Pete — he offered me good money to help out on a job. Some guy had been taken for half a million bucks by his former business associate. He'd lost the court case and his ex-partner was laughing in his face. He wanted the smile wiped off. The order was specific: the jaw was to be broken. So we paid the guy a visit, stormed in and trashed his place. Then I went to work on his jaw. I picked up three grand.

Pete had plenty of work and was always looking for a helping hand. He teamed up with a lot of different blokes but I only worked with him. He showed me the ropes. And so my grim apprenticeship began, learning how to leave people in very, very bad states, by all manner of means.

The stock tool of my new trade was a baseball bat. You'd get two to three grand 'baseballing' someone, just working them over badly. You might crack some bones in the process, but breakages were normally subject to demand. Jobs were custom orders. Clients would specify what they wanted done — jaw, teeth, finger(s), thumb(s), kneecap(s), leg(s). These jobs paid up to five grand. Some dealer stiffs another. Says he got busted by the cops and lost the gear. Has no money to pay for it but is now offline because he has to keep his nose clean, with his case coming up and all. Can't say, exactly, when his court hearing is. Is spotted cruising Surfers Paradise in a Lexus with a metre maid, both shielding rays through Gucci shades. Stiffed dealer wants the fuckwit fixed up good. Both legs. 'How? Dunno. Knock him out and jump on them for all I care.' I asked around. Somebody recommended a metal pole. Baseball bat doesn't have the grunt. Even with the pole, you've really got to put your back into the swing. Especially legs. Efficiency matters — you don't want to be there all night.

Kneecaps, I'd come to learn, required particular attention. If you didn't have a real go at the patella, all you'd do is inflict an awful lot of pain but not break anything, and then you wouldn't get paid. Clients would wait a week or more to make sure the job was done right. Only once they were satisfied would you get your money. But even then I sometimes had to beat it out of them.

There was no need to place an ad in the Yellow Pages. The lust of anger and vengeance spurs the wits — hate found us. This was the main and sometimes only quality our paymasters shared. There were ethnic mobs and bikie gangs who wanted anonymity and so outsourced their work. There were a few jobs from mainstream Australian types, but they tended to shit themselves at the last minute and try to call the job off. For the most part, though, we were hired to issue the type of punishment I'd courted but never received — the infliction of pain and injury and fear to speed up the payment of drug-related debt. But it wasn't all about drugs. Not everyone's pursuit of justice stops when the law doesn't deliver. Some people press on. There were, say, fathers who wanted paedophiles turned into jigsaw pieces; guys who sought muscle to avenge wounded pride or the sting of a business deal. And then there was the white-collar mob — corporate and legal contractors. But I had to work my way up to them. Theirs was high-end stuff paying up to twenty grand. That's when things got really heavy.

The money I'd traditionally worked hard for was in very short supply. Ring appearances were few and far between and the drugs had all but killed my inspiration to train and fight. My career was just about shot. And, as I was about to find out, the same went for my parents' marriage. The news of their break-up came out of the blue and rocked me more than I could have ever imagined, since

I'd long felt such an outcome was inevitable. Mum called one day and said she was leaving Dad. She was upset, though not in tears. She'd finally decided she'd had, and given, enough. I was like, 'Yeah, okay. You've got to do what you've got to do. I'll support you 100 per cent.' Dad's response? 'Yeah, sure. Go on then.' He thought she'd never go through with it.

After she left he stayed in denial for months; he was so sure she'd come crawling back. I know he was hurting bad, but he never deigned to show it. The past few years had brought a series of failures he took as inflicted fate: the demise of the gyms, the fruitless treasure hunts in Zurich and South Africa, and now this. All the work of external forces. I don't reckon failure weighed lightly on Dad at all, despite appearances. And, as I've said before, he never took pride in his successes and never strived to sustain them, so he was doubly defeatist. How could he possibly win? He never really allowed himself genuine hope or anything as silly as optimism or as spurious as self-belief.

When Mum moved into an apartment down on the Gold Coast, he wanted to do the right thing. She'd asked me to help her move and, while I didn't need reminding, Dad rang me to say, 'Paul, you make sure you're there for your mother today.' He still believed she was going through a phase. Actually, I can't say I know what he believed. Nor what, if anything, he really believed in. But he sure didn't fight to save his marriage — didn't lift a finger — even if it was unsalvageable. Again, he let his life hurtle onwards with his hands off the wheel.

Mum was gone. She'd done all she could and, with all the children grown, she knew she had to get on with her life if she was to ever find peace. She lost weight, got a new hairdo and began dating to get herself out and about, even though she was not ready for intimacy. She'd put enough of herself into others; it was time for her to give back to herself. She was amazing.

Then, by some twist of fate, she came into contact with an old friend. She rang me with even more surprising news: she was seeing Wayne, the guy she'd left thirty years earlier to marry Dad. It was at this point that Dad really went off the rails. Not only had the fact that Mum was gone for good been rammed home, he felt deceived and insulted. He was convinced Mum had run to Wayne, but that was clearly not the case. Even though Dad had won Mum's heart and had her for so many years, he felt cheated and degraded, as though Mum had set out to compound his pain and was dancing on his bed of woe. He became a real arsehole. He made nasty threats. He hit the grog and indulged in all sorts of destructive behaviour. He was a man in a tailspin.

God, divorce. Even when you think it's just what your parents need, it can tear them — and even their grown-up children — to pieces all the same. It was brutal, emotional turmoil for all of us. Donna was a real trooper, trying to remain impartial and loyal to both Mum and Dad. I was spending a lot of time with Dad at the gym, where he'd unload bitterly about Mum. He wanted to lash out. And now that he was drinking again, he was only ever one slug of bourbon away from going nuclear.

It wasn't too long after Mum and Dad split that my kickboxing career finally ended. My last fight unravelled in a chaotic churn of violence like some disintegrating freak show. I'd gotten onto the 'roids to beef up for jobs, taking a course of stanozolol and a shot of testosterone. I was so inflammable, I scared myself. On the road I'd put my fist through windscreens for no less than a frown. My opponent, this Croatian kid, took an absolute pounding, especially in the first round. In the second, something in my head cracked and fell like a broken cliff face. Out of nowhere, Nathan appeared. I hadn't seen him in months; hadn't wanted to. And here he was, this emaciated mess, the ghost of my brother. He was bone thin, his eyes black and his body white and out of it on whatever it was he was into, and he jumped up on the corner and started yelling at me what to do, how to fight. I stole glances at him and it was such a shock to see him so bad, I was shattered. Dad was screaming at him to get down — this is in front of a packed venue — and I just thought, *What am I doing? Why am I doing this any more? Why am I here?* I'd had this anger brewing and brewing and brewing inside me and at that point I felt it totally engulfed me. Here I was in the ring, living my lifelong dream, and behold: it was a complete and utter fucking mess. *I'm still the man, am I? What bullshit.* I was a drug-fucked phoney — once a warrior, now just a rudderless vessel of rancid fury. Look at my brother, at my father, at this whole fucking gutter circus around me. I hated the man in front of me, I hated the man beside me, my father, and I hated my drug-fucked brother. But, most of all, I hated the man inside me. This was what my dream had become.

There was something evil in the air that night, and much of it, I knew, flowed through me. When the main event was under way, the promoter came to me and said, 'Paul, I'm sorry, but we've done our arse.' He told me he couldn't pay me straightaway but that he'd get me the money in two weeks. I was seething: 'This joint is packed and you're bust?' I had guys beside me. One has gone, 'Let's cut the prick up.' And I'm like, 'Fuck it, man. You're off.' He was shitting himself.

Word quickly spread and soon all the trainers and fighters rallied around, the wind of a rort fanning their tempers. I got the promoter to repeat what he'd told me and this one bloke exploded, as I knew he would, and king-hit the promoter. His head slapped on the ground and he was out. He was taken away by an ambulance and ended up in a coma. Outside, a massive fight erupted and someone got knifed. I went back to this nightclub with a mate and said, 'That's it, I'm retiring.' I did get my money, though — I was the first guy the promoter paid. Whether the others got theirs or not didn't concern me.

I was of a mind to adopt a terrible outlook. The way I saw it, violence made the world go round; it was the universal language. Everyone was trying to do you over. You had to constantly watch your back. I thought it was such a cesspit of a world and I hated my place in it. And since I was hurting, I wanted to hurt people in the worst way I could. I'd done several jobs by then and I was thinking, *Yeah, this is a good way to go. I can do it by stealth, take it out on these scumbags who've pulled one slimy con too many.* But I had to slip off the radar. I needed to dwell where no victim could easily finger me. So I vacated the spotlight of the ring, went slinking into the dark recesses of club land and took more jobs. I could justify it to myself: these fuckwits had justice coming and I was going to serve it up to them. I was going to be their judge, jury and executioner. Delusional, cock-pulling bravado, that's all it was. But in my mind I was a man on a mission. I was setting out on some indiscriminate rampage like someone who, having destroyed his home and his loved ones, ventures out onto the street to take his war to the world.

Bigger, riskier jobs came my way, paying ten to fifteen grand. Some heavy might want another heavy cut up or his drug trade handicapped. They might get us to do them over while they're holding big amounts — like fifty pounds of dope, duffle bags full of the stuff. Other times you might be collecting gear that was being withheld for whatever reason. We usually took half of what we found, even as much as 70 per cent, because our clients would never have seen the money if we weren't on the case, and 30 per cent was better than zip. To meet these kinds of orders we'd pack knives and guns — anything from 9 millimetre pistols to assault rifles and sub-machine-guns. Mixing it with this crowd, you didn't go in with the safety catch on. You knew you had to shoot first — and, hopefully, last.

For the most part, though, my mission was enlightenment: my clients wanted their victims to be made painfully and shockingly aware they'd fucked up. But they wanted them kept alive. One, because their aim was to recoup money or drive a point home; two, dead bodies are problematic — they're hard to get rid of and they talk to cops. No one runs to the police saying, 'These guys kneecapped me because I owed so-and-so a hundred grand'. Not in those days, anyway.

The jobs took a little planning but we weren't launching rockets. We just had to find the right time to move. We'd do some basic homework, like finding out who the mark lived with and when all the occupants came and went. We only wanted to deal with our target. Things can get really out of hand with other folk around. When the time was right, we'd just rock up and knock on the door. It's funny how people who'd screwed the likes of our clients would just open the door to strangers. And we'd just walk straight in. Or else we'd kick our way in. And while they were trying to work out what the hell was going on, we were breaking and smashing things, warming up the terror. Then we'd close in on them, make sure things were done and leave. We'd say nothing the entire time. We'd said it all, really.

Nine times out of ten something would go wrong. We might have lobbed to find the mark not home, or the presence of someone we did not want or expect to see would force us to bail. We might have had three jobs in a day planned and none of them would come off. So between these bursts of violence there were long hours spent sitting in a car with Pete. The boredom kind of made the whole sordid business even grubbier — I'd have plenty of time to think what a dreary, shitty, evil little life I was leading. I was working for some of the scummiest people you could imagine: murderers, rapists, dealers and hardened crims. And sometimes I'd have to crack them to get my money off them. But what made it hard to live with myself was the knowledge of what heinous things I was doing to people with knives and fists and clubs.

I saw some pretty gruesome goings-on. Like I say, the object, mostly, was to scare people into paying. We had to put the fear of God into them. We didn't want to walk out and have them disappear. They had to be terrified of the consequences of further noncompliance. I'm telling it cold and plain because that's the way I fixed my mind to handle it. These shits had asked for it. They'd crossed the wrong guys; they'd figured they'd wait and see what would happen. Sound familiar? Unfortunately for them, we came knocking and something bad did happen. And I was a pitiless son of a bitch. In those sadistic moments I was the dominator, the tormentor. I held the power to deny mercy, to unleash brutality and to turn up the agony. To me, this was what it meant to be a real man — a hard, scary motherfucker who would do anything to people and not bear a scrap of conscience. A man of stone. But I wasn't immune to what I saw and heard. No cold front could prevent my mind seizing on the bloody and graphic scenes I witnessed and enacted.

I took plenty of speed before doing the jobs. We even did the odd job on acid or ecstasy, just for the hell of it. That's how fucked up it got. But I'd always take plenty of dope and pills to numb myself afterwards. That's what drugs were all about now — to smash myself. They were my antidepressants, I suppose. They helped me to live with what I'd done.

And, for all my front, I was far from impervious to fear. The hairier jobs showed me that. I'd be standing outside someone's front door with a baseball bat up the sleeve of my bomber jacket and a gun tucked into my jeans, readying myself to charge through, and I'd be scared shitless. The weapons I carried were a good indication of the type of reception we could expect. So if I was carrying a machine gun, the fear was all the more intense. Given what I knew about a target on the other side, stepping through that door might well have been the last thing I'd ever do. It was at those moments that I realised I wasn't as hard-core as I thought. I was a pretender. Every time I was as nervous as all hell, trying to get my shit together, clenching my teeth hard and growling to steel myself. I'd end up resorting to the type of thinking I'd struck on in Tokyo before my fight against Samart: I had to tell myself, *Instead of sitting here shitting yourself about what might happen, let's check out what's going to actually happen and then we'll see if we're afraid of it.*

One time Pete and I lobbed on the doorstep of some junkie dealer. He'd broken into some guy's house, tied up his wife, stolen everything and then cut her up, leaving her alive but permanently disfigured. We were the revenge. We had knives, bats and guns to pay the dealer back in kind, plus a tip. We'd found out he was a bit of a loony who liked his guns and was trigger happy. He had a bit of form. So we had to be ready for the worst. When we knocked on the door, his girlfriend answered. That hadn't been in the script — we'd thought she'd gone. One look at us and she freaked. Besides finding two mean-looking skinheads on the landing, she could see how agitated I was. She slammed the door shut and bolted the inside, screaming out to her boyfriend. Pete grabbed the locked screen door and ripped it clean off. We kicked in the front door, stormed inside and attacked the bloke. He wasn't armed at all; he was just plain terrified. Most people would be, I guess. But moments before, I had been the one trembling. And for all my rationale concerning fear, what really got me through the door was that I didn't value the consequences. Standing out front, I knew my life could soon be taken by the bullet of a nervous junkie and I didn't care. I was a desperate man — a lost, scared little man who considered his own life worth risking for as little as three dirty grand.

In the thick of my standover days, I got a tattoo done across my lower back. It reads 'Hurricane' in large Old English lettering. Took the guy five excruciating hours to complete and I was in shock by the time he was done — pale and weak, and I had to get someone to drive me home. But I had my tough sticker. It showed everyone just how hard I was. I was still the Hurricane, still a force of destruction. But it was, in truth, a prop and symbolised nothing I could be proud of. I'd made Hurricane an irremovable part of myself and now that tattoo is significant for a reason other than the macho whim that inspired it. Now it's a sign of my worst times — a period in my life I can never delete, a reminder of the godforsaken world in which I once dwelled.

# XX

## *Backing Out*

Now that the ring was history, I had two lives, each one a waste. My open life as deejay drug dealer was a quickening treadmill of fast nothings and synthetic highs. My closed life as a thug for hire was a road to oblivion. I was one twisted, two-faced unit. One moment I was numb and hateful, the other I was high and beaming; I could be the life of the party or the face of terror; I could be talking tunes one minute and sticking knives into hamstrings the next. My rave scene friends knew a little about my standover work — only the grim larks I chose to share with them, of which they no doubt took two-thirds for bullshit. They had no idea of the extent to which I'd given myself over to my hateful urges.

My nightmares were now based in violent fact rather than the macabre fiction spawned by my rape. The things that haunted me most were the sounds: of screams, of body parts cracking and tearing. I remember lying in bed with a head full of horror, a suitcase full of guns and ammunition under my bed, a pistol under my pillow, knives throughout the house and a loaded shotgun at the front door, and in a high state of anxiety. I'd been thinking of all the people I'd fixed up or sorted out. Someone must surely be coming for me. And I had every reason to believe they would. Undoubtedly, the drugs exacerbated my angst. But so did the knowledge of what savagery men were capable.

I was always led to believe that there were prices on my head. After just about every big job, I'd go to get paid and they'd say something like, 'Nice one. Here's your ten grand.' And then, 'Oh yeah, by the way, they put a hit out on ya.' And I'm like, 'What? What do you mean? How the hell would *they* know who I am? *Do* they know who I am?' 'Well, no, but they've put a hit out on the people who did it. So now people are going to be looking for ya. Just letting ya know.'

'Yeah, cheers mate. Ta. Thanks for the heads-up.'

*Shit! What does that mean — a hit out on me? Knock me or just break my legs?* I could only reassure myself that they wouldn't be able to finger me. For many jobs I'd walked straight in but for all the big jobs I'd worn a hood. Still, everywhere I went I'd always be looking over my shoulder. I'd be out shopping with Leah and some steel-head would walk past and look at me strangely and I'd get on edge. I was always on guard. A horrible bilge slopped about in my guts constantly.

Physically, I was sliding. Having abandoned all pretence of being a professional athlete, I indulged in what once had been taboos. I stuffed my face with comfort junk food — pizza, Macca's, KFC, takeaway — and washed it down with Wild Turkey and cola stubbies or chocolate milk. In no time I had blown out to 96 kilograms, almost 30 above my former fighting weight. But I didn't look obese as much as very solid and very scary. Heavy in every sense of the word. A total thug, from clean-shaved head to head-kicking toe.

Between jobs I figured I had a pretty cool lifestyle. I had plenty of time to kill and, usually, enough money and drugs to make a good fist of it. I'd start and finish the day with a bowl of mull — a bowl being made up of many cones. That would get me ripped enough to get bogged in the lounge all day. A coffee laced with half a gram of speed would soon get me going. My teeth would start grinding, my feet would start tapping, my blood would get racing and I'd be out the door armed with a few joints for the road.

I'd get in my gold Ford Telstar and go do some rounds, drop off a quarter ounce of speed here and there. I'd visit a friend. He'd go, 'I've got these new pills, really solid — just try a half so you can get on with your day.' So I'd drop a half, continue my rounds, then go home, get on the phone and invite some people over to spin records and drink Wild Turkey. They'd come over. I'd be like, 'Oh, so-and-so's got some new pills. You haven't tried them? I've had a half and they're great.' 'Well, whack up, mate, let's go.' So I'd get my pill guy over and it would be on, the party's started. It would be barely afternoon. I'd ring more people, they'd come around. More pills. Racks of coke. And on and on and on it went.

I had mates with nine-to-five jobs who'd come around for cones after work. They'd rock up to a house full of people on E with the music pumping. And they're like, 'What have you been doing all day?' 'Oh, dropped off this and that, checked out this guy's new pills, came back and it's just erupted and we're going to rock on until tomorrow.' They'd go, 'When are you going to get a real job?'

Time took on a whole new meaning: it didn't exist. There weren't even days. It was just this ever-flowing *now*. Night and day, night and day. *What day is it today? Who cares? Today's the day after yesterday and the day before tomorrow. And what's tomorrow? Tomorrow may be the day we eat some food instead of substances.* The way I saw it, the friends who got angry with me weren't big enough to live their life the way they really wanted to. They did their nine to five. *Well, you go for it, Kool and the Gang. I'm doing okay here with mine.* I was always comfortable with not knowing how I was going to pay my rent or eat. Money was always there. Something always came up — a deal here, a job there.

For a while it was kosher. Then it wasn't, because I was digging myself a massive hole of drug debt and getting deeper into a heavy scene because of what I owed. I needed to do jobs more for income than to satiate my sadistic nature. I dwelled in my own twisted little world and saw little of my family. It was drama that usually brought us together.

One day I got a call from Dad's new girlfriend, Andii. She was hysterical. Dad was pissed and armed and threatening to shoot himself. I got in my car thinking, *It never stops with this bloke! It never ends.* By the time I arrived Donna was already there, comforting Andii. And there's Dad sitting in a chair with a pistol in his hand. My heart sank with sadness, with fatigue, with pity, with anger. The poor, sad fucker. The bastard. My father. My poor, fucking father.

Tears began to spill from my eyes. I was weeping for all the things I knew about him and all the things I didn't. It broke my heart to behold what an utter mess he was. But I hated him for seeing to his own ruin so thoroughly. And now here he was, this wretched shell of a man. I began thinking, *Do yourself a favour. If it's that bad, end it. Put yourself out of your misery. We're all grown up now, we've got on with our lives and you're still there, you're still stuck in that miserable place. If it's torturing you that much, just get out.* But he didn't have the balls. Everything with him was front; I knew that more than ever from that day onwards — I could see it in his eyes. There was no way he was going to stick that gun in his mouth and pull the trigger.

'You don't want to do that, Dad,' I said. 'Give me the gun.' I stepped towards him. We were looking at each other through tears, two sad-fuck reflections of misery. I lifted my hand. He came out from wherever he was and, resigned, offered up the pistol. I went to his safe and got the remaining rounds, and then we put him to bed. Everyone was calm. Yeah, everything was all right. Just sweet. We could all trundle off home now. Roll those *Waltons* credits. Crank up the Cat Stevens.

And the thought wasn't lost on me that, despite wanting to be everything my father wasn't, I'd ended up just like him. The apple really hadn't fallen far from the tree. I was cultivating my own ruin just as effectively as he had, if not more. It formed part of the ingrained despair I carried within me and which no amount of drugs could obliterate. For a long while I'd been winning hands-down a battle I was trying to lose. Drugs could never beat me. I wanted to take leave of my conscience but it never happened.

I was popping up to thirty E tabs over a two- or three-day binge — I'd start off with four then drop one every hour or so, downing them like Tic Tacs. Still, that wasn't enough and I'd be adding coke and whatever else I could to the mix. I did everything but stick a needle in my arm. And I knew that if I did that, I'd end up dead. No matter what I took, the complete abandonment I craved was denied: I just could not switch my brain off. Despite all the orgasmic rushes and booming highs I'd experienced over the years, I'd always retained this rigid grip on reality.

I once spent an afternoon alone snorting line after line of premium coke after being up for a couple of days pilling solidly. My friends had all fallen by the wayside and I kept on racking up. I was on a mission to break myself mentally, to incite some powerful neurosis that once and for all would shunt me into the realm of the unhinged, and I couldn't do it — I mean, the drugs couldn't. So I stopped. That I didn't hoover up every fleck of coke I had on me speaks for itself; that's a landmark right there. Something was getting through to me about the futility of my destructive life choices. They would fix nothing. So I couldn't help but respect my cursed strength of mind. It simply refused to give way, entrenched in my head like some unwanted chaperone. There was nowhere to hide.

There was no kidding myself into feeling good, either — I couldn't erase the bleak knowledge that I was fundamentally screwed up and deeply unhappy. I could never shake that sense of floating on black water and feeling the cold brush of leviathans beneath — things loathsome, empty, loveless and predatory. I'd tell myself that I only broke people who had it coming. I'd tell myself that things would work out with Leah. I'd tell myself that I had stuff going on. But deep down I knew I was full of shit. Literally. I used to be champion of the world. Now I was nothing but a contemptible drug-fucked leech making scum out of my life.

If I used violence to ease my pain, the relief was short-lived. After about a year of being in the game, I started to really assess where I was at. The nature of one particular job meant I had to lay low for a while; all I'll say about it is that it wasn't so much violent as daring and it paid extremely well. I had pause to think. I was just 23 years old, and I could see that my life was on a fast track to ruin. Over the time I'd been doing jobs, the rules of the game had begun to change. There were home invasion laws that — if I was ever found guilty of them in court — could put me away for twenty years. Now, that's a fine recourse for regular members of society, but for me the problem was that crims started to hide behind them. It was weird — I couldn't just walk in and baseball bat these people. Over the phone I'd be calling in money on behalf of somebody and making threats to pay them a visit, and these heavies would say, 'Do that and I'll get the cops on ya.' What?! This was bullshit. These outlaws were supposed to be hard-core. They were like, *Yeah, I'm real hard-core, until* you *threaten to come see me.* Things were getting untenable and, during my enforced hiatus, the message began to sink home. If I kept on doing what I was doing, and lived long enough, I'd land myself in the one situation in which, I knew for certain, I would have no exit strategy. If I went to jail, I could not see myself ever coming out — and I don't mean because I'd top myself.

I was still full of anger and reacting violently on the street and the road, but I knew I had to give up the jobs. Then came the heaviest of offers: a job to murder some guy. He was talking to cops and was a severe risk to the freedom of some very influential people if he ever took the stand as a witness. I was involved in discussions about how the body would be dismembered and buried. But I knew that if I crossed that line there was no turning back. Something clicked in my mind; it should have clicked a long time before then. *Shoot the guy. Cut up the body. Logistics of a murder. This is insanity! Where am I? What dimension have I slipped into here?* I was like, *Can you live with this? Are you really going to be able to live with this?* And the answer was, *No. This is not who I am.* I turned down the job. And from that point on I started to back out. Just baby steps. But together they would constitute a giant leap from the fire. This world was not the world I wanted to live in. Enough was enough. And once I'd made that call, I had to stop myself from running. Just quietly, I urged myself, slowly back-pedal and ... get the fuck out of there.

It's not easy to excuse oneself from that scene. I'd come across so many very disturbed men. Men who could laugh as they told you of a friend who'd had a row with his girl and cut off her head with a shovel. Men who'd had unthinkable cruelties inflicted upon them repeatedly as boys. Men who'd long grown so cold, so desensitised, that they chilled rooms. The walking dead. Men who wanted me to help them kill the world together.

The first thing I did was gather up all my guns and get them out of the house. I filled a big bag with machine guns, assault rifles, a shotgun, a sawn-off shotgun, sawn-off 22s with silencers, a 9 millimetre, a 38, knives and knuckledusters — something for everyone. I looked at it all and went, *My God: this is my life*. Not every tool was mine — it was more a team kitbag. I thought, *Look at this — I'm minding someone else's nightmare. I don't even know what half these guns have been used for. And I do know what the other half have been used for*. I went and left the bag with Pete.

Pete took offence: 'What are you doing? Where do you think you're going? What do you mean, you're getting out? Think you're better than me, do ya?' Others displayed genuine puzzlement; they thought they led a normal lifestyle. 'Come on, get real, Paul. This is your life, man.' It was like trying to get out of quicksand.

I felt so naked without the guns. I already lived with a great deal of paranoia for all the jobs I'd done — any number of people could be coming after me. Now I could be seen as a risk by my former associates because of what I knew. Those guns were my security blanket. Without them my confidence was gone.

But I was glad, too. I was so sick of the fact that my whole life revolved around talking about one of three things: drugs or hurting people or money. I needed to change. Desperately. And it was all I could do to conceal from certain people just how anxious I was to leave. I wanted to give no one the jitters. I had to back out nice and slowly.

Within months I had an amazing stroke of fortune. Not that I deserved any such grace. It happened when I was down in Byron Bay, in the thick of a drug binge, waiting for a mate of mine called Jim. He was about to finish work and we were going to go score some coke. I was languishing in that 'there's nothing wrong with my life except everything' kind of mood. I'd split up with Leah for the umpteenth time and, as usual, had immediately veered into a monster sessions, ingesting anything that came within my vicinity. No drug was safe around my black hole of an appetite. And as supplies in Brisbane dried up and momentum around me slowed, I headed for Byron to stay on my roll. The night before Jim, a couple of mates and I had had a hoot dancing in the street to this mob of bongo drummers. We were on the pills and these guys sounded awesome. I put fifty bucks in the hat and told them to keep on playing and for an hour we went right off, drawing a crowd of people who wanted to get a look at the twisted freaks dancing up a storm. Finally the drummers said they needed a break, so we moved on. Byron had always been good to me drug-wise and this trip was proving to be no exception.

So I was sitting on Watego's Beach when up from the water walked this hippy. He sat down at a picnic table in front of me and we began chatting a bit. He said his name was Ramé. To look at us you'd say we were complete opposites. He was the archetypal herbal dude whose every gesture, every tone, was mild in manner. But he was no sap: he was really switched on, and I found him interesting. I told him a little about myself, about breaking up with my girl, about being off my head for days, about wanting to stay off my head for a few days more. He asked if I wanted some acid. I said yes, very much so. He gave me a tab. He asked if I fancied a joint. I said a joint sounded like a fine idea. I liked this hippy.

Jim arrived and it turned out that he and Ramé knew each other. Ramé handed Jim a tab and the three of us walked up to the headland below the lighthouse to enjoy the trips. The sun behind us was low enough to have lost its glare and it began enriching the colours of the beautiful coastline seemingly for our benefit, as the acid had begun to turn our vision into something more sublime and tactile than mere sight. More like deep sensory inhalations. The effects were enhanced even more when Ramé began playing his didgeridoo. We smoked joint after joint and talked. To hear me, you'd think I was enjoying a coffee as opposed to a solid trip and spliffs of resinous buds. That was me, though — only volumes of drugs could begin to touch the sides.

I sounded so normal. I spoke about myself, things good and bad, with candour. Ramé said, 'Man, you're a pretty full-on dude.' I was like, 'Yeah, whatever.' But he knew full well that I had issues I needed to deal with. Not that he said any such thing. What he did say was, 'You've got to come out and meet this woman with me tomorrow.' 'Who?' I asked. 'This American Indian woman. Her name's Grandmother Windhawk. I'll take you out to meet her.' I was like, 'What for?' All he said was, 'Trust me. It will be an experience.' An experience? I was up for that. 'Sweet. Yeah. All right. I'll come.' 'Cool,' he said, and he began skinning up another hottie.

The three of us crashed at Jim's place that night and in the morning I found myself in a car going to some place called Drake, thinking, *What the fuck am I doing here with this hippy? Where's this tripper taking me?*

To the beginning of the rest of my life, as it turned out. To my life's very axis. Of all the choices I'd ever made, this would prove the most pivotal. Upon this vague decision everything would come to hinge. A small, clear light was about to shine upon the confounding sweep of my fate: a tiny diamond of truth.

# XXI

## *Illumination*

I had half a mind to wrench the wheel back towards Byron Bay. While I was tripping and stoned, the name 'Grandmother Windhawk' sounded so goddamn profound and the American Indian shit really, really cool. Now, in the bright wash of daylight, the whole thing seemed like some daft hippy wank. Need I remind anyone that we were in northern New South Wales, Australia, not frigging Wyoming? And *Grandmother Windhawk*? What's with that? I was picturing some loopy old bat with magpie feathers in her hair mumbling hash-cookie gibberish under a totem pole made of beer cans; some dislocated white Aussie chick who'd lost it in the '60s and disappeared up her own arse laying claim to spiritualisms that weren't hers and former lives she'd never lived. I liked the whole idea less and less with each elapsed kilometre. And old mate Ramé said this was a two-day gig. God help me.

I looked at Jim — he looked perfectly chilled. I kept my reservations, so to speak, to myself. There'd be no pulling out. Besides, it was a top day for a drive. The warm sun set off the green grass and bush and hills around us as we motored through Nimbin and beyond. We had sunnies on, good music, an open road and a pile of buds. Things could be worse. I relaxed a little, took in the scenery and toked hard on the scoobs that came my way.

The three-hour drive took closer to five. The dope messed with Ramé's bearings and he took a few wrong turns. Still, it gave him plenty of time to elaborate on what the hell we were getting into. He told us that Grandmother Windhawk was a very wise woman who conducted sweat lodges, some American Indian purification ritual where you sit in a hot sauna and come out with a steam-cleaned soul. At some level I liked the sound of that. At another, I thought it was a crock.

When we got out of the car, my worst fears were realised. It looked for all money that we'd crashed some corporate bonding weekend. Standing around was, on face value, a small party of flabby businessmen and pasty Motor Registry dweebs. And here was I, this 'fucking look at me and I'll kill ya' misfit, coming down off a lot of drugs. I was like, *What am I doing here? Who are these knobs?* The first sign of a group hug and I was gone. I wasn't about to spend a weekend with a bunch of lost twits turning gay.

But what was I, if not lost?

Every fatuous notion I'd had about Grandmother Windhawk evaporated the moment I saw her. What a compelling woman: she was every bit the real deal. I knew it the moment she caught my eye. In a second, I sensed that my past and present had been studied and grasped completely. And by the time the brief exchange broke, she seemed to bear knowledge concerning my destiny. I felt utterly naked before her. But she started talking about how she was going to teach us about the Earth and its wisdom. At first I was like, 'I don't give a shit about the Earth. I don't give a shit about anything at the moment.' Then, as she continued, my resistance began to slip. She spoke in soft but firm tones and every word rang with significance. She explained the sacred ceremony of the sweat lodge, what would happen and what we had to bear in mind. She said we would leave having learnt some fundamental truths about ourselves, about how we work, and how to better align ourselves with how the Earth works. She was unbelievably grounded. There was nothing airy-fairy about her. This old woman was as hard as stone yet as peaceful as a breeze and as wise as time.

After listening to Grandmother Windhawk's introduction, we pitched our tents, ate some dinner and then crashed. She told us we'd do the first sweat lodge later that night, although no time was set. She'd have to seek permission from the spirits of the land, and would conduct the ritual at a time of their choosing. At about one in the morning she came and woke us. We were on.

Seven of us crammed into this small hut about 3 feet high. The floor was covered with green gum leaves. We sat in a circle with our legs up against our chests and our heads bent forward. Grandmother Windhawk placed a red-hot volcanic rock in a little pit in the middle of the hut. She doused the rock with water, gave thanks, sprinkled some more water on, and then closed the door to leave us to the scalding steam and pitch-black darkness. The heat grew very intense very quickly.

Then Grandmother Windhawk opened the door for a little while and we got a breather. Then she added another damn rock. After she'd placed seven of the fuckers — one for every man in the hut — round one was complete. Then she would begin the second round, then the third, then the fourth. Such hell I'd never known.

After just a couple of rocks the heat was so brutal that it felt like my skin had been peeled off. My body felt like an open wound. I could have sworn my flesh was cooked through and ripe to fall off my bones.

Very early on it was panic stations. We all flattened ourselves against the ground to escape the high heat. We scraped up a handful of leaves and sucked at the meagre scented oxygen they seeped. We pushed against each other to position ourselves better while trying to keep our feet from burning on the rocks.

I started freaking. *I'm burning to fucking death in here! I need to get out! And it's so so dark! And it's ... oh, my God! GOD!* And so began the manic search for help.

The idea of the sweat lodge is to force yourself inwards, to reach inside yourself for the strength to endure, because there's nowhere else to turn. The fundamental rule was that you remained in the hut.

By the end of the very first round I was reduced to a tortured mess. I might have vomited, I might have pissed my pants, but I didn't care. One part of my being was trying desperately to find a way to cope, to endure, while the other was screaming at me to end it. And I realised I was essentially holding up a mirror to myself, and I saw all my demons and all my strengths reflected. I almost gave in to my panic. But Grandmother Windhawk stood guard outside and talked with me and calmed me down.

After forty minutes we were done. I came out crawling on all fours; I could hardly stand. We headed straight for this big dam and dived in. I was so dehydrated and depleted I started seeing things. I was completely numb. I don't think I can describe exactly what it was like. I felt as though I was not in my body but in another place, that I wasn't in my present but was aware of it. I felt as though I was just out there, somewhere else, as though my spirit and consciousness had somehow escaped the confines of my body, but what they experienced still registered with me.

By the end of the sweat lodge I had completely surrendered because my body had made me surrender. I came out stripped of ego. Nobody said a word for probably two hours afterwards; everyone remained silent in their own space. Eventually, it was back to bed. It was one of the most painful experiences I've ever been through, but also one of the most profound.

We did another sweat lodge the following day and then left. There wasn't much talk going on in the car. I'd never been so fully contemplative. It was as though the sweat lodges had aired the rank confines of my soul. I felt cleansed and lifted. For the first time since I could remember, a nugget of peace was housed within me. It was beautiful. I was thinking over a powerful new thought: *If I change the way I look at things, the things I look at change.* The notion was rich in possibility and hope.

In one way or another, anger had governed my entire life. So I tried very hard to contemplate myself in a state of not being angry, and it was like warm sun striking frozen earth — small, good things seemed to sprout. Traces of love came to life. I could actually believe that, at heart, I was a good person. I had a glimpse that I was a good guy, that I was capable of good things and making people feel good around me. It was a scrap of reform — and a significant one.

I'd had a good talk with Grandmother Windhawk about my drugs and violence. I thought, in the case of the drugs, she wouldn't know what I was on about. But she knew all right. She knew the lingo and everything. She'd been a heroin addict and an alcoholic. She'd been there and done that in life. I didn't tell her about my rape, but I felt in some way I had. She seemed to know everything I was going through.

When I got back to Brisbane I was talking spiritual stuff to Ben and he was like, 'Man, I saw you stomp on some guy's head last week.' 'True,' I said, but now I was all set to do a little meditation and light some incense. And for the first time in my life I picked up a book to read — Paulo Coelho's *The Alchemist*. But this was not my salvation, or a rebirth. Within days I was back into the deejay lifestyle, necking pills and amphetamines all night, sleeping through to the next afternoon and awaking to cones and speed and a full tank of rage. I'd lost none of my violent impulses. Save for not doing the jobs, I was back in the old loop. But I couldn't shake the notion that some transition had been set in train. I knew that to deal with certain issues, I had to go deep within. I knew I'd find no peace if I just settled with making do on the surface of things.

Screwed up as I was, you'd think I was in no position to help anyone. But my father needed me. He'd regressed into lost-child mode and was hitting strip joints and doing all sorts of self-destructive stuff. I would think, *What's all this about — your childhood? What, twenty-nine years as a husband and father doesn't change you? Come on. You didn't want to change. You don't want to make an effort.* And what about me, you ask? Who was I to judge? Well, I had an excuse, didn't I — I was young. He, on the other hand, was beyond 50. Hadn't he learnt anything? Maybe he was convinced to the depths of his soul that change was impossible. I really can't say, because he's never spoken about it.

He did make one significant change, I'll concede, however belatedly. He came to me and said, 'I've joined Alcoholics Anonymous.' He was wanting this great big 'Oh, good on you'. But I was thinking, *What? You go and fix yourself now? You want to think about it now? Bit late, isn't it? What about when it meant something? The family's finished. It's all over, man. The damage is done. Thanks, you bastard. It means nothing now. It means something for you only. You're doing it for you. What about before, when you were terrifying your wife and kids? Why didn't you do it for us?*

But what I said was, 'That's great, Dad. I'm proud of you.'

It was around this time I first saw one of Dad's papers, some classified military document. I was over at the house — our Algester home that he now had to himself — and he had all this paperwork scattered around. When he was in another room I noticed this one sheet, picked it up and started reading. It had 'classified' on it and looked really old. 'David Robin Briggs' was up top and there was all this information on him. Honourable discharge due to wounding, it read. And it indicated he'd been a bodyguard to some South Vietnamese general. There was mention of the money spent to train Dad up and, I swear, it was in the millions. I was blown away. But that's all I got to read. Dad came up and snatched it from me without saying a word. He gathered up all the papers and walked into another room. He came back and made a coffee. Still not a word. I didn't question him. It was like, *You weren't meant to have seen that.* But now when I think about it, the whole Vietnam stuff doesn't add up. Dad was in the New Zealand navy. As far as I know, they saw no action in Vietnam. At 18, he was married and living in Christchurch, and he did no more service for any branch of the military. So maybe all this 'Nam talk was stuff he appropriated from army guys he trained in self-defence. Was he that delusional? That good an actor? Could he have invented all those stories he raved on about when he'd drunk himself into another crisis? Were those details of nights spent in foxholes under the noses of the Viet Cong and him replacing the innards of a dying buddy all the product of a warped mind? They may well have been. But they could also be nightmares borne of his civilian deeds that he'd recast into the theatre of war. Maybe. But what was that document I saw? I remember it vividly. I swear, I just don't know what to believe.

Whenever my own self-loathing weighed heavily on me, I'd find myself thinking of the sweat lodges. Finally, I decided to go back — and I took Dad with me. Whatever truly lay in his past, he needed cleansing as much as I did, if not more.

Seeing Dad attempt the purification ritual taught me something and nothing about him. For the first time, I saw him fully let go of his aggressive front. That was all well and good, but I was interested to see how he'd handle the inner battle the sweat lodge would force upon him. Because that's what it is: a place of confrontation. You are presented with such powerful, raw and undeniable aspects of yourself, it's frightening. You face your truth. In trying to endure the incredible physical pain, you find yourself desperately reaching into your spirit for strength, and hoping to find merciful refuge in your very own soul. Yet as you strive to draw on that pure force, you are harassed by extremely powerful demons — your darkest thoughts, your deepest fears, your blackest feelings. It's a profound test of mental strength and will; an amazing journey of self-knowledge. But Dad couldn't cut it. When his hellspawn arose in force, he panicked and fled the hut.

I was pissed off. I thought, *You're supposed to be this hard dude but you can't face up to yourself.* I said to him, 'You're going back in there. You must confront this stuff.' But he was crying like a little boy, saying he couldn't go back in, swearing he'd go mad if he did. Grandmother Windhawk was far more annoyed than I was. She said nothing but glared at Dad: *How dare you leave.* She knew exactly what all his stuff was about. This incredible woman — or, should I say, poor woman — channelled everyone's crap; she was a medium through whom all our experiences passed, and Dad's episode left her in a furious state. It was as though she'd been defiled. She had to go away for an hour or two. She was still visibly upset when she returned for sharing time, where all the men would sit in a circle to listen to one another's sweat lodge experiences. She began saying how angry she was about what man does to himself, what men do to other men, and she went on about all this killing. She said to me afterwards, 'He's big enough to do this but he's not big enough to face it.' And that's what Dad's whole life had been about — 'I'll do this but I'm not going to answer for it. No way. I'm not taking responsibility for anything. Nothing.' I've never heard him say, 'I was wrong.' I've never heard an apology from his lips. Never. He has acted as though he was perfect, as though he was always right, but what a sham that is — and not just for him but for every soul on this planet.

Your troubled past — I know this only now — is like an arrow embedded in your soul. To have any hope of healing yourself, you must pull that arrow out. Conscious acknowledgment and extraction is an extremely painful yet vital part of the process. You can bandage around that piece of steel all you like but it's not going to work. Emotionally, that's what Dad tried to do. All this patching. Band-Aids and disinfectant for mortal wounds.

Later we were all sent into the bush to have some reflection time alone. I was sitting in long grass looking over the dam when I turned and saw Dad standing 10 metres away. I hadn't heard him — which was surprising because the long grass made a real racket when you walked though it — and he hadn't seen me. We were not meant to be anywhere near another person and I thought I should move. But I was intrigued by what Dad was doing, and I wanted to keep observing him without him knowing. Then I looked down to brush an ant off my leg and when I looked back up he was gone. Vanished. I never heard a thing. It was freaky; it reminded me of the time a bunch of us played paintball and Dad was like a commando spirit of the bush, appearing out of nowhere to drill us. He wiped everyone out. If it had been everyone against him, he would have won, no question. I know paintball ain't war, but where did he learn that sort of shit? Vietnam? Gove? Through his army mates? All my life I'd developed these ideas in my head and think, *Man, he's full of shit.* And then something like that would happen and I'd just go, *Whoa — what am I to believe?*

As for me, the sweat lodges that weekend brought me closer to the idea of committing myself to turning my life around. But at that time it was more to do with firming my thoughts than taking action. I spoke with Grandmother Windhawk about how I hated so much about myself and my life. She knew that I aspired to better things and that I couldn't see how to achieve them. The sweat lodges showed me clearly that I'd refused to confront the greatest obstacle in my path: my rape. I'd never spoken about my rape in share time, so the nightmares it triggered in the sweat lodges were my demons and mine alone. But in our one-on-one, Grandmother Windhawk began talking to me about it. I hadn't told her a thing, but she came out with details that shocked me. I began crying openly as she spoke. As usual, though, she was not one to indulge in emotions. She knew I was hiding, that I was avoiding dealing with what I'd blocked out so long. She knew I wanted to be better. She asked, 'When are you going to walk your talk, Paul? *When are you going to walk your talk?*'

I had no idea. It was like asking a school kid, 'What do you want to do with your life?' I used to know that. Now I was like so many other people my age: I didn't have a clue as to where I was headed. Through a stream of ephemeral highs and horrors I carried a dull need for something of purpose to take root in my life. But I was so lost to violence, I'd even begun to think of it as therapy: I was sharing my pain, communicating my own hurt. The specific effect of each force at work within me was not clear to me but it did occur to me at one point that I'd been inflicting pain upon men as I would have on the guy who'd raped me, if I had the chance. If I told you the things I've dreamt of doing to this bloke you'd be physically ill, I'm sure. Not that I was ever conscious of it at the time, but so many other people copped it instead of him. Don't mistake my actions for mindful vengeance or think that I sought to analyse my motives in the thick of my job days — I was immersed in a formless hatred and for the most part I hurt people simply because I wanted to hurt them. I'd even forgotten what that guy who raped me looked like until recently, when I saw him in a family photo. And he should know this: it's my choice that he's alive today. He should thank God for every breath he takes.

I knew I had to deal with this rage, somehow. No amount of violence was going to release me from my own suffering: I had to make an effort to change. There's no innate ballast guaranteed to right stricken lives. Happiness doesn't simply come to the unhappy. That was made patently clear when I got the news that Adrian, the guy I used to wag school with, had killed himself. Turns out he never found his niche in life and opted out. Apparently, he'd taken an E a few years back and was never the same afterwards. He ended up on medication that, one day, he decided he wasn't going to take any more. He bottomed out and gassed himself in his car.

With severe remorse, I thought about the last time I saw Adrian. He came to watch the Vella fight and I brushed him; I was too busy being the champ. At the funeral I gave my world title belt to Ray, Adrian's stepfather. I'd known Ray a good while before I met Adrian — he used to come to Dad's gym. He was a big fight fan and was so proud of me winning that belt. A wonderful man, Ray. And he was so good to Adrian. He was utterly devastated to lose him. He loved that boy so much and yet was powerless to save him. Just as there was no one who could save me. That, I was starting to realise, was my job.

# XXII

## *The Price Of Vulnerability*

My capacity to reflect upon things was a fairly new tool. Still, it was blunt from neglect and wasn't busied much with fresh work. Putting it to some use, I could see the madness of my life. I was running at a thousand miles an hour in total darkness, hoping not to crash into something. I was living with zero awareness and zero care; I was a totally reactive being. The root of the problem, I realised, wasn't that my life was out of control but that I had thought it beyond my control. And obviously, unless I was somehow incapacitated, that notion was utterly false.

Slowly, I came to embrace awareness as a gift of illumination. There was nothing sudden about it, no light-bulb moment, no jolting epiphany. Perception came flickering alive like a globe fed by a sketchy current. Slowly it grew steady, but it was energy I had to sustain. It took years for me to see where things were, to find my way. Awareness became my excavation tool. Layer by layer, I began to strip down through my thoughts and feelings until I struck upon the stone of my truths. It was a sordid business. Never had I faced an opponent full of such awful and stubborn might as my self. Don't expect I ever will.

Since doing the sweat lodges, I'd felt ill from awareness. The memory of my rape had been dug up to become my constant companion. It had felt better suppressed. But while I may have

187

acknowledged the value of reflection, I didn't apply it to any great degree. Eventually I vowed to put things into practice: I'd start walking my talk. But you tell yourself a lot of things, don't you?

I knew I needed to talk to someone. That was a big thing for me to come to grips with — sharing my burden. I muttered convictions out loud to spur myself on: 'You are not normal. You are not well. You need help. Put out your hand. This doesn't mean you're a pussy.' Being this Paul 'Hard Man' Briggs made it very hard to admit that I was in dire need of rescue. How was I going to do this? Where was I going to start?

Leah. Who else? We'd split up — again — but there was no one else I could turn to.

She was onto me immediately, thinking I was trying to soften her up to get back with her. Still, as always, she cared and was open to listening. I lost it before I even started talking. I'd barely got two sobbing words out when she said, 'I know what you're going to say.' She said she'd noticed how I got funny whenever the subject of rape came up. She'd long suspected something wasn't right. I went ahead and told her anyway. I wanted to tell her what had happened in detail. I grew hysterical, ending up on the floor in a foetal position, howling and rocking back and forth.

Leah was freaked out. She called for back-up and a friend came over and the two of them put me in the shower to try to calm me down. I regained my composure at last, and then proceeded to tell Leah that I wanted us to be together, that I loved her, and I regurgitated all the pleading crap I'd wheeled out so many times before. This time she didn't roll over. She said she wasn't going to even think about having me back until I got professional help. She found me someone to see. And while her charity kicked off the long process of my healing, it would ultimately seal the demise of our relationship.

I did seven weeks of counselling. That's not much but the effect was fundamental and lasting. I found that talking about all my inner turmoil was a healthy start. The messages I took from those sessions struck home, as though I was in a process of revision rather than learning. I started to honestly fathom the enigma of my own self. I had a clean-up job on my hands and I recoiled at the scope of the mess before me. It was like, *I've got problems. Yes, okay. I've got to deal with my rape. Okay. I'm angry. Yeah, all right. I know that. I'm angry because of my rape. Okay, cool. I'm angry because I had a father who stood over me all my life. Check. And I've got a few addictions to deal with as well: substances and sex and violence.* One particular drug wasn't my vice — it was a cocktail of speed, ecstasy, cocaine and marijuana. As for sex, three roots a day wasn't enough; I'd have to have a couple of DIYs as well. And the violence ... well, that was a twisted kind of lust in itself, a smutty primal urge that could only be relieved, not expunged. All up, I could see I had some major work ahead of me. Things looked better with the lights out.

The counselling was full-on. I was doing group sessions with people whose problems dwarfed mine. There was the father who'd lost his baby, a figure of profound grief who was lifeless but for the tough strands of courage and dignity he showed. There was real strength, right there. The weight of other people's sadnesses tore me up. What was this I was feeling — compassion? I couldn't help but be moved by these people, inspired by them.

For the duration of the course I was forbidden to take any drugs — no stimulants or emotion-affecting substances. Not even coffee. I obeyed. It was so hard, not so much for the forces of habit I had to resist, but for all the feelings that surfaced. And for the first time in my life, because I was instructed to, I paid close attention to what I was feeling. I forced myself to stop and reflect on what was happening when emotions surged. Not react, not snuff them out with drugs, not demean them as useless sensibilities or weeds in my character; I tried to simply experience them and let them come out in whatever way. If I cried, if I got lonely or sad or insecure or guilty, I wouldn't fight or react. I had to acknowledge and embrace these things until they subsided. Then I had to think over why they arose and what they meant to me and rationalise them. They could mean nothing of consequence or they could be important. I was becoming aware of what lay beneath and beginning to accept aspects of myself I'd been striving to kill off since I was eight — those soft, oily and suspect emotions that gave me such a disturbing sense of frailty. I was beginning to welcome my sworn enemy: vulnerability.

I really struggled. For months and months after the course finished, I nursed a riot of conflicting thoughts and feelings. I had gained insights into why I was the way I was, but that didn't mean I could change overnight. I didn't instantly turn my back on the drugs, the dealing and my violent behaviour. And I remained stuck in the destructive cycle I'd developed with Leah. The counselling had made me aware of co-dependency, and suddenly there was a perfect description of our dysfunctional relationship. To think we thought it was love! We were torturing each other. Every time I wanted to change, I got her out of my life. Once alone, I'd get scared and would tell her that I couldn't cope without her, and I'd win her back. I was petrified of being alone. She always thought, despite a mountain of evidence to the contrary, that somehow it would all change. She was unable to set the boundaries for her own life — what was acceptable for her, what was not; what was healthy for her, what was not. Neither was I. We were no good for each other, but because of history and naivety and misguided hope, we remained trapped in this sad, abusive flux. I would blunder in and out of her life like some drunk bumping off corridor walls and into wrong rooms. It was driving me nuts and holding her in chronic denial. And vice versa.

So I was onto something — but I wasn't. I was opening doors and slamming them shut. Oh, what a glorious path was self-discovery. It was a muddy, seemingly limitless trek at the end of which awaited something intangible. All I knew was that I had to keep going forward, no matter how many stumbles back or sideways offset my progress. Though I may well have been the last person on Earth to deserve it, I wanted to cleanse my soul. And such a state seemed remote and complex, a prize matted in impossible knots that would eternally confound me.

Happiness. Love. Peace. These were mere words. I wanted them to have real meaning in my life. Why? Because for all my lessons in hate, blood and violence, I knew this deeply: there was no other reason for living. I had made up my mind; I was not going to live my entire life as a viperous wretch, to know nothing other than the dark arts of drugs and violence. I was not going to remain at the mercy of external forces; I was going to lift myself out. I was a better man than the diseased, delusional piece of work I'd fashioned myself into. I realised that I was very much the product of my own handiwork and the perpetrator of my own misery. But I could do so much better. This, too, was something I knew deeply.

Perhaps my lowest point came in Drake. I was back doing sweat lodges and we'd done one at dawn and another at sunset. Both were very intense. The first seemed to give me strength for the second, and I needed all I had because the second was an amazing but gruelling process of release. Physically, emotionally and mentally, I was purging all manner of waste from my system. I was dry retching and spent, mentally broke and full of nothing but the emptiness of sorrow. Then the visions came to me.

I saw myself as a little boy who walked up and stood before me. He was beautiful in the way that innocence is simply beautiful. He reached out and took my hand. I was looking at a sweet child and an old soul. There were no words spoken but it was clear his purpose was to comfort me and to teach me. He had come back for keeps; he was home, which in itself was a gift of such consolation and grace as to fill even the weakest of men with hope, the most guilt-ridden, the most condemned with forgiveness of themselves. He was a vision of pure love. I felt I'd received something priceless: I had been given back to me.

The second vision seemed to be a coda to the first. I saw myself walking with a woman, who was obviously my wife, and two children. The potency and promise of that image, with its sublime sense of family, of belonging, stirred up feelings of such purpose that I could dare to believe that this was not mere fantasy but a glimpse at my future.

I was not so sure afterwards. Outside the hut, I felt horribly soulless — gutted in the most literal sense. Once it might have been an appealing notion to have my soul stripped bare, but the feeling was of being suspended above a void. I am describing vulnerability. Grandmother Windhawk told me that I must begin to fill that void with love, to look at the world through the eyes of a child, with love instead of hatred and anger. And the first recipient of my love must be myself. This was daunting — I could barely stomach the idea of liking myself. But to know love, I had to become love itself. I had to be strong enough to stand defenceless before the world and embrace whatever experiences — good, bad and ugly — such openness brings.

Damn. Was that ever something to mull over on the trip home. Me, Paul Briggs — the monster on your doorstep — a vessel of love? If you knew me then, you'd have thought the idea ludicrous. For the good of society, you'd have believed I was fit for nothing but wholesale removal. And you'd almost have been right. But I dared to believe otherwise. I felt there was some good in me. I was going to try to wrench my life around. No, I was determined to. Confronting how my rape was affecting my life was where I had to start.

First there was the relationship with my mother. I had to tell her what had happened all those years ago. I wanted her to know there was a reason for me being such an unfeeling and wayward child. That I wasn't malicious just for the fun of it, and that if she ever thought of me as being unhappy or disturbed, she could at least consider what underlying forces were at work. My misbehaviour wasn't a nasty campaign to win out over my twin brother, who was bigger and more ideal than me. My life was not simply a twisted response to Nathan.

And what of Nathan? He'd become someone I knew less and less. What I did know was that drugs were destroying him. Then he started with these stupid robberies. I mean, he'd had his own little Hail Caesar complex going as well, but he abused the privilege wantonly. He believed he could get away with blue murder. He was busted for this and that — like the time he smashed the front window of a skateboard shop and the cops arrived to find him passed out at the scene, just-used skateboard at his feet. Dad had leaned upon his influence with the cops and lawyers to keep Nathan from jail. When Nathan pulled an armed robbery, though, there was nothing anyone could do to save him. He was locked up.

I never visited him, at least not initially. The gravity of his plight didn't compel me to break our estrangement.

To be honest, when Nathan went to jail I felt that our relationship was essentially the best it had been for a long while — because we were further apart than ever. And I know it sounds heartless to say this, but I profited from this definitive separation. For once, we didn't have to deal with each other. In a very personal sense, Nathan's incarceration liberated me. I thought about him a lot but unlike Dad — who, all credit to him, visited Nathan constantly — I didn't go see him. As much as it shames me now to admit, I got on with my life.

So the timing wasn't great to hit Mum with bombshell news. She was really down about Nathan, feeling like she'd failed as a mother. I should have known my revelation would be too much for her. But my need to have her know outweighed all other concerns. I took courage from a bottle of red before Leah and I went around to Mum and Wayne's for dinner. After the meal I approached her in the kitchen while she was tidying up. I said I had something to tell her and then I was out with it. She didn't react at all; she just went on packing the dishwasher. Didn't miss a beat.

I felt like a complete idiot. News of my life's greatest trauma could not dislodge my mother's attention from dirty dishes, cutlery and soap powder. I whirled out of the kitchen, volcanic with remorse. *How could I be so stupid?* She'd just shunned me. Totally.

Mum followed me out and sat down. I could see she was struggling but was unable to handle it. She held up a front. She did not, or did not want to, believe me. She seemed to resent being lumbered with more baggage to take ownership of and was having none of it. Her attitude was like, 'Why tell me? What can I possibly do?' She missed the point entirely. I was thinking, *Why tell you? You're my mother!* But I said: 'This is not for you to handle. I'm telling you so you know. Not to blame you. You did a great job as a mother.' But she took it like the only reason I would tell her was to attack her, to get an apology, to demand her sympathy at gunpoint. She was so far off track but there was no resolving chat afterwards; she dug herself a trench of denial. She obviously found it easier to think I'd stooped to a vile play for her affection. There was no progress to be made. Leah and I upped and left.

Fill yourself with love? Be strong enough to make yourself vulnerable? Fuck that for a joke. It had taken all my nerve to open up to Mum like that. And what did she do? Made me a fool, cast me as a liar, withdrew in disgust. Needless to say, things between us deteriorated from that point on. I never sought to fully hide the anger and bitterness I held towards her after that. She, on the other hand, really tried hard to keep the relationship open. Every time we'd speak I'd employ this venomous tone and she'd say, 'Why are you so angry with me?' She came up to see me once, crying, saying, 'I don't understand what I've done. Why are you blaming me?' I would tell her that I wasn't blaming her but I had no inclination to help her by elaborating. *I'm blaming you, but not for that,* I thought. *I'm blaming you for your response to my reaching out, to my needing you. All I wanted was for you to validate me, to hug me and tell me that everything was going to be all right. That's all. And you couldn't bring yourself to do that — it was all about you. I've talked to people about my rape and I'm in a stronger place with it. But I do need you right now. I'm struggling. I'm struggling with my life, with my addictions.* But I kept my mouth shut and her shut out.

I got a better result from Dad. He hugged me and comforted me, just like all those years before. But then he broke down, fell to the floor and cried at my feet, talking about some horrible abuse that had been inflicted upon him. What? What was this? Was this another one of his improvised stories or was it for real? Well, whatever. Good on you, you bastard. If your story was true, you still then stood over me all my life. Like Mum, it was all about him. He couldn't protect me, he was saying. He'd always thought he could protect me. And it was like, *This ain't about you, man. It's not about what you could or could not have done. It's about me.*

Still, there was no question who was in my corner out of my parents, and whose corner I was in. Mum could go to hell. Actually, the whole fucking lot of them could go to hell.

I could have thrown myself back into the jobs but I didn't. Yet the fury I harboured was as powerful and volatile as ever. I ended fights with strange men brutally and showed them no mercy. I'd been afforded none. Gone was the compassion I'd felt in the counselling rooms.

# XXIII

## A New Way Of Thinking

I was living in a dump. Everything was clapped out, from the paint to the carpet. I had money to burn, from dealing, but I was living it up in squalor. The one saving grace — that I'd given up the jobs — didn't colour my world with sunshine. There were short-term hitches — withdrawal symptoms, you could say. I'd removed certain people from my life, but Brisbane is not a big place. I kept running into former associates and thinking, *God, I'm never going to escape them.* I'd be filled with paranoia, as if being sighted by one of these outlaws would remind them that I was at large and outside the fold. I'd imagine a call made, a job offered, a job taken, and any minute some gorillas would burst through the door with triggers pressed. I took drugs to allow me to sleep through my constant thoughts and memories of violence; they also sharpened the fugitive complex I had going.

But the more I took, the more into my head I went. And that was the last place I wanted to be. It wasn't nice being asleep; it wasn't nice being awake. Given my head space, I was constantly in bad company. Finally I decided, once and for all, that I was going to completely lose my mind. As ridiculous as it may sound, it was like I was filing for divorce — I was determined to part company with my brain. I was jack of the fucker. The perfect date loomed: a bush doof being held on a property down near Drake. It was a three-day rave that would be full of hippies, trippers and weirdos. Perfect. They'd be playing primarily Goa trance, which was tailor-made for acid. I went with a mate. We were armed with a sheet of acid. I kicked off with six tabs.

There were about 6000 people and all of them freaks — nice, mellow freaks. I was too out of it to talk, so I just wandered about and watched. Really tripping hard. I saw trees grow from saplings to full size in seconds and then suddenly disappear altogether. Birds came swooping down and just before landing turned into people walking past me. The grass changed colour constantly. A dog came up, turned into Satan and started talking to me — fancy picking *me* out of the crowd! — then turned back into the dog. For two days I kept taking tab after tab, although I never felt I'd lost the plot entirely — I was hallucinating heavily but I still retained awareness in my head. I could always tell the fake from the real. God, it was annoying. My brain was my constant guardian, my ever-present wowser: *You're not going anywhere, Paul.* On the last day, when we ran out of acid, we got hold of some E. That was pretty intense because all the residual acid in my system ramped up the effects of the Es — candy flipping, they call it. The music was unbelievable — we just danced and danced. Over the whole weekend I ate little more food than a couple of hash cakes.

As far as losing my mind went, the mission was a flop. I was stuck with it, till death do us part. But it sure cured me of acid. I didn't get back to normal for two weeks afterwards and I haven't touched the stuff since. The weekend was a landmark of sorts, though. I think from that point on I was just about ready to consider giving drugs away.

The thought of a drug-free existence didn't sit easily with me. I thought there was no way I could stop having that coffee in the morning, let alone the filthy meth I spiked it with or the pills or the coke or whatever else. Drugs were my life. I couldn't see myself stopping. But I knew I had to; things weren't working for me. I'd think to myself, *When's this all going to change for me?* I began waking up to the fact that it was me creating my own universe. *I am the god of my world. I create my reality.* I had been stuck in the mind-set of being a victim of my surroundings: *Why does this always happen to me? Why does my car always break down? Why do these guys provoke me to road rage? My life sucks.* I'd sit there and feel sorry for myself. Often. But it was *me* tormenting me. Not anyone else. Not the guy who raped me; not the drugs; not the evil intent of the world. I needed to step up and take responsibility for my circumstances. Get a job. Start sleeping at night. Eat some food. Start acting like a normal human being and maybe things might start going a bit better for me.

The power of the mind is unbelievable. What you think is the blueprint of your reality; that's where you create your reality. Here I was jammed within certain ideas, taking all these drugs, living this crazy life, and then wondering why everything else in my life was going to ruin. *My life's fucked. Well, you're making it that way. Any tick of the clock you can stop and say, 'I want to be a different me. I want my world to be different, therefore I have to be different.'*

I contemplated my life a lot. I examined my experiences for lessons I could learn, to see what I was doing wrong. It's an attribute I honed while fighting, and it becomes a powerful exercise when done with honest awareness. If something's not working, try something different to fix it. But I had to be able to accurately pinpoint what I was doing wrong to be able to do something right. I had to understand what wasn't serving me to know what would. In that way, my faults could serve a valuable purpose: helping me create and live the sort of life I wanted.

However, I had to not only become aware but also stay aware. And the conviction of that changed everything. I thought, *I need to change the way I'm acting by changing the way I'm thinking about the world I'm living in.* And there's the key: awareness. Being aware in every sense, being aware of myself, being aware of people around me, what I was doing, how I was thinking, what I was thinking, what things meant to me. Blundering along as I was, I didn't care whether I was hurting anyone, affecting anyone or changing anything. What could I reasonably expect in return?

I remember, as a 96 kilogram thug who had little more than vice and a pocket of fleeting cash to his name, sitting in my humpy thinking, *This life isn't serving me any more. I want what I feel I deserve.* And what did I think I deserved? A beautiful wife. Kids.

Millions of dollars in the bank. Me? Paul Briggs? How *dare* I! But that's exactly what I dared to believe. And I vowed I was going to put every single cell of my being into making that a reality. Once and for all, I had to start walking my talk.

Incentives sprang from unlikely sources. Over the years I'd become a chronic road rager. Taking as much speed as I did every morning, I'd be out behind the wheel constantly looking for trouble. I was bad enough when I was pumped with speed and so much worse coming down off it. Some guy would mouth a snarling word at the lights; he'd think he was safe in his air-con cabin with his favourite morning radio crew. Seconds later I'd have smashed through his window and bashed his face into a bloody pulp. This was nothing to me. The road was just another field of conflict, an extension of all the forces at war with me. Or so I thought, until I realised fully that it was I who was at war with them.

One day I was in the car with Leah and this truck driver behind us started up with his horn. I was in the passenger seat and I shoved my arm out the window and gave him the bird. He leant on his horn again and that was it. Leah broke a couple of nails trying to stop me getting out, but I was gone. I walked around to the driver's side, trading abuse with this fat little bloke wearing glasses, and smashed my fist into his door with such force that the whole cabin rocked. I stepped back and this guy was waving an iron bar at me. 'Come on, arsehole,' I shouted. 'Get out here and have a go.' And I realised I hadn't stepped back but staggered. Something ran down the side of my face; I put my finger to it and saw blood. The trickle turned into a flow and I realised that the guy had clouted me as I punched the cabin. As I was standing there he shouted out, 'Get back in ya car or I'll fuckin' clean ya up!' And with that he shifted gear and drove off.

Once the steam had stopped coming out of my ears, I thought, *I would have shot that prick if I'd had a gun.* That was the response I had programmed myself to make. Once that urge had subsided I began thinking, *Maybe I shouldn't be jumping out of my car to belt people. What happens if next time the bloke's got a gun and he's so shit-scared, like that guy was, that he uses it? Then I'm dead. And what if I'd had a gun? I would have shot him. Then*

*I'd be doing twenty years. That's my whole life gone, right there, in one stupid incident that was entirely my fault. My life gone. And for what?* How many times would I ask myself that over those twenty years? I would be sitting in a jail cell thinking, *I don't really care about being a tough guy any more. I just want to see the sun go down. I want to see the sun come up. I want to see the stars again. Big fucking tough guy. So hard. That's not hard. Ending up in the nick's not hard. It's pretty easy to get yourself stuck in jail. What's hard is not. What's hard is thinking first, and thinking about other people.*

I soon realised that all those guys on the road weren't out to get me. They were not bringing violence into my life — I was. I was the cause of this. This blood trickling down my head began with me. How could I fix it? It started with me, not anyone else.

About a week later, I saw the guy from the truck in a video store. I was on the phone to a promoter from Sydney who was trying to force me into a deal regarding these German deejays. He was trying to do the standover thing, saying, 'I'll get lawyers. I'll come down hard on your arse.' My normal response would have been to say, 'Listen, motherfucker, I'm about to jump on a plane and come down to Sydney and cut your fucking head off.' But I was biting my tongue. And then I saw this little fat truckie. The dude on the phone was rattling on about suing me, that he had the money to do it and that I didn't know who the fuck I was dealing with. And I was eyeing this guy who'd clocked me on the head. My ego wanted to drag him outside and bash the fuck out of him because he'd gotten away with something no one else ever had. He saw me looking at him and turned pale. The universe had presented me with the perfect opportunity to react violently again — a double whammy. But I simply told the guy on the phone to piss off and hung up without threatening him. And I walked out of the video store and got into the car beside Leah.

I was thinking about the truckie all the way home. *It was my fault. Why should he pay for decisions I make?* Leah was going, 'What's wrong? What's wrong?' Because whenever I'd get pensive we'd split up. I was thinking, *It's time to make some changes. It's definitely time.*

Not long after the bush doof, I'd moved in with a mate of mine called Clint. I'd known him on and off for a couple of years. Very early in the piece, Clint saw straight through me — this intense, angry, dodgy, try-hard who had everyone about him on edge — and believed I was capable of great things. And I could see he was searching just as hard as I was. We quickly became good friends who seemed like old mates. We saw each other as fellow travellers, so to speak — he was someone with whom I traded answers and raised questions regarding life. He was one of the few people I could engage in deep conversations with, where I'd open up about my anger, frustration and unhappiness. I could confess to him that I wanted a more purposeful life. He got it. He'd been facing some serious issues since his father was killed in a tragic accident. And that spiritual connection between us formed the platform of a lasting friendship. We'd lost touch for a while but he looked me up after he heard I was producing music. He was building a studio at his place and was keen to see if I liked the idea of us working on music together. When he visited me, he was shocked by the filth in which I lived. Not long after he said he had a room at his place if I wanted it. I told him I did.

So I found myself in a beautiful house in Annerlie. I should say we, because Leah moved in as well. But we were so on and off, no one knew where we stood at any one time. I was still doing my deejaying and was renowned for being this full-on, crazy dude — 'The Hurricane', the posters would read, 'the Brisbane Madman'. I'd play what they call Gabba, which, at about 200 beats per minute and God knows how many decibels, was kind of the thrash metal of dance music. The young hard-core speed freaks loved it, just going all night. But as I started chilling out, the sort of music I was playing changed. I got into epic trance, which is quite soft. And it was like I'd gone Celine Dion on everyone. People were coming up going, 'What the fuck's happened to you, dude? Listen to this shit you're playing.' But I loved this new music. It really moved me. And the change was no coincidence: something new within me was finding voice.

The biggest step was to get off the drugs. Clint and I made a pact to give everything up. The dangerous thing with drugs is that you think you're all right up to the point when you realise you're not. It's when you try to stop that you discover you're an addict. You suddenly become aware that you're not in control. And I always thought I was. I could look at my drug days as being the best times of my life. I was living in what young people imagine heaven to be: plenty of money and plenty of time, no rules nor responsibilities, no one to answer to, do what you want, when you want. And I had plenty of those nights where to be sublimely out of it was exactly where I wanted to be. I couldn't possibly, then, have thought my time was being wasted. And, overall, I would have said my drugs period was far from being a horrid, tortured existence. But honestly, drugs had long since stopped being for fun. They'd become painkillers, deadeners — shields against the experience of real life.

Clint and I quit for eight months. Out of all the drugs, the most difficult to shake was pot. Whenever I'd get a little edgy or aggro I'd have the urge to punch a couple of cones and smooth my head out. So we still smoked a bit but stayed off everything else. Being drug-free was so at odds with the rave lifestyle; there were so many cues to take drugs. There were some new pills just in or some new drug or some premium coke. And my Pavlovian response was to pounce and devour. Staying straight in the rave scene was like asking an AA member to stay dry in a pub. At its very simplest it was like, *How am I going to stay awake all night at raves without drugs?* And I began to think, *So what? I don't even like these raves, these people or this music any more. What am I doing here? I don't need this shit.*

My earlier drug-free stint during my counselling made me a little nervous about all the raw feelings I could expect to surface. But, far from being scary, they made me feel more alive than I had for such a long time. And one of the most amazing things was that my nightmares became less frequent and less severe. These horrors had haunted me for years. Now, mercifully, I was at last becoming free of them.

Clint and I really focused on our music. The studio wasn't complete, but enough was in place for us to record some tracks. We were very serious — we were aiming to do no less than change the face of dance music. We called ourselves Journey, and our idea was to make killer tunes that contained messages of love. We thought how cool it would be to sew seeds of love into the minds of kids pilling off their heads, and maybe six months down the track the seeds would bloom in their hearts and they'd be on their way. I was so into it that I went and got my forearm tattooed with 'Journey' written in runes. I wanted a new tattoo to mark the change in my life, my transition into a new phase.

A letter from Nathan drove home the timeliness of and sense in me getting my shit together. He'd been inside more than a year and I hadn't seen him once. I broke down when I read his words. He wrote about how close we used to be when we were younger and how when he got out he hoped we'd get back there again. The letter inspired me to visit him. I find it hard to relate what it felt like to be sitting opposite my brother, him in jail, me a free man. It was terrible, heartbreaking stuff. I felt so low for not having visited him earlier and I wished I could have led him out then and there. It was an utterly sobering experience too, because, while I was really sad for Nathan, I couldn't help but feel fortunate that I wasn't inside with him. Both our lives had spun out of control and I also knew that little more than luck had kept me from sharing his fate. I knew that he thought the same.

I'd tested the patience of both the law and the lawless. But I was Joe Cool. I had everything under control, didn't I? Running the gauntlet of the underworld, I'd be like, 'No worries. Everything's sorted.' But the truth was that I had an equal chance of being on the receiving end of a bullet or a prison sentence. I might have been savvier about how I conducted my deeds than Nathan was, but I was also luckier. As far as he and I went, relations were somewhat restored, if not mended, after my visit. I'd go to see him once in a while before he was released, even though it just seemed to reinforce the separateness of our two lives.

And that 'Journey' tattoo proved to mean more than a symbol of change. I was indeed about to set a new course in life but it would have nothing to do with the music Clint and I planned to produce. This would be a far more personal and profound journey than I had expected. In seeking to change my life, I'd opened myself up to an unexpected new destiny.

# XXIV

## *Fire*

Did I say I'd opened myself up to a whole new destiny? Initially, it seemed anything but. I saw no glinting pathway rolled out before me. More like I found myself on a used car strip choked with traffic and beige with smog. My direction was anybody's guess, and if promise was the ride of my dreams then this looked an unlikely place to find it. I didn't feel alive with fresh prospects; I felt grounded in the most mundane way. Having given up drugs and violence, I was hit with an alarmingly drab dose of normality.

I earnt money doing deejay work but I also had a gym down in a plain-Jane Brisbane suburb called Moorooka, where I traded on my spent name and taught kickboxing classes I could barely tune in to. This gym had been up for months and had been built around me. Yet for the most part it had had to get by without its questionable drawcard. I don't know how many times I'd called in sick or with car trouble at the last minute because I'd been pilling all night and was too ripped to lick a stamp, and so twenty students would again be left standing and vowing to quit. Now, at least, I was fronting up, but I was hardly floating in there on a wave of enthusiasm.

I was also in the fight game by way of training a couple of kickboxers. But to keep money coming in, I took a job with Clint installing air conditioning into an office block. I didn't feel I had a hell of a lot going on.

Was this my life — this little outpost of a gym? These classes? These fighters? This music stuck in the pipeline? Air conditioning? I did wonder. Was I restless or just an agitated ex-addict? Was I impatient or just looking for an excuse to shirk and relapse? I lacked something solid within myself on which to grasp — a purpose, a sure mind-set that I was happy to lock and load. Deep down, I hankered for something beyond mere contentment. I wanted belief.

What I got was an honest look at myself. And it was utterly humiliating.

I had one of my fighters on a card of a Brisbane event. At the weigh-in this guy came up and said, 'Hey, Paul. Remember me?' It was Wayne Parr. We hadn't seen each other for four years. I'd stopped following his progress through kickboxing magazines a couple of years back. Last I'd read he was living in Thailand and kicking arse, true to the fight name the Thais had given him — 'John' Wayne Parr. I was shocked by his appearance. He was a total, in-shape, ready-to-rumble warrior. Just like I had once been. He was lithe and brimming with vitality. A fist of muscle. Little Wayne Parr. I was lost for words. I just stood there thinking, *My God. Look at you.*

He didn't have to say what he was thinking. He wouldn't have dared. But I knew — you could see it in his face — *Geez, man, what happened to you? You've sure let yourself go.* Last time he saw me I'd been a fit, strong champion. Now I was this shaven-headed thug who weighed almost a hundred kilos. I was such the ex-fighter — a real blowout. I'd gone Maradona. What on earth had happened to the legend?

I felt so self-conscious and ashamed. Seeing myself through his eyes crushed me. I couldn't talk to him, so I brushed him. But I walked away thinking, *God! Look at me!* The guy I once thought of as Mini Me hadn't been able to hide his dismay. His reaction had left me reeling. It had dawned on me exactly where I was at, just how far I'd slipped from my prime and all my promise.

At the fight itself, Wayne approached me again. This time I was more at ease. He told me about all the Thais he'd fought, about living in camp. He said, 'I just want to let you know that you've always been a role model for me. I followed in your footsteps. That's one of the main reasons I went to Thailand. Every time I had a hard day or a hard fight I'd think about what Briggsy would do and that would give me heart.' I damn near cried, I was so honoured. And I was amazed at what he'd achieved. I was like, 'Man, you've done it. You've fought at Lumpini Stadium *three times*. Just to *fight* there, let alone win.' And he was rattling off a list of superstars he'd knocked out. Whereas I'd fought, and lost to, Jomhod — that was it — he had a frigging roll call. He'd lived in Thailand for *four years* and could speak the language fluently. I'd spent three months and could do little more than order a green chicken curry. I was looking at him in awe, thinking, *I used to be your hero. Now you're mine. You've done things I only dreamt of doing.*

A couple of weeks later was River Fire, a festival on the Brisbane River where they set off a whole bunch of fireworks and sent jet fighters shooting overhead with afterburners cranking. Someone I knew from the kickboxing scene had booked a hotel room overlooking Storey Bridge, the focal point of the event, and had invited me to come along. Clint, Leah and I walked in and straightaway I saw Wayne. And he was already pissed. I thought, *Wayne Parr likes to party!* I immediately felt in the mood to get on it but I was in two minds. Clint and I were still clean and both of us were in this full-on spiritual contemplative mode. Clint took one look at the party and bailed — he knew that if he stayed he'd just be tempted to get amongst the gear. I was so stoked to see Wayne, all I wanted to do was talk with him. Next thing I knew, I had a few pills in my system — but I didn't care. I was away.

After a few beers, Wayne suggested we have a light spar for a bit of fun. So we stood up and got into it — just tapping, nice and light, moving around. This was the first sparring I'd done in years. We were just playing, but he was amazing. He was showing me what he knew and his technique was flawless. He'd come a long way since those Saturday sparring sessions where I used to drill him. People gathered around to watch and suddenly Wayne cracked me on the head with an elbow, the little shit. Everyone froze, thinking I was going to lose it — they'd all seen me explode over nothing more than a murmured word. Tears were pooling in my eyes — the bastard had really stung me. Wayne was nervous and apologetic. I've gone, 'Man, it's sweet.' But the sparring ended then and there.

We took seats out on the balcony and talked until the sun came up. We covered everything — all that he'd been through, all that I'd been through. He told me more about his fights in Thailand. He'd had about thirty, eleven of them televised, and he'd fought in a few King's birthday events — the absolute top honour for a Muay Thai fighter, where 100 000 people turn up to pay homage to their revered monarch and watch the finest practitioners of their national sport do battle. At one point Wayne said, 'You used to be my hero. You still are, but I can't believe how you look. You look like shit.' He said, 'Don't you ever miss getting in the ring? Don't you miss that adrenaline rush, being in the magazines, and everything else about fighting?' I told him I did. I also told him that I couldn't kick any more because of the varicose veins on my legs. I pulled up my jeans to show him all the blue-string webs and welts I'd accrued. I was talking like such a has-been. Wayne was having none of it. He goes, 'What about boxing? You've got really good hands. You used to KO heaps of blokes with your hands. Why don't you just box?' This time, I was more honest: 'Nah, mate. The fire's gone.'

That morning Wayne had a photo shoot down on the Gold Coast and he asked me to come along and said we could watch videos of his fights. That sounded great. We hung out the whole day and he kept at me. He said, 'Paul, you're only twenty-four. You're so young. Why don't you come back and box? You've done it with the kickboxing.' And he grabbed a jar of *namamoy*, this Thai boxing liniment, and said, 'Here, smell this.' I inhaled the old familiar scent and I smiled. I said, 'Mate, it's over. I'm retired. I just don't have it any more.'

But that wasn't entirely true. Something had begun to slowly kindle inside — the faintest heat of belief. Next day I went back to work, putting air-con ducts in place. But my mind wasn't totally on the job. I began visualising myself back in the ring. It was like, *Maybe I could come back and train with Wayne.* Then I'd shake the fantasy — which was exactly what it was — out of my head. *Nah, Paul. Get real.*

A couple of nights later I found myself standing in my kitchen drinking coffee after a 14-hour day on the site. Clint and I had this routine where we'd work from four in the morning through to six in the arvo, then come home, smoke a doobie and get in the studio. I was thinking, *There's got to be more to life than this. This isn't me. This isn't Paul Briggs. I'm a fighter. I'm not a producer or a fucking deejay — I'm a fighter. That's who I am.* And I felt this outrage rise within me. *There's got to be more to life than this.* And I began to get angry and started yelling it out. 'THERE'S GOT TO BE MORE TO LIFE THAN THIS!' And I repeated it several times with growing intensity. I felt as though I'd been deep underwater for so long that I'd almost passed out, and I'd swum so hard for the surface and then finally just broken through and filled my lungs. 'AAAARGGH! THERE'S GOT TO BE MORE TO FUCKING LIFE THAN THIS!'

Clint came bounding in, looked at me and said, 'You've really lost it now, dude.' Leah came up the stairs going, 'Are you all right?' 'No! I'm not all right!' She was thinking it was one of my frequent outbursts. Clint said, 'There's something going on.' I said, 'Yeah! There is something going on! I'm not happy with my lot in life.' And I had this rumbling deep inside me. It was back. That fire. That drive. After the counselling and the sweat lodges I had started addressing all my issues, but I had felt so sedated, so fucking geriatric. Now, a powerful force had returned. And it wasn't rage. I had life surging through me again.

The next weekend, the IndyCar race was being held on the Gold Coast. A friend of mine, Simon, said to come down. I told him I wasn't sure, that I was in a really weird head space. Leah and I weren't together but we were still living together and I was feeling that, once and for all, I wanted to move on. Clint said, 'Just come along and chill for the weekend, let your head relax a bit.' So I went, and Leah came too because she was good friends with Simon's girlfriend, and it was like, *Oh, man. I'm stuck in this thing.*

Come Saturday night, I was in Simon's apartment and he was describing this girl, Tash, to me. She was a friend of his brother Marcus and was by all accounts a babe. Simon was saying that, although she was a stunner, she was really full-on, really outspoken. And I'm like, 'Whatever.' I'd dropped an E — my drug ban had gone out the window the previous weekend and I was in a state, churning all sorts of ideas around in my head. I was glad to be out of it and, numbed again, happy not to be thinking too hard about anything, least of all women. All I wanted to do was to chill out.

So I was sitting on the lounge, pretty wasted, down in the dumps, having a beer and talking crap when the door opened and in walked Marcus. I'm like, 'Hey mate, how you doin'?' Then in came Tash. I was like, *Damn! Look at that! Oh, my God!* I stood up and this beautiful, beautiful, amazing-looking woman strode over wearing a slick black dress and heels, and I had to do my best not to fall back onto the lounge. Here's me: overweight and wasted in my boardies and some grubby old shirt. She walked straight up to me and said, 'Hi, I'm Tasha.' And I was like, 'Of course you are.' Her handshake was strong. What a wonderful force she was. Then more people filed in and the party started. My legs were in a bad state — I couldn't stand up for too long — so I parked myself back on the lounge. A little while later, Tash came over and knelt beside me. 'So you're a kickboxer,' she said. 'Oh, I used to be.' She looked at my mess of veins and said, 'Is this all from kickboxing?' 'Yeah.' 'I do boxercise at the gym,' she said with pluck, as though she was half in the fight game herself. 'Really?' I sounded politely impressed but I had to stop myself from cracking up.

Tash went back to the kitchen and I couldn't take my eyes off her. All these tossers zeroed in on her, trying to chat her up, and I just kept on staring. And she'd be talking to someone then look at me and give me this gorgeous smile that struck me like a wand. When about four guys had milled around her, she figured the time was right to sort the wheat from the chaff. She said, loud enough for me to hear, 'My next boyfriend's going to be the man I marry. I want to get married. I want to make a commitment for the rest of my life.' When the smoke had cleared, and three tossers with it,

I was still staring at her, saying to myself, *And that's going to be me.* I was looking at her, thinking, *I could have kids with you. I could spend the rest of my life with you.* Then I'm like, *What are you thinking, you imbecile? You're still attached, in whatever way, to a girl you don't want but won't let go. Wake up to yourself.* So I kind of slapped myself out of dreamworld and told myself not to take any more pills. *Just relax and enjoy the view. This girl is way cool.* I liked her spunk. I liked her attitude. I liked the way she was making these guys look like idiots.

I watched her all night and it wasn't until the sun started to come up that I made my move. I got up out of my chair and went over and sat down beside Tash. We started chatting and she lay down and put her head on my lap and was looking up at me as she talked. I don't know how long we were there. Seemed like eternity and no time at all. I could not believe this was happening. This girl felt so good to be with. She was incredible. And we were so at ease with each other. I wanted to hold her, and to hold onto a moment I dared to take as a beginning. Could this really be the start of something? I couldn't believe such a girl had walked straight into my life. Then reality hit home. Tash said, 'If your girlfriend walks in, just tell me and I'll sit up.' 'My what? Huh? What do you mean?' I didn't want her to think I was with anyone. Finally I conceded: 'Don't worry. It's okay, Leah's gone.'

A lunch was being held in another apartment upstairs, so we all rested, got changed then headed up. Tash and I didn't know anyone else there initially so we hung out together. She started punching me, like play-fighting, but she was really laying into me. She had to show me how hard she could hit. As we fooled around, I drifted off into my own little world with Tash. No one else was in the room.

Then Simon came in and dragged me into a bedroom. He goes, 'What are you doing?' 'What do you mean?' I said. 'What are you doing with this girl?' And I'm like, 'Man, she's the one.' He's like, 'Paul, you haven't slept, we've been partying all night, so don't get too far up in the clouds.' I said, 'Simon, I'm telling you: this is it, she's the one.' 'But Leah's here!' he said. 'So what? I never invited her down! She's not with me, so what does that have to do with anything?' He's like, 'Fine, fine, I just don't need the grief.' He knew that if Leah got upset he'd cop it from his girlfriend. I said, 'I'm just doing my own thing. But I'm telling you, this girl's the one.' I was levitating. I said, 'I don't know where she's at but I'm telling you she's knocked me for six.'

We got back into the lounge room and there was this big smile waiting for me — 'Where have you been?' And we went back to our play-fight. It was so cool.

That night we all hit this bar and I felt like I'd known Tash for ages. I pulled her aside and said, 'I'm going out on a limb here for the first time in my life. I'm going to be really blatantly honest, put myself up to be smashed big time.' I said, 'You've got the power to really crush me as a man.' And I'm thinking, *Shut up, you fool! Why tell her this? Why give her such power over you?* I ignored my fear and said, 'You have severely knocked me off my feet.' She was like, 'What do you mean?' I said, 'I think you're amazing. I think you're awesome.' I was ready to tell her then and there that I was in love with her. But I couldn't. She'd think I was insane. As it was, my outpourings were a bit much for her. She was very flattered but wary. She'd obviously asked around about me. She said, 'Aren't you engaged?' And I started to get nervous, thinking, *I'm going to get slapped down like the other guys.* I said, 'No, I'm not engaged. Leah's my ex-fiancée. We've been on and off for years.' Then Tash said, 'Listen: lose the girl, give yourself two weeks and call me. All right?' And with that she grabbed her drink, turned around and went off to dance with her girlfriend.

*Lose the girl.* Man, I guess I had to take that as a good, not a bad.

We all headed off to another bar. When we entered, I did my normal thing — asserted my authority — and scoped the place for no-necks. I noticed that there was only one guy working security and it looked like he had no idea. I got some drinks and came back to our group to find a ruckus going on. Simon was swearing at this Ferrari driver and Tash was in a slanging match with his girlfriend. I saw the Ferrari guy grab a champagne bottle and I looked at the security bloke, who didn't know what the hell to do. I'm going, *Great, I have to take care of this.* So I leant forward and whispered in the driver's ear. I essentially told him not to bother. I said something along the lines of, 'You're out of your league tonight, mate. You don't want to do this because I'm not going to stop at smashing a bottle over your head.' I think I told him I'd bite his face off and dislodge a few body parts. Guys usually pick up on how serious you are. He let go of the bottle and hustled his crew out. Meanwhile Tash was still going off. I'm like, *Man, this girl's got some real go in her.*

I had to go outside to get some air and cool down. I couldn't just turn on and switch off. Once I was calm, I went back inside and sat next to Tash. I said, 'Do you want to get out of here?' 'I'm not going anywhere with you,' she said. I started rubbing the back of my hand against her thigh. 'Stop that!' she said firmly, no smile. I was like, *D'oh! You idiot! You've blown it!* Then she said, 'Keep going.' So I start rubbing her leg again. 'Stop that', she said, a little less firmly. It was our little game and I thought it was all very cool. There's contact here. I said, 'Come on. Let's get out of here.' This time, she agreed. This Marcus guy really had his nose out of joint. He said, 'Where are you guys going?' I said, 'Dunno, see you back at the unit.' He was like, 'Tash, are you all right?' 'I'm fine,' she said. And we were off.

We walked for a while and then stopped and kissed. It was amazing. I would have stood there all night, even with my dodgy legs, but we hadn't slept much over the past two days and all I wanted to do was lie down with Tash and hold her. I didn't want to let her go. But back at the unit I had to avoid a scene with Leah. Tash and I took a lounge each and passed out. When I woke up, Leah was sitting in the room and Tash was still on her lounge, watching me. Leah was giving both of us looks. It was really weird. I was utterly infatuated with Tash. And I wished I could make Leah disappear.

'Come on,' Leah said, 'I'll give you a lift back. It's time to go.' And I'm thinking, *Why are you acting like we're together?* But I didn't want a situation on my hands. Then I thought the lift back would be a good time to tell Leah it was all over. I remember getting to the door and I said, 'Hang on a sec', and turned around and ran back inside. Tash was looking at me and I said, 'I'll call you.' She just gave me this look like, *Yeah, right.* I remember thinking, *I know you think I'm not going to call, but I am.*

In the car, Leah was asking what happened between me and 'that Tash girl' — 'Was she with you?' 'Yeah, of course.' 'So you were partying with her?' 'Yes.' I said, 'Why am I not asking you where *you* were?' 'I don't know,' she said. 'Because I don't care. It doesn't matter because we're not a part of each other's lives.' 'What do you mean we're not a part of each other's lives?' 'Because we're not. This is it. I'm going to move out. There's been nothing there for so long. We've been torturing each other for ages.'

Man, I'd been with Leah for nine years, and this is how we ended up. It was all like she was my burden — as if I wasn't hers. As if I wasn't to blame, always being so damned needy when my chips were down that I had to con my way back into her life. Leah was not a bad girl, not a hopeless person. I'd manipulated her for so long and, knowing I had that power, I had wielded it selfishly. But when I was flaying at her, I was attacking my own pathetic weakness. All respect between us had dissolved and I loathed our sham. At those times, I had no heart for kindness, no care for her feelings. I felt so righteous because I believed that what was right for me was right for both of us, and she'd never have the strength to take the initiative and ditch me for good. She was so reliant on me that I always felt responsible for her happiness. So no matter how I treated her, I continually had the guilts, the lamest kind of tenderness. And she knew she had this psychological control over me, and used it. Meanwhile, I'd done horrible things to try to hurt her worse and worse, hoping she'd reach the end of her tether and flick me. I'd put the ball in her court and lose more and more respect for her because she always hung on. I guess I always thought it would be less hurtful for her if she made the call. But how gutless is that? Why didn't I be a man and shoulder that responsibility? I had always taken the easy way and left it to her. Until now.

Leah was in tears, saying, 'You can't leave. You can't.' I said, 'This isn't even a relationship. You don't respect yourself enough to kick me out. You let me treat you like shit. I'm hating myself because of how I'm treating you.' 'What happened last night?' 'A lot of things happened last night for me.' I said, 'This is it. It's over.' We were only halfway to Brisbane and I said, 'If you want to stop the car I'll get out and find my own way back.' She said, 'Don't be silly.'

We got back home and she ran inside saying to Clint, 'He's leaving me.' And Clint's attitude was like, 'Well, you two aren't really together, are you? Are you? No one can keep up with you guys any more.' Leah spun back out, got in her car and drove off.

This was Monday morning. Some start to the working week. I was late clocking on at the site and copped a serve from the boss. I climbed up a ladder carrying a high-powered rivet gun and started punching brackets into concrete, but I couldn't stop thinking about everything that had happened over the previous week. Fighting, Wayne, Tash, Leah, Clint, music. And the bottom line struck me: it was time to start living my truth. That was the big thing Grandmother Windhawk had tried to drill into me for two years: start walking your talk. Now was the time to do it. *Now, Paul.* And that was it. *I'm going to fight again*, I said to myself. I must have stopped still for 10 minutes because one of the dudes walked over and said, 'Paul, are you all right?' 'Yeah, I'm all right. I quit.' 'What?' 'I quit. I'm going to fight again.'

I stepped off the ladder thinking, *I'm in love with this girl. She has seriously done some damage to me.* And Leah? I felt sorry for her but this was *my* life. The best thing I could do for us was to stay out of hers. And I really wanted to get out of Brisbane and leave the criminal shit behind me. I had a couple of heavy mates down the Gold Coast for back-up if things followed me down. I was covering all my bases. I thought about the future. Here I was, feeling like an old man who was slowly dying and I was twenty-four years old. Twenty-four! I went downstairs and told the boss I was quitting and walked off the site.

I went to find a payphone. *I'm going to fight again.* I was all emboldened but then I felt how heavy I was as I walked. *God, I'm so fat. Getting back into shape is not going to be easy.* I rang Wayne. He was up at Noosa Heads on holiday. I told him I'd just quit my job and that I was moving down the coast. I said, 'I want to fight again.' And he was hooting, 'You fucking beauty!' I said,

'I want to come train with you at your gym. Do you mind if I live with you?' He goes, 'Are you kidding? If you were a girl, I'd marry you. You leaving now?' 'Yeah,' I said. 'I just have to go home, pack a bag, tell Clint, then jump on the train.' He said, 'Man, I'm getting in the car now. I'm checking out and heading home. I'll see you tonight.'

Telling Clint was tough. I said, 'I've got to go for it, man. And besides, it will be good to get out of Brisbane. I've got to get out of this scene, the music scene. And there's a whole other part of my life you don't really know about.' He goes, 'I know.' I said, 'No, you don't. You might have an idea, but I need to get away from some very fucked-up, nasty people. It's not running — it just makes a whole lot of sense on so many fronts not to be here.' Clint was gutted. We'd shared a dream; now, suddenly, it was all his. He took some time out in his room to meditate. A short while later, he came out and said, 'Mate, you've got to follow your heart. I know that. If you have to do the kickboxing, you do that. I'm not going to let this harm our friendship.' The guy was rock solid. I rang my old man. I told him I was leaving, that I was going to fight again. He went, 'No you're not.' 'Yeah, I am. And no one's going to tell me what I am or I'm not doing.' He said, 'You're kidding yourself. You're retired.' I said, 'That's you talking. I'm fighting again.' 'Oh, okay. Then I'll train you.' 'No, you're not training me.' He goes, 'Where are you going to train?' I didn't want to tell him where I was going. I said, 'I'll let you know. I'll ring you eventually and tell you where I'm at.' Then he got upset. 'What, you're just leaving me?' I knew he needed me but, again, this was not about him.

This was not a whim; this was real. I could feel it in my body. I felt this breath of life revive me. I'd had such a long break from drugs and I'd partied two weekends in a row. So for a second I thought, *What am I doing? I'm slipping again. I'm not thinking straight. This is a huge call and I've made it on the back of a couple of nights on the pills.* Then it was like, *No, I'm not slipping. Not at all.* I realised then that I had both clarity and belief.

I jumped on the train and felt unbelievably free. No feeling like it. I couldn't stop thinking about Tash and about getting fit again. I was like, *Man, what I know now. No one's going to be able to beat me.* Every time I thought like that this flame inside went VRRRROOOMPH! It was like, *Yee-ah! I'm not done yet! Paul 'Hurricane' Briggs ain't finished yet!* I had 30 bucks in my pocket and I'd get two grand from work in two weeks. That 30 bucks had to last.

As soon as I got to Wayne's place, he showed me my room. My bed was a dirty old mattress on the floor with springs sticking out of it. I said, 'Mate, I haven't got money for rent at the moment.' He said, 'Don't worry. Old school. I'll look after you and I know you'll look after me some time down the track.' I couldn't help but be reminded of the Spartan conditions of the camp in Thailand. And that shitty little room was perfect. From here I'd start again with nothing but my experience. And that was plenty. I could have been standing in the foothills of Everest gazing at the summit I would soon set out to climb — I had that pleasurable edginess of great expectations. I had next to nothing, but my life was in my hands, and I felt the wealthiest of men.

Wayne couldn't stop smiling. 'I can't believe you're going to fight again,' he said. 'Not just fight again,' I said. 'I'm going the whole way.

'But,' I said, 'I need to hook up with this girl.'

# XXV

## Shock Of The New

In the morning Wayne suggested we go down to the beach for a swim and some breakfast. Get some food into us before we hit the gym in the arvo. Sounded good to me. Treading water in the ocean, I looked back at the beach and the curtain of high-rise buildings gilded by the early sun. From those towers I would have appeared as just another nondescript figure in the sea. But from my viewpoint, I was a man enjoying a glorious baptism. I suffered no delusions: I was still struggling with a lot of what I had done. But I had begun to like myself, to think a little more fondly of myself, for the first time since I was a boy. I felt, right at that very moment, that the regeneration of my life had commenced. I was so happy, I could have cried with joy. *This is it. I'm doing it.* I had chosen to live a clear truth. I was thinking, *All I have to do today is go and train.* Beneath all my muck I had struck upon something of immeasurable worth. That it would always require polishing was something I'd never lose sight of. I had so much work ahead of me and, believe me, I was up to the task. And I mean working on *everything*: my self, my life, my fighting — they were all part of the same project. I had to live with my past but not in it. I was not about to deny my history, but I was certain of this: my future was mine to mindfully craft, a gift of my own making.

I had a hell of a road ahead of me. For a start, I had so much weight to lose. Sixteen kilos, if I wanted to reach my former fighting weight. I knew that even to get to a point where I could train seriously would take months. In the afternoon Wayne led me out of the gym for a warm-up run. I trod so heavily that the pavement slabs just about yielded. I didn't even get halfway around the block before pulling up and telling Wayne I'd catch him back at the gym. Hitting the pads and bags, I had good technique but no staying power. Still, I raised sweat. It was a start.

That night we went to eat at a Thai restaurant called Boonchu. I knew the owner, Richard, from way back. He was a huge Muay Thai fan and always used to feed me for free. Now he was doing the same for Wayne, to whom he had become a second father. He'd been a huge support for Wayne during his time in Thailand and had helped set up Wayne's gym. For Wayne, there was only one name to call it: Boonchu, which means 'blessed by the gods'. Richard was so pleased to see me again and even more so to hear that I was getting back in the ring. He gestured to the wall — the pictures I remembered he had of me were still there. He welcomed me as family. It went without saying that I'd never need money in his restaurant.

I'd invited Simon to join us, plus a mate of mine, Damian. We'd done a few jobs in the past and I needed to run a couple of things past him. First, I wanted to know if he had my back if need be. He was like, 'Of course, mate. No worries.' That was reassuring — although he looked as mild-mannered as they come, Damian was one of the hardest blokes I'd ever known. I considered myself a try-hard next to him. Second, I needed work. Not that kind of work — something legit. I told him that I didn't want to be partying or deejaying. Something very low key. I just wanted to keep my head down and collect my cheque. He said he could get me a job at The Breakfast Bar, a nightclub that was called a day club because it got going at four in the morning and went till midday. A cleaning job, Damian said. Real easy. Everyone's wiped before they even get there. I'd just have to mop up — move them along or kick them out. I said it sounded, well, perfect.

After the meal, I told Simon that I needed to know where Tash was. He pulled out a card with her number on it; he knew I was going to ask. He said she worked in one of the retail shops in the Jupiters Casino complex, which wasn't far from where we were. I borrowed his phone and stepped outside.

'Tash, it's Paul.' Silence. 'You know, Paul from the weekend.' Silence. Then she was like, 'Oh, hi. Look, I'm really busy. Can you call me back in ten minutes?' And I'm like, 'Yeah, sure.' And I hung up going, 'Noooo! Noooo! She's brushing me.' The silence. Man, that wrecked. She was thinking, *Who's this freak? Desperado. Stalker. Eject button. Quick! Flick the loser!*

I went back inside and sat down all glum. Simon goes, 'She didn't brush you, mate.' I said, 'She did. She was really quiet.' He said, 'Dude, you caught her off guard at work. Don't stew over it. Just call her back.' So I waited ten minutes and called again. She said she was about to finish up. I told her I was just down the road at Broadbeach and asked if she wanted to meet up for coffee. Silence again. Fuck! She said, 'What do you mean, you're at Broadbeach?' 'I've moved down here.' 'What do you mean, you've moved down here?' I wasn't about to go into that. I needed to cut the talk before the blackout struck. I said, 'Just come and have a coffee with me.' She agreed. Then, a ray of light. She said warmly, 'I didn't think I'd hear from you again.'

The second I saw her, I hit cloud nine again. Her smile and 'Hello', relieved me of my worst fears of rejection. She looked stunning and graceful and there was an allure to her entire being that, then and there, I'd have volunteered lifetimes to fathom. I was utterly gone. I didn't lose it, though. I managed to keep my cool — a feat helped no end by the fact that she was clearly pleased to see me.

We went and had a glass of wine each — at seven bucks a pop, they stung like wasps. Quelling the terrible prospect of having my poverty exposed, I told her what had gone on. It was all too impulsive, too full-on, for her liking. Coming to see me seemed not to be such a good idea. She'd met me three days before and now here I was like a stray dog. She started telling me she had a lot on her plate and I was getting the picture — there wasn't much room for me. She was in the process of completing her degree in industrial design. She had exams and assignments to focus on. And then she was going to move to Sydney. She'd recently been down there for work experience and she was keen to go back and make her mark. There were no work prospects for her on the Gold Coast. She was jack of the place anyway and couldn't wait to get out. She was primed to become a dynamic professional woman. She was single, independent and had plenty on the go. A boyfriend wasn't really in the frame.

We got onto relationships and she said her inspiration and guidance was coming from the Bible study she was currently absorbed in. She was so enthusiastic about it, and she didn't come across like some born-again God-botherer. She was feeling inspired and empowered after having been exposed to a spiritual template she could apply to her life. She was saying she had all this new knowledge and faith and she wanted to start putting it into practice. Her line about her next boyfriend being her husband had been totally for real. She'd broken up with some guy three months earlier; she'd had a handful of dud relationships since she was 15 and she was fed up. She'd just turned 22 and she was done with the partying, the bullshit and marking time with the wrong guy. And although a boyfriend wasn't even on her agenda, the bottom line was that she wasn't going to settle for anything less than love and marriage. She put everything on the table: her ideas about how she wanted to live her life, her thoughts on relationships and her plans for the future. To everything I was going, 'Cool. That sounds great.' She must have been thinking, *It's going to be damned hard to get rid of this guy.*

But I understood right then that things between us might not work out. Not because the marriage thing scared me off — far from it — but because Tash seemed so admirably set on her own path. She wasn't scouting for a co-pilot. For the first time in my life, though, I'd really fallen for someone. But I could live with that not being the prelude to a fairytale. My desire to fight was so intense that rejection from Tash would not have set me back. I was ready to take on the world again, to be someone again. Become something. If solo was how it was going to be, then so be it. Our talk was such a reality check for me. I figured I could just cultivate a friendship. If she moved to Sydney, good luck to her. But I thought she was just so amazing.

Tash finished her wine. I asked if she wanted another — that would be the rest of my money gone. Thankfully, she said no. Relieved, I paid the bill. I left bugger-all for a tip. It's a dog-eat-dog world, my friends.

We stood on the pathway and looked out over the ocean. I so wanted to see her again but I didn't want to come across as too heavy. I told her that I was looking for female companionship. Someone to go to the movies with. Catch up, have a coffee. Just a friend. But I was thinking, *You click your fingers, babe, and I'm there.* She said she couldn't see me for two weeks. *What? You don't want to see me?* She said, 'I'll call you when I'm done with uni.'

She gave me a ride home. Drove like a lunatic. All the way, I was thinking, *I've kissed her before. Does that mean I've broken the ice? Or has it re-formed?* When she pulled up at my place, I walked around and asked if I could kiss her. She said yes.

It was a good kiss but weird. A let's-be-friends kiss? A goodbye kiss? I didn't know. And in some way, that was fantastic. It was real. Whatever happens, happens. I did want more, but I felt buoyed just to be at that point. We knew each other better. At some level, that was reward enough. I floated up the stairs and into my little hovel. A whole new world was opening up.

The flat was a two-bedroom job in Hedges Avenue, right on the beach. There were four apartments in our building. We had a drunk next door, and below, nutters on one side and surf rats on the other. Wayne's Thai trainer was sleeping on the lounge and his girlfriend slept over as well. We had a cardboard box for a bin, a toilet that was never cleaned and a gangrenous shower recess for which thongs were mandatory. It was cool, though. The austerity echoed the deprivations of my Muay Thai camp. *Forget about a social life*, I told myself. Training was all that really mattered. My quarters were solely to provide rest. And I was doing a lot of sleeping — the training was killing me.

I was going as hard as I could, and while my mind was strong, my indignant body filed one complaint after the other. The fat was stubborn, as though it refused to be convinced of my purpose. That I was still on the Elvis diet didn't help. I kept the local

Macca's and KFC busy and would smuggle ice creams into my room so Wayne and his trainer wouldn't see the resilience of even my small vices. My main concern, though, was the condition of my legs. Despite Wayne's encouragement for me to box, I saw myself returning to Muay Thai, for which the ability to kick well is obviously vital. Not only impaired by varicose veins, my shins had gone soft, and they'd take years to harden again. Some fighters endorse rolling bottles against the tibia or getting nerve endings taken out. I think that's garbage. Nothing beats kicking hard leather pads and bags to condition your shins. Skin on skin kills the nerves and builds up that calloused strip better than anything. I once wielded my shins as crowbars — I could kick anything and bump my legs and take skin off without noticing. And now, they were totally normal — which in Muay Thai means useless. During sparring, blocking kicks with my legs was excruciating. There's no pain quite like shin on shin when you come off second best. My legs swelled up during every session. I'd have to focus on other aspects of training and fitness until they settled down, then I'd start kicking again and they'd blow out, become tender, and I'd have to rest them. I had serious doubts they'd ever harden up again.

Two weeks into training, Wayne said he had a fight for me. A promoter friend of his was looking for a boxer to match against this Kiwi. Wayne didn't even ask me. He knew I'd jump at the chance to get in the ring, not to mention that I needed the cash. He told the promoter I was in. Too right I was. Wayne told me the Kiwi was pretty dirty, had only a half-decent record but could go all right. I didn't care who he was. I'd been paid to fix up blokes outside the ring for a couple of years — it would be fun to get inside the ropes again and do it for a more respectable dollar. I wasn't in great shape but I was rearing to go. The set date was a month away.

The mere prospect of a fight injected more sprite into my training and I got my mind totally on the job. As it was a boxing match, I could rest my legs and concentrate solely on my hand combinations.

My job at The Breakfast Bar was ideal in that I only worked Saturday and Sunday mornings, so I had the rest of the week to train. Other than that, it was a shocker. Clubbers filed in who'd already spent half the night twisted and then wanted to party on into tomorrow. A lot of very bent people got up to a lot of loose and seedy things. It was a total meat market — newly hooked-up couples would be all but shagging each other; blow jobs, hand jobs, tit sucking, you name it. Every recreational drug known to man was being consumed — the worst for me was Fantasy, because I'd have to clean up after it. You only know you've had too much Fantasy when you pass out, and I'd have to sweep up casualties who'd nodded off and pissed themselves on one of the lounges.

From the outset the place was a real test for me, though, because I was being offered drugs left, right and centre. Not the ideal environment for an addict trying to stay clean. But I had all the wolves of temptation onto me. There were chicks I could have pulled but I kept my hands to myself. The hardest part, though, was that I was getting job offers. 'Paul, I need this done, that done. There's five grand in it for you.' I was broke and still in transition, still discovering my own personality after leading such an intense, drug-numbed existence. And I was being seduced into regression. It was like God was saying to me, 'How serious are you about changing your life, Paul?' As in the sweat lodges, I had to keep my focus and stay strong. To think that my purging and cleansing was being played out in the thick of this sleazy day club. I'd leave the place and walk out into midday sunshine with my head spinning. It would take a while for me to adjust to the real world again.

Tash helped enormously. I didn't wait two weeks for her to call me. I rang her a few times and she didn't brush me. I just really wanted to talk to her and hear her voice. She didn't know then what strength she gave me, what clarifying oxygen her friendship fed my heart and mind.

When she finally rang me, she sounded amazing. She was done with uni and was so relieved and excited and free. She said she had money in the bank and was going to sell her car to get more, she had no obligations but her shifts at the casino and a whole summer ahead of her. She sounded like she really wanted to let her hair down. I was stoked she'd thought of me straightaway. Wayne and

I had just moved into a big old house that had a pool out the back and I told her to come over. She arrived light and relaxed and happy. And she wanted to hang out with *me*. I dared to think that this awesome girl might be a little keen. *One step at a time, bro.* We just sat out back, enjoyed some wine and swam. Man, it was good to see her. Life felt grand. We hung out together day after day from then on. Within in a week we were lovers.

The more time I spent with Tash, the more I felt for her. From the day we'd met I'd wanted to tell her I was in love with her. This was no infatuation — I was in love with everything about her: what she stood for, the way she looked at things, everything. But for all our deep conversations about relationships, Tash was insisting ours was all just fun. And she was so spontaneous, so wanting to enjoy her new-found freedom, that I believed her. I felt so strongly, but I really didn't know where I stood. I was hanging out for the official stamp of approval but she kept on telling me we were just friends. I was like, *All right, we're not acting much like 'just friends'. We're spending every day together, she's staying over most nights and we're having amazing sex.* Damn, we were good friends.

I sensed she was struggling with her feelings, so I never pushed the issue. Crunch time came when we bumped into Leah at Simon's place. She saw Tash and I together and it was really awkward. After we left, Wayne was driving us home when his phone rang. He handed it straight to me. It was Leah. She started having a go at me, saying I'd lied to her about Tash and that I'd run out on her for another girl. I gave her the official line: Tash and I were just friends and I could have whatever friends I wanted. There was nothing I wanted to say to Leah more than, 'Hey, I'm sorry, but I've found my future wife.' Not to be cruel for cruelty's sake, but to tell Leah — and to tell Tash — that I was getting on with my life, that I wasn't just fumbling around in the dark. I still felt a little protective over Leah but I was in love with Tash. Sitting there in the car, I was cramped — I couldn't display either feeling.

When we got back to my place, Tash hit the roof. She thought I was keeping Leah hanging, saving her as a fall-back option. I couldn't believe my ears. I simply didn't want to overstep the mark.

If I'd said to Leah that Tash and I were more than friends, I was
sure Tash would have protested. Now here she was, having a go at
me for talking us down. Seems I'd spurred her ego into play. She
wanted our relationship to be respected for what it was by other
people, not to hide it. But between us she still wanted to sail under
the friendship flag. I didn't get it. *She can't have it both ways*, I
thought. I put it on her: 'What are we? I want to know. I want the
medal on my chest. I want the seal. What's going on? We're not just
beach buddies, are we?' Tash conceded that there was a lot more
than friendship going on. So that was it — I got the official seal.
From that day onward, there was no more 'just friends' nonsense.

A couple of weeks later was my fight. I'd got my weight down to
86 kilos for the weigh-in. Cruiserweight, as it's called. I still felt fat,
though, and on the night I was pulling up my shorts to hide my roll.
But I didn't have to be a *Men's Health* cover model to fight. I knew
I could hit very hard. I was excited that Tash was going to see me
fight. I could really impress her. But it was she who impressed me.
Before the fight she got right into it and was so supportive. She was
very affectionate, and was saying little things all the time by way of
encouragement; she got me totally revved up. I felt I was fighting
for something far greater than myself, as opposed to finding an
outlet and target for my rage. So much more of substance was on
the line. I took courage from that. And I felt invincible.

I jumped into the ring and smashed this Kiwi halfway across the
Tasman. I was pretty much street fighting, but I didn't need razor-
sharp technique against this bloke. I stopped him in the fourth. It
felt so good to be back. And all the more for having Tash there
with me.

The next weekend I was doing a shift at the day club when the
manager came up and said he'd been to the fight and had taken
along a guy called Rod Waterhouse. He said this bloke was a
trainer and that he'd been pretty impressed by what he'd seen. I
didn't give a toss. I knew enough about this manager to know that
his friends or associates were the kind of guys I wanted nothing
more to do with. But he fed me the story of how years ago this
Waterhouse bloke had trained a boxer named Russell Sands to

within an inch of a world title, before Sands was killed in a car accident. Waterhouse had been so devastated that he'd turned his back on the boxing game. It had taken a lot of persuading just to get him along to my fight. After he saw me, he said to the manager, 'Tell Briggs that if he wants to become a world champion to come and see me.' Touching story, but I wasn't in any hurry to meet him. An offer had come through to take part in a kickboxing event in Japan over Christmas and that was exactly what I was going to do.

The Japan fight was put together by Ray Matsumura, a local kickboxing promoter, and he was stoked to be heading back to Japan with both 'John' Wayne Parr and Paul 'Hurricane' Briggs. No question, Wayne was the superstar, but I was the old superstar, so there was a bit of a buzz around the event when we arrived. They put me up against the Japanese heavyweight champ, and when I came into the ring the place just erupted. It was weird — I hadn't been in Japan for five years and there was this *Groundhog Day* element of living through the experience a second time, and the fresh touches to an old story made the whole thing very strange.

In the first round this dude kicked me hard in the leg and it killed. I could feel the damn thing swell up immediately. He kicked me again. And again. And again. With each blow, I felt my legs disintegrate more and more. If I didn't get busy and knock this guy out, he was going to cripple me. My legs were shot; that left my fists. I stepped up, knocked the guy clear across the ring, then ran after him and unloaded. Again, I was street fighting — there was nothing clinical about off. I just gritted my teeth and smashed him and stopped him in the third.

Afterwards the Japanese promoters were frenetic, talking up all these fights they could get. But even before I left for home all their promises had fallen through — no one wanted to fight me. I was right back where I'd left off. That was it — I was over kickboxing. Enduring a rerun of all that crap was not what my journey was about. I'd had a lot of fun boxing and I hadn't enjoyed the kickboxing at all. As the old merry-go-round began to swing again, I decided to step off. I was in a lot of pain, my legs were a mess and I just thought it was time to move on. Kickboxing was history; my future was boxing.

\* \* \*

I'd been away from Tash for almost a week and I hadn't spoken to her once. We'd been training in the countryside outside Tokyo, and making an international call was nigh on impossible. And when I was in Tokyo I couldn't get away from all the fight palaver. So I called Tash from the airport before we flew out. I was sitting there hurting and drunk — because it was Christmas and I just wanted to be with her — and she gave me a royal serve. She was furious that I hadn't called and dismissed my pathetic excuses outright. She then told me she'd been out with Simon and a few bods, that she'd ended up at some guy's penthouse where everyone was on ecstasy and this guy had put the hard word on her, and Simon had intervened and stuck up for her and ... *What? What?* ... 'And meanwhile you're over in Japan just doing whatever you want, not even thinking to call ...' I was on my feet and pacing. Useless. Low. Agitated. Thousands of miles away and sorry-arsed.

The conversation eventually came good but this had been our first real fight. We spoke a little of the road trip we had planned down the coast for New Year's. Thankfully, Tash didn't pull the pin on it. I couldn't wait to get home. Now that business was out of the way, we could chill and spend some quality time together. As the plane lifted and took me back to Australia I could think of nothing else but being with her again.

# XXVI

## It's Going To Be A Boy

A lot can happen in a summer. Still, when I look back on early 1999, I'm amazed by the speed at which my new future was installed. When we set off for our trip down the coast in early January, I'd known Tash for two months. A fortnight later, we'd vowed to spend the rest of our lives together. Then — twice — we concluded we were mistaken. Then all doubt was dispelled. And then, before the summer was over, Tash was pregnant.

I know how it sounds: a dime-a-dozen tale of an impetuous, naive young couple giggling their way through a fog of weighty concerns with their wits on low beam. The type of story that starts with Jack and Jill in the dizzy throes of lust and ignorance and ends with Jill on the happy pills and in tracksuit pants flying solo with a cargo of kids and Jack in the pub drinking his life's bitter piss, eyeing ungettable skirt and stiffing Jill on payments.

I'll admit, it was a wild and fantastic ride, but the last thing you could say was that we didn't think things through. Man, did we workshop. We wanted to be absolutely sure about each other — we utterly rejected the popular blind hope that marriage itself will right any concerns you may have about a partner. But we did so much groundwork on so many key issues, I'm surprised we had time for fun. We even ended up writing down a mission statement featuring the trouble spots each of us had to address. I look back now and think, *What on earth were you two on?* We were so serious and honest about our feelings. For many young couples, marriage is the last thing talked about for fear of spooking the other half into doing a runner. We wanted to discuss marriage; it was something important to both of us in the context of the new lives we sought to create. Very early on, I believed we were ready to commit. Tash, though, wasn't so sure. She was more circumspect, and with good reason.

The summer was primarily meant to be a time for her to relax. And although she wasn't even contemplating the idea of marrying me, the way she saw it, if I couldn't engage with her in conversations that mined deep feelings, I was a waste of bloody time. Her heart was enjoying our romance but her head was telling her she was making a silly mistake, that she was straying from her resolve to make responsible and firm life decisions. She was struggling between her present and the vision she had of establishing a successful career and financial independence. Her faith gave her guidance and strength, and to stray into a summer fling seemed to be a pointless and possibly regrettable indulgence.

Over the first couple of months she tested me. She sussed out my ideas on everything to do with marriage: commitment, faithfulness, honesty, parenting. She would ask how enthusiastic I'd be about marriage during the really hard times, when most couples get divorced. I'd say that I understood marriage wasn't all bliss, that you can fall in and out of love, that a marriage takes more than love. And I wasn't pulling these things from the top of my head or bumbling through rehearsed spiels. There was no way I could bullshit Tash. I did have ideas on marriage. I believed in it. And from watching my parents I had formed impressions of how it could and should and should not be. Moreover, my thoughts were similar to hers. Those hard times might seem a worse way to live compared with being single and free and having less responsibility. But by entering a marriage, we believed, you make the decision to stick out the bad times. You must be willing to look at them as instructive phases. And when two people are changing constantly in their own lives, there will be times when you grow apart then back together. You can't always have love and passion peaking. This was how we talked. When Tash started to believe that we saw eye to eye, she began to relax and even to entertain the possibility of me being her husband.

I was upfront with her. I told her I wasn't much used to having feelings, let alone airing them. I explained where I was at in my life; that I had come out of a very intense, heavy time. She didn't fully understand — how could she? — but I opened myself up to her and was willing to take whatever consequences came of my honesty. I'd been a closed vessel for so long, but she was someone I trusted implicitly and I wanted to risk allowing her to know me. Whichever way we were headed, she was quickly becoming my best friend.

We were both children of divorce, so we were equally determined not to repeat history. Tash's father had split when she was nine and she grew up thinking that so many things were keeping him from contacting her and her two sisters. Later, she discovered the hurtful truth that he'd chosen not to include her in his life. While it's not fair to say that he simply went on with his life while Mum had raised three girls single-handedly, that's how it appeared. But Tash would later grasp that, when it came to communicating with his daughters, her father was all but paralysed by the uncertainty of his place and fear. Like my old man, Tash's father seemed to be a prisoner of his own demons. Anway, the upshot was that Tash had resolved never to be reliant on any man, never to compromise her independence only to find her life royally screwed by some lame gonad. She wouldn't tolerate guys who had the asinine urge to make out that being a man meant they were stronger and smarter than her. She knew that was all pretence and fakery. And she certainly had no time for dick-led boys whose idea of relationship responsibility ended at agreeing, under duress, to wear a condom.

Tash was adamant that she would take charge of her destiny. She'd laid out her life's path all the way to the gates of the retirement village. She wasn't going to be caught unawares, to find herself years down the track going, 'This is not the life I wanted to live.' She was all about due diligence and was not afraid to put me through some hoops.

Being so methodical, she naturally grappled with my willingness to trust my instincts. I may have been new to caring and sharing but my gut instinct was an old ally. When I felt something strongly, I didn't question it — I knew it was right. If I said, 'I think we would have the most amazing life together', she'd be like, 'How do you know that? How can you be sure?' True, I was coming out with some big guns early on, but I never swayed. I *was* sure. And eventually she started feeding off my energy, my conviction and my optimism and began to tune into her intuition and trust her own instincts more.

Finally, I decided I had to tell her that I loved her. I was enjoying a time in my life where I was pushing the envelope. I wanted to start learning what I was on about and pushing my boundaries and mastering myself. I had to risk telling Tash all that I felt. So I booked a table at this cool little restaurant called Getta India. She loved the place as soon as we walked in. But she knew I had something on my mind. I was normally pretty intense, but that night I was tight as a sprung trap. Once we were settled I said, 'You know my feelings for you are so strong. Tash, you have no idea.' I said, 'I really want to tell you how I feel.' She looked at me calmly and intently: 'Okay.' Then I said, 'I am totally in love with you. You have all the qualities of someone I could spend my life with and I want to do that. I want to spend the rest of my life with you.'

She blushed a little. Actually, she radiated. For a second my words were out there hanging — but not precariously. She'd caught them with grace and savoured them. I could see she was happy to hear what I was saying. She then told me she felt the same, and all the joy I'd ever experienced being with her was nothing compared to how I felt at that moment. It was so much richer than a fairy tale because this was so real — the sublime affirmation of mutual, passionate love. Man, what does not seem achievable amid the delirium of such a moment? But I knew full well that the deal was not done, that everything was not tickety-boo, that once I'd paid the cheque all that remained was for me to gather her up and steer my steed into the dying sun. The gravity of what we'd declared — given all we'd discussed — weighed upon both of us, but it was a beautiful and invigorating burden. Our shared journey had begun in earnest. Now did I ever have something to fight for — personally *and* professionally.

\*    \*    \*

Having made the decision to go from Muay Thai to boxing, I knew I needed specific training. It was like taking up squash after a career in tennis. Muay Thai and boxing may well be played out in the same arena, but they are fundamentally different activities. Having eight weapons at my disposal in Muay Thai, my combinations were permutations of left or right kick, knee, punch and elbow. Say, a left jab and straight right would be the lead-up to a left kick, so my body position starts forward then moves back to steady for the kick. But I'd spend most of the time with my weight back in Muay Thai as I found my range by throwing kicks, the way a boxer uses the jab. In boxing it's all hands, obviously, so you're always weighted, or at least poised to weight, forward. And in kickboxing I'd drop my hands and trust my eyes to read which of the eight missiles was coming at me. You can't do that in boxing — your hands are as much shields as they are weapons. So I'd have to get better at both offence and defence, because I'd be coming up against guys who'd only ever used their hands and were far more sophisticated than any kickboxer I'd faced. Lower your guard in boxing and you get clouted, which is why making a show of dropping your hands amounts to such cocky derision.

Then there was movement. In kickboxing you have to keep your body quite still for the sake of balance, so you can quickly transfer weight from one leg to the other. Try to fight while bobbing and weaving about in kickboxing and you'll fall over like a drunk. There's so much to body movement in boxing — it's an entire language of deceit and evasion devised to dupe and expose your opponent into your range. There was a lot I knew about boxing, but there was more I didn't know. And it was time to learn. I had a lot to unlearn, too — I had to kill off the instinct to kick. So I needed a good trainer. But I wasn't interested in Rod Waterhouse.

One day after work, the manager offered me a lift to my place. On the way to the car he said he just had to duck home first. He lived miles away; I was ten minutes up the road. I said, 'That's insane, I'll get a cab.' Then he insisted that he needed to talk to me about something. So we drove out to this house with a huge gate and security cameras, and I'm thinking, *This is not your place.* I said, 'Dude. Where the fuck are we? Whose place are we at?' He said, 'Paul, I really want you to meet Rod.' I went, 'Oh, for Christ's sake.' He said, 'Mate, just come in and have a chat with him.'

This big Aussie guy answered the door. His name was Boofa. He was 160 kilos, much of it fat. Big mo and goatee, long hair, tatts. I sized him up — sure looked the part, but not a whole lot of go in him. We were shown into a room and there was Rod Waterhouse, sitting at a table puffing on a durry. Rod would have weighed as much as Boofa. He had trimmed silver hair and the physique of a truckie whose daily workout was getting from cabin to roadside diner and back six times. He didn't look hard; he looked like a character, like one of those big, full-of-wind blokes you see starring in their own budget TV commercials. I felt as though I'd been summoned to appear before him and I resented it. I'd stepped out from the underworld and I knew the manager was a try-hard in that scene. I was not going to warm to Big Rod anytime soon. But, since I was there, I wasn't in a hurry to leave. I wanted to see what he knew.

Rod started talking, saying he'd seen my fight and was of the firm opinion that he could make me world champion. I sussed him out on a few things and he sounded like he had half an idea. He did know a bit about boxing and he knew what he was talking about training-wise. He liked to talk hard but I could tell he had a big heart, and I could see myself working with him. He said he had a four-year plan: three to get the title shot, taking on all comers; one year to defend and cash in; then retire on top. That sounded fine to me. So I said, 'Okay, let's do it.' He said, 'Great. We start Monday. I want you to run here in the morning from your place, and we'll get stuck into it.' I was like, 'Sure. See you then.' *Always good to start with a nice little run*, I thought.

On the drive back to my place, I started to realise this would be no light jog. I figured it must be 10 kilometres. The last decent runs I'd done were in Thailand. And even with the training I'd already been through, I knew that running wasn't my strength. I hated it. Once around the block was enough for me. Come Monday morning, I set off feeling anxious. Three and a half hours later, I arrived at Rod's thoroughly broken. I was upset, angry and demoralised, feeling myself at the soft, fat-slug end of the fitness spectrum. All that I'd hoped to prove and gain and earn by my comeback was being shown up as nothing more than a fantasy belonging to a boy, or a fool of a man.

Turned out the run was 16 kilometres long. And I was told to do this every day. The go was for me to run to Rod's, where I'd do an hour's worth of exercises, then Rod would come down to the gym for the afternoon session where I'd do pads, bags and sparring. But that run — or, should I say, walk–run — was a huge mental hurdle for me. Sixteen kilometres, every day. Whatever distance I covered on the road, I doubled in my head. I dreaded the alarm going off. I kept at it for a week or so but it was too much. I started getting Tash to drive me halfway, which meant I had to lie to Rod about how my running was really coming on.

I paid the price for such a sudden resumption of intensive training. My body tried every trick in the book to make me stop, or at least ease up. But I couldn't afford to — I wanted and needed fights. I was willing to take anything going and I always had to be rearing to go. And so I entered the fundamental purgatory of fighting: preparing for bouts that never happen. The cycle of teased and broken promises had resumed: promoter rings up, says he needs a fighter; I say I'm in; all good, date is set, and I get super-enthused, focussed; three weeks before the date, fight is cancelled. Pay cheque remains a figment of my imagination. Back to the gym, heavy with lost hope, training for training's sake, taking and making calls. Another promoter rings — fight's on; rings again — fight's off. Back to the gym, forget the cheque, ride out the downer. Over the first couple of months I trained with Rod, a few fights fell through. But until they were cancelled I'd train as though they were set in stone. My body wasn't coping — my back, my knee and my hamstrings all downed tools on me several times. One day my back seized up and the physio, whom I'd come to know pretty well, said I had to rest for three weeks. That was impossible — I had a fight on. Well, at the time it was on.

Then I was put onto a doctor called Craig Berry who sorted me out quick smart. In no time Craig became an integral part of my program — sorting out all my injuries and devising calisthenics routines that were a bit left of field but helped round out my fitness, sharpen my speed and increase my power. Eventually my body started cooperating, allowing me to train consistently. I began to feel like a fighter again. Except I had no fights.

Meantime, Rod was teaching me some basics. With his help I started to rid myself of a lot of old kickboxing habits. We had to spend a lot of time on my footwork and my stance, because the way I was accustomed to carrying myself was denying me power in the hands. He also drilled me about keeping my left hand up. I went to school on the old peek-a-boo pose. But the biggest thing Rod did was bust my arse. That was really his forte — although a few times I was tempted to crack him as he went on about my weight, ridiculing my gut and calling me a fat, lazy this and that.

To be honest, my body was no temple. My diet was still terrible and I hadn't stayed off the drugs entirely. I'd been clean for eight months then lapsed over the week that I'd partied with Wayne and met Tash. I kept the good times rolling until Tash feared I was in danger of regressing. I wasn't taking much, but I was stuck in old behaviour patterns. Then one day I told Tash I'd cast drugs from my life once and for all. That was meant to be that. Then the Big Day Out came to the Gold Coast in late January, and I blew it big time.

Tash took a job at the event doing a Red Bull promotion. I had a ticket and went along with Damian. When I got there I visited Tash but she was busy, so I went off and hooked up with a bunch of deejay mates from Brisbane I hadn't seen in months. Then the pills started coming out, the dance music was cranking and I figured, *What the hell — I'll just have a half.* What a joke.

Four halves later I was pretty wired, and I decided to go and see Tash. I rocked up with a cigarette in my hand and she knew the only time I smoked was when I was wasted. She didn't even have to see me smoking to know I was out of it, though. She said, 'Why are you smoking?' I'm like, 'Ah, I just feel like a smoke.' She didn't ask me if I was pilling; she just gave me every opportunity to be honest with her. I held my bullshit stance. A part of me was slapping myself over the back of the head: *What are you fucking doing? SLAP. You idiot! SLAP. You're bent. You're lying. You're doing — SLAP — it — SLAP — again! SLAP.* And I could see her thinking, *You know what? I don't need this in my life. I've been through this type of bullshit before and I'm not going through it again.* She gave me the cold treatment. Conversation over, relationship over, the love of my life traded for pills. I drifted off reeling. Now I really needed drugs because ... *SLAP — you're a fucking tool. She's the only good thing that has come into your life and you're blowing it. You're blowing it, you moron!* The only way I knew how to cope was to get off my face. So then I went and necked a couple more pills. I returned to Tash to walk her to her car. She said, 'What have you had tonight?' I'm like, 'Nothing.' *SLAP.* From that point on she couldn't bring herself to speak to me. I was trying to talk to her but she was barring me, like, *Whatever.* I went back to the party and got myself royally twisted.

I was terrified to go home and have Tash tell me to fuck off. As I made my way to her place, the self-hatred started again. Just like that I was back in the pit, having done a lot of work to dig myself out. I cursed myself aloud all the way to her door. I went into her room and climbed into bed.

'Tomorrow,' she said, 'just get your stuff and go. I don't want to see you any more. I'm not doing this again. And I'm not interested in second or third chances.' The floor fell away from beneath me. Desperately, I reached for all my old tricks. 'Look, we can talk about this. Please, Tash ...' But it was no use. In the morning we talked things over rationally but Tash was adamant: game over; we were done. And I knew she was right; I could understand her. We'd had an honest work in progress and I'd gone and trashed it. She said we could be friends but she told me she didn't want to hear from me for a good while. 'It's time to call it quits,' she said. And that was it. I was out.

That big fat rosy moment in the restaurant was now rendered a puff piece, total Ramsay Street schlock. So this was the happy-ever-after. For all my noble words, I was nothing but a cheap snake-oil huckster. Was I? Did my word mean nothing? I believed otherwise and I had to convince her. A week after she flicked me,

I called. She could tell my remorse was genuine. I admitted I had a problem, both with drugs and lying. I said, 'I know it's not your problem and I know you don't feel like dealing with this. It's my problem — I'll deal with it. I'll never lie to you again.' I laid it on the table. I said, 'This is what I was used to doing in my last relationship. But that's not the sort of relationship I want.' I swore to her that I would change. Finally, she relented and took me back. But I was not about to forget this lesson. She'd shown me that I had to be real. I had to grow up. If I was going to be a certain type of man, there were things I had to address, and honesty was a big one. My whole life had been a lie. But the honest truth was that I wanted a new life and I wanted Tash right in the heart of it.

Things were great for a couple of weeks. The workshopping didn't stop, though. We were both wanting to scrutinise matters that might break up a marriage if they weren't addressed beforehand. The subject of faith brought us to a new cricital point. I believed in God but in a different way to Tash. I was into runes and a few things that were part of the Celtic heritage my father had enlightened me about before he went gypsy. But I was into learning about Christianity by reading books like *Conversations with God*. Tash thought I was ungrounded, a bit of a dabbler. When we spoke about each other's spirituality, we always clashed. But it was healthy arguing.

For me, though, the issue wasn't faith — it was acceptance. I said to her, 'This is who I am, what I've always been, and I don't know how to be any different in my faith. If you can never accept and love my take on the world, then this isn't going to work.' Because when you do fall out of love — and you do in marriages — there has to be that respect, that endearment, that friendship. If you think your partner's an idiot, what do you really love about them? I wanted someone who was going to be open about working together on this. I didn't think Tash had that in her. As soon as I said this to her it was very strange. I felt so empty again but I was ready to move on. I'd come to that place where I had to stake our relationship on the issue. And I meant what I said. This was so hard for me to do, but I had to, because I knew I couldn't settle in a co-dependent relationship like before, to stay with Tash chiefly because I needed to have someone there. Like Tash had done earlier, I had to be prepared to set a boundary. And she blew me away when she said she was willing to work at it.

We were so back on track. The result of all our talks, however, was that I never proposed to Tash formally. The spontaneity had gone. We'd covered all the potential obstacles to us getting married and cleared them. We'd agreed that we wanted to spend the rest of our lives together. So if I'd asked her to marry me I would have been posing a rhetorical question. The closest thing to a proposal came when we were lying in bed early one Sunday evening and, after we'd been talking of our love for each other, I said, 'Why don't we get married?' And there the decision was made. We talked about what kind of wedding we wanted; that we should just elope. I didn't want an engagement party — I'd been through all that. I just wanted to get married. And that was fine with Tash.

In February there was a kickboxing show up in Brisbane we were planning to attend. I wasn't fighting but I was going to be brought into the ring to say a few words, to let everyone know I was back with the intention of winning a world boxing title. On the day of the fight I returned home from a trip to Sydney and walked into my room to find Tash there, crying. I felt winded. I was thinking, *Oh, no. She's decided to back out. She's going to tell me she can't do this. It's over.*

I said, 'Babe, what's the matter?' She was so upset. She looked at me and said, 'I'm pregnant.' I didn't need to hear any more. I was out of there.

I bolted down the hallway jumping up and down, screaming and hooting and cheering and carrying on like a lunatic let loose into the sunshine. Tash came out wiping her eyes and said, 'You're happy?' 'Well, of course I'm happy! What did you expect, babe? You're pregnant! And I'm stoked. It's a bit sooner than I expected, but what the hell. I want to spend the rest of my life with you, so what difference does it make? This is awesome.' Tash started laughing. I had no idea of the extent of her relief. I found out later that while she was watching me, she was thinking, *He's not running off.*

I had no idea how freaked out and scared she was about falling pregnant. We both knew it was on the cards, though. Tash had gone off the pill before I'd met her. She'd been on it since she was 16 and came to believe she was better off healthwise not to be tampering with her body's normal functioning. She wanted to get her body back on track and, man, was it back on track. We used condoms once but then we did without. Knowing we were playing with fire, we had talked about the prospect of her getting pregnant and what we'd do. And in those discussions we decided that if it happened, it happened. But that was talk.

I'd been reassuring Tash with my intentions for three months by that time, but when reality struck Tash began thinking, *Am I putting myself into a position I never wanted to be in? Am I going to be a single mother?* So she was elated and heartened by my reaction. And this allowed her to enjoy all the wonderful feelings the thought of having a baby stirred up within her. Then all the practical issues flooded her mind. It was very strange for her, as though she was standing still and the rest of the world was bustling around her. In a second she'd learnt that her life was about to change for ever. That's a very hard thing to fathom. Contemplating having a baby, contemplating that in eight years' time we'd have an eight year old, that we needed a baby seat, that we needed to move in together — it was all, naturally enough, a bit overwhelming.

'It's going to be a boy,' I said before we left the house. And during the trip up to Brisbane my mind went into overdrive. I was experiencing a daunting but beautiful sobriety: I was going to be a father. Yet I was such a kid myself. I had a hell of a lot of growing up to do before I could teach a child anything. The desire to better myself escalated. I wanted to become a good man for my son, to be as good a husband as I could be behind closed doors, where it matters most. I needed to start setting principles for myself. I wanted Tash to know she was safe and that I was loyal to her. I wanted to show her how happy I was and let that rub off on her. Maybe that would ease her mind a little, because I could see she was freaking out. Here she was — my future wife, the mother of my unborn child, a young woman with mature, wise values. She was a woman I loved so much and was willing to die for.

At the fight, the announcer called me up, saying Paul 'The Hurricane' Briggs was back. I got up there, and during the interview I found Tash in the crowd and connected with her over our wonderful new knowledge. 'Yeah, I'm back,' I said, looking at my future wife and unable to stop smiling. 'I'm back,' I said. 'And I'm going to be a father.'

# XXVII

## *Speechless*

In early May we took a small townhouse in Bundall, just behind Surfers Paradise. After our whirlwind summer, the pace hadn't slackened — we'd both sought meaningful change in our lives, to shed old for new, and we had a revolution on our hands. In seven months' time we were going to be parents. Before the birth we had to get married, and I had to fire up a career that could support my wife and child. Tash and I were daunted but incredibly happy, buoyant and confident.

The prevailing mood of both our families was not so chipper. To them, we appeared foolhardy. The last thing Tash's mother Vicki had known was that her youngest daughter had been determined to forge a career, see her independence to full bloom and insure herself against her mother's tough, sole-parent fate. Now Vicki's great hope was up the duff and shacking with a start-up boxer who had little more than a head full of long shots. As for my family ... I wasn't on great terms with any of them and hadn't had much contact of late. As far as they were concerned, I was still the old selfish, impetuous, belligerent, pipe-dream Paul they knew so well. I'd made a flash trade of Leah, music and partying for Tash, boxing and fatherhood. They took my optimistic outlook with a grain of salt — time would tell whether I was living convictions or whims. They hardly knew Tash, having met her just a couple of times before we told them about the baby. Dad seemed to suspect that Tash was out for my money — of which I had none — but I guess in his own way he was showing he cared. Mum, I'm sure, would have wanted to become more involved in our lives, but I still had my teeth bared at her. I can't blame them all for being less than thrilled, as much as it annoyed me. But what they thought didn't matter: Tash and I had huge faith in ourselves. We didn't need anyone to bless our good fortune. Would have been nice, though.

We spent a wonderful year in that house. Naturally enough, it was a formative time, as we had so many things to adjust to and work through. There were the small domestic issues, like me learning to tidy up after myself, and big-picture things like the life we wanted to make for ourselves. Tash and I would lie in bed at night and talk about what was good for us, our family and our future. Money loomed as a major concern. Tash was still doing her shifts at Jupiters and I did my couple at The Breakfast Bar. I hated working there but I couldn't afford not to. Together we pulled in just enough to get by. The money for the move came from a fight, the first since my comeback bout five months earlier. I made two and a half grand.

I'd hooked up with promoter Bill Mordey, the slim and savvy godfather of Australian boxing who carried the air of a bygone era about him. Mad about horses, he always dressed for the members stand but was happy to sit out the day in a pub with his middies, form guide and smokes. Dry as outback iron, he'd helped put Australian boxing on the map by guiding Jeff Fenech, Jeff Harding and Kostya Tszyu to world titles. By the time I met him he was phasing himself out, but he was still the best and, I believe, straightest operator in a ramshackle business. I told him I'd fight anyone; he matched me with an all-or-nothing Fijian named Mosese Sorovi. This guy rarely tested the judges' maths — all but six of his thirty-five fights had been won or lost by knockout. Two months earlier he'd broken form to go the distance in his loss to Glen Kelly, the Australian light heavyweight champion who everyone reckoned was a gun. I had sparred with Sorovi as he prepped for Kelly, so I knew what he had. I also figured a knockout might be a nice way to announce that Kelly had company. The fight ended in the seventh after I rocked Sorovi with a solid left hook. My follow-up punches kept him cradled in the ropes and on his feet. The ref stepped in before he fell. It was a bad knockout — Sorovi never fought again.

My next bout came seven weeks later. Bill priced my purse at $3000 — enough for a wedding. Tash and I set the date for 1 July, the day after the fight.

The prospect of the wedding raised a few curly issues. My parents were still relatively fresh from their divorce and both wanted to come, but only if the other wasn't going to be there. Tash and I considered eloping but decided we'd do the next best thing: we'd invite no one. Our families were disappointed, but they understood, and offered to help where they could. We went about our plans with full hearts and keen eyes on our tiny budget. Tash picked the celebrant out of the phone book and when we met her she was perfect. We went to a jeweller and selected the most basic rings we could find — 200 bucks for both. We put them on lay-by. I believed we'd treasure this time, it was so cute and special. We wouldn't always be poor. We both saw beauty in the unadorned nature of it all, and never lost sight of what lay at the heart of it — the very idea we were getting married contained a thrilling grandeur all its own.

After I'd beaten Sorovi, Bill had said to me, 'Okay, you've got past a big puncher. Let's see how you go against a hard man.' And he lined me up against Jamie Wallace, a tough journeyman with a workbench of a jaw. Wallace had lost two-thirds of his thirty-odd fights but his medal of honour was that he'd never been knocked out. I decided to take his body out (I do have half a nous). A good shot to the head can short-circuit the brain, but the brain can clear to marshal the body again. You don't get over good body shots during a bout. They can hurt for days; in the ring, they do cumulative damage. Under repeated assault, organs become more and more sensitive and acutely painful. Eventually, the body becomes paralysed — the opponent can barely tense up his torso to save himself. From the opening round I banged rights into Wallace's sternum and solar plexus. I rattled everything inside him until, in the third, I fired a rip into the keel of his right ribcage, finding the liver. The fight was over.

A hard liver shot is one of the most devastating in boxing. It can bring the toughest man down, particularly if he doesn't see it coming and the strike catches him relaxed or breathing in. There's not much pain felt in a knockout punch to the head — you're just gone. With the liver shot, a fighter will be writhing in agony, looking for all the world like he's been shot by a gun. It takes the feeling of being winded to a horrible extreme. Wallace was mortified, and sore. He told me after the fight that he'd never been hit so hard.

That night was my buck's night. I celebrated with a couple of beers at Simon's place with Nathan, Clint, Dad and a few others. The guys were pushing for us to go out and get on it but I said, 'No, I really want to experience tomorrow. I really want to be there.' So we drank a bit, passed a few joints around, then I went back to Clint's place to crash.

It had been storming for three days straight and Tash and I were freaking because the venue we'd chosen was outdoors, a lovely garden up on Mount Tamborine, just inland from Surfers. Thankfully the clouds had scattered by Saturday morning and we found ourselves blessed with a superb day. But my money took a little while coming and once I got hold of it I had to get busy — pick up the rings, buy myself some shoes, organise a limo for Tash and get myself ready. We arrived separately, Tash in a dress made by Mum, and me in a Briggs tartan kilt. I wasn't nervous until I got up there. It was so quiet and serene, and the only other three people there were our celebrant, Dierdre, her husband, Ian, and the photographer, Christine. Actually, there was another precious soul there, and we were so pleased to have him in our presence, kicking away inside Tash's belly as we exchanged the vows we'd written. We thought the simplicity and solitude lent a wonderful intensity to the moment. We weren't distracted by food or drinks or guests — all we were focussing on was the person in front of us. I became Tash's husband. Tash became my wife. It was so profound, so genuine.

After the ceremony, we headed to a small A-frame rainforest cabin we'd rented. We lay down together saying, 'We're married.' It felt different. It was a spinout, to tell you the truth. We had a little cry together. We were so happy. We made love, ordered pizza and then fell asleep, exhausted. Overnight, storms closed in for another three days.

*        *        *

My training had been going well. I'd been running the full 16 kilometres to Rod's every morning with Wayne, who'd decided to box and so joined in my training, and I came to value that run as a time for reflection. And I had a lot to think about. There was no doubt that the fire was back in my soul again. I was on a mission. And as I ran I'd think about where I was going as a man, a husband, a father and a boxer. I'd learnt that a major part of becoming more aware and gaining more creative power over my life was to be thankful for the gifts I had. I used to thank every hill I was running up for the strength it was giving my body. Wayne and I would push ourselves hard up those hills and get inside the pain and find gratitude, and our bodies took more strength again. To improve my boxing and win a world title was a massive goal in itself. But my central desire was to become a better man. I knew I wanted to change myself, but knowing it and living it are two different things.

I experimented as I ran. For all that had happened in my past, I still had the comfort of knowing that we are all pure of heart. I needed to build on that goodness that had always been there. For me, change had to start with my thinking, because I still thought violently. Although I wasn't reacting violently as often, the thinking was still there. I'd make judgments about people and life and react angrily: that's how I still saw the world. I had to go to work on my thought processes and reprogram myself. I talked to myself, posed questions to myself. I pulled up a chair and listened not only to those questions but where they were coming from. And answers and insights started to come from within.

God was there. Not a figure or someone else's voice, but a channel of universal truth I'd tapped into. Once I'd found it I realised that it had always been there. It could never have not been. I thought, *I've spent my life drowning out a true voice within me with the clamour of my rage.* I hadn't realised how much time I'd spent thinking violently. Every situation didn't need to be read in a violent way. I had to start listening to myself, my inner self. I had to start listening to Tash and other people. If I was to be a man of substance, my word had to start meaning something. To change, I had to not only think but react differently. I had to learn to react with patience, understanding and love. I found that such thoughts were calming, for they were clear and liberating and encouraging and inarguable. And they were a challenge. They would mean nothing if I did not apply them to my life and those around me. To sustain change required work.

I need to say that these thoughts evolved over the many months that I did this run from home to Rod's. It was literally a step-by-step process of reprogramming myself. In my car I'd think, *That motherfucker just cut me off! Didn't even indicate!* And I'd feel like forcing his car over and caving his head in, as I had done numerous times before without thinking. This was me, day in day out. At lights, *What are you looking at, prick? Smartarse. What's he thinking?* Walking along: *What are you looking at?* Day in, day out. I had to ask myself, *What is that going to attract to you?* I had to think about the answer. These guys had picked me? No. What had I ever done wrong? I thought and reacted with such anger that it blocked out true reason. I'd feel like I was this negative magnet that drew all manner of shit towards me. And I had to stop thinking like that. I had to start thinking like, *This guy doesn't want to use his indicator. That's his prerogative. And you know what? It's not making any difference to me. I can see he's changing lanes, so who cares?* I ended up having guys rocking up next to me going, 'Motherfucker!' And I'd just laugh at them — 'Yeah, you're the tough guy and I'm not. I'm going home to my wife.'

When I began to really understand that I was the creator of my world, I also began to understand how I could control it and bring into my life whatever I wanted. I would come to realise that I was so in control that it became a bit of a game. *God works through us. We are the physical manifestation of God experiencing himself. We are God, so we are gods ourselves. We have the same creative power that the source of the universe has. We can have in our lives almost whatever we want.*

I've even timed it. Going from a thought to a physical manifestation of a change I want to bring into my life used to take me two years. Now I've got it down to three months. But, as I said, I am saying that today looking years back to the point where I began to really become responsible for my own actions. The process was a gradual one, but one that I could definitely feel working.

One day when I was at The Breakfast Bar, I went to grab a coffee and a guy came up and said hello. I was shocked and instantly on edge. This guy had been a victim of mine. I barely nodded my acknowledgment of him. I just looked straight ahead. I wanted him out of my space. His pregnant girlfriend was with him and he was telling me that he'd really cleaned up his life. I was getting really annoyed. *Why the fuck would you want to talk to me? I don't want to be your friend. Good on you — you've turned your life around.* I didn't tell him to fuck off, but I said next to nothing to him. I got back to work, angry that he'd approached me and reminded me of what I'd done. I was heavy with guilt and I sunk back into self-hatred. But I checked myself. I was like, *Hang on, hang on, hang on. This is a good thing. You didn't know him then. He's cleaned his life up and good on him — that's a good thing. It's a good thing for you to see that.* And I felt kind of humbled he'd wanted to befriend me. *He's getting his life together. What you did wasn't right but maybe that was a big wake-up call for him.* I was doing the self-counselling, self-therapy thing. But it worked. Not magic-wand worked — I mean, it helped me reflect and gain a healthy perspective, one that didn't condemn me for eternity, nor damn the other guy, nor pollute the future for either of us. It was a real take on the present. A small but instructive event in my life, if I choose to use it as such.

After Wayne and I arrived at Rod's each morning we'd do our hour's workout and then Rod would put on a big breakfast and we'd sit around and listen to him tell stories from his colourful past. I developed a great bond with Rod. He is a very kind and loving man. And generous to a fault: he could never say no to people. And during that year my career went from strength to strength. Bill got me fights in July and then October and I won them both. The first paid seven and a half grand, the second eleven grand. I'd give Rod 20 per cent, that was our deal.

After each win I'd have an excuse to party. I'd go out, have a few drinks, a pill or two, and hang out in clubs till the early hours of the morning. I wasn't taking drugs like I used to, but on those occasional nights when I'd given myself the green light to indulge I'd end up feeling as though I was clinging onto a lifestyle I needed to break with cleanly. Tash was okay with me letting my hair down a little, but a post-fight night on the pills was becoming part of my routine. This could not continue into my fatherhood. Tash and I would talk about it in bed and she just said, 'You have to find a new way of celebrating your fights.' I thought, *I've got to stop this.*

All up, though, things were ace. Tash had started doing volunteer work at Paradise Kids, a grief counselling service for children that had been founded by our marriage celebrant, Dierdre. Since before we'd met, Tash had wanted to find something more than a professional career. She'd been thinking how wonderful it would be to find a charity she could devote time to. And she prayed she would find something she felt so deeply about and inspired by that would become her lifelong passion. As soon as she heard Dierdre talk about Paradise Kids, she wanted to know more and more. So after we married Tash completed the training and began working as a counsellor. The experience was, of course, both upsetting and rewarding for her, but we both loved the fact that through our humble little wedding her prayers were answered.

The baby was due in late November. After my win in early October, it was time to go to the next level. Glen Kelly had vacated the Australian light heavyweight title and I wanted it. So did a bloke named Adrian Bellin. Things were going so well for me, I made a few assumptions. I figured Bill would want to promote the fight and that I'd stay on my upward pay curve. But Bill only wanted to act as co-promoter, which I couldn't understand at all. The result was that I had to take a pay cut to eight grand. This fight was vital: I needed the belt to advance my career, and we needed the money. Soon we'd be down to one income, and suddenly it was seeming all the more unreliable.

I left The Breakfast Bar to train for the fight — I wasn't going to work in that freakzone while training for the Australian title. Everything was riding on this fight. The date hadn't been fixed but the location had: Melbourne. Tash was due on November 26 or 27.

She was going to have a home birth and I had a major role. We had everything planned — the inflatable spa, the music, the lighting and, after consultation with Tash's naturopath, a bunch of essential oils and teas. Tash wanted no drugs, no epidural; she wanted to feel the whole thing. And my place was front and centre. A midwife would be there in the background supervising, jumping in when needed. But I was going to help Tash bring our child into the world. We'd even decided on the name. I'd had a dream in which I was playing with my little boy and calling him Isaiah. I asked Tash what she thought of Isaiah as a name and she loved it. So we were all set.

Then I was told the date of the fight: November 24. I couldn't believe it. Tash wasn't impressed and she turned on me. A lot of strong feelings were coming to the fore, understandably. But what could I do? I had to fight. When the time came to leave I said to her, 'I'm going to go fight and I'll be on the first plane straight back. Just hold off.' And the minute I got on the plane I knew I wasn't going to be there.

November the 24th was the weirdest day of my life. My phone rang at five-thirty in the morning. 'Hi,' said Tash. 'Hi, darling. How are you feeling?' 'You should be here,' she said. 'I know, darling.' 'You should be here. You're supposed to be here.' And she started to get really pissed off with me. I tried to reason with her, going, 'It's silly doing this, babe. I'm down here now. I'll just get the fight out of the way and then I'm coming straight back.' Then I thought, *Hang on a second. Why is she ringing me at five-thirty in the morning and chewing my head off? This isn't like Tash. We're blueing in the morning.* But it was a weird sort of aggression; senseless: she was whingeing about things that a logical mind knows can't be changed and it wasn't like her at all. I said, 'What is wrong with you? I'm not going to fight with you. What's this about? What's wrong? Are you in pain?' 'A little bit,' she said. I said, 'Darling, are you having contractions?' 'Yes.' 'Since when?' 'Since about one o'clock in the morning or something.' 'So you're having a baby?' 'Yes.' 'Tash, why are you arguing with me? I'm ringing your mum.' 'Don't ring my mum.' 'I'm ringing your midwife.' 'What for?' 'Because you're having a fucking baby!' 'Don't ring my mum.'

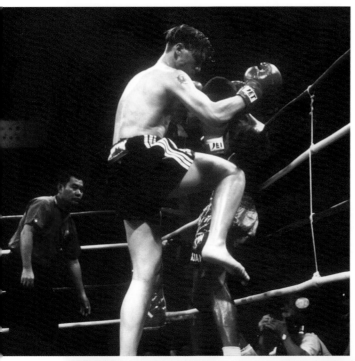

I won the world title in one of the most pitiful fights you could imagine. Winston Walker was happy to do little more than stay in the ring with me and avoid getting knocked out. But he had to throw something, BELOW, or else the ref would have stopped it as a no contest.

RIGHT: Second fight in two nights. Same result — second round knockout. This time it was Shane Dalton.

BELOW: Who's next? Another second round knockout, beating Jeff Tupu and defending my Australian light heavyweight title.

My unsuccessful WBC world title bid against Poland's Tomasz Adamek actually reminded me of why I fight: I love it. Here, it was close but no cigar. It was a loss, but it was a gold mine.

LEFT: With my brother from a different mother, world champion 'John' Wayne Parr. He inspired me to fight again.

BELOW: My first speaking engagement, talking to schoolkids about achieving your dreams. I was scared stiff.

The best move
I ever made —
marrying Tash
in 2000.

ABOVE: 2 + 1 = 3

RIGHT: Words are
just so limiting!
Isaiah Darius Briggs
at two weeks old.

LEFT: Nothing compares
— this is moments after I
delivered Aramea Shanti
Briggs. My children are
the greatest achievements
I'll ever make.

TOP: Multi-tasker.

TOP RIGHT: Enjoying some downtime with Aramea two days after beating Stipe Drews.

ABOVE: Our favourite time of the year.

RIGHT: Having a ball at Disneyland — woo hoo!

ABOVE: My world — my family.

LEFT: My anchors to sanity in Los Angeles as my world title fight kept getting put back and our lives entered a mind-bending period of uncertainty.

'Darling, I need someone to get there. You're at home by yourself.' 'You should be here.' The endorphins had obviously kicked in, and Tash was flipping from drowsy silliness one minute to lucid anger the next. Then she started crying and I was just gutted. I couldn't hold her nor comfort her. I told her that I had to hang up and ring the midwife and her mum and that I'd call back straightaway. I hung up, feeling so anxious and low. 'I'm not there,' I said to myself. 'I'm not there.'

So I hung up and rang the midwife. She said, 'No problem. I'll give Tash a call.' There was no sense of urgency. I was freaking. I said, 'You've got to get there.' She said, 'Listen, Paul. It's a long process. She'll be fine unless her water's broken. Did she say her water's broken?' I said, 'I don't know. I think so. Sounded like it was.' 'She'd know, Paul. She would have told you.' The midwife said she'd get back to me.

When I rang Vicki she said she'd already spoken with Tash. She said she'd get there soon, in a couple of hours. 'No, you've got to get there now!' I said. 'There's no couple of hours! What's wrong with you people? She's having a baby.' 'Paul,' said Vicki, 'she's okay.' Then the midwife rang me back and said everything was under control. She said, 'Relax. Tash is fine. This is just the beginning.'

I looked at the clock — six-thirty. Nathan was in the bed next to mine and he congratulated me. He'd been out of jail for more than a year and had followed me down to the Gold Coast, where he took up boxing and trained under Rod with Wayne and me. I tried to dissuade him from taking it up but he wouldn't listen. I just knew he didn't have it in him to make a real go of it. I think, though, that Nathan wanted to prove that he could overcome that fear he'd experienced all those years ago in Perth. Regardless of us not seeing eye to eye on his boxing career, he was very supportive of mine. And at times like these, when I was freaking over my wife going through labour without me, without anyone, it was really cool to have Nathan there. He was such a support. He was fighting that night too, but he was there for me.

Suddenly I realised I had a fight on. Normally I'd wake up on fight day — much later than five-thirty — and straightaway switch on to it mentally. But I'd woken up and I wasn't even there. I wasn't even in Melbourne. My mind was up on the Gold Coast. I reassured myself that I'd fought enough to know that when the time came to step into the ring, I'd be good to go.

I became psychic, I swear. I knew what time movies were on. Nathan and Dad were talking about seeing a movie and I rattled off titles and times. Rod came in saying he had a punt on a horse and it won. I said, 'Yeah, but it got disqualified.' Rod looked at Dad — 'Did you tell him?' Dad said, 'No.' I said, 'Did it?' He nodded, 'Yeah.' Then Dad's phone rang. I said, 'That's Diego.' He was a Spanish friend of Dad's. They hadn't spoken in ten years. I went down to the shops then back up to my room and the whole team — Dad, Nathan, Craig Berry, Rod — was following me around, annoying the hell out me. Rod was panicking. I was just like, 'Just fucking leave me alone! I'm a fighter. I fight.'

I kept ringing Tash. I couldn't bear to be apart from her. I was a wreck.

When it came time to go to the venue, I told myself I had to get my head together. When I was gloving up, the phone rang. Nathan answered, then put it to my ear. It was Vicki. She said, 'Listen to this.' I heard crying. It was my son. Isaiah. For a few seconds, I listened to him wailing away, then I lost it completely.

Bill walked into the dressing room, looked at me crying my eyes out and said, 'What the fuck's going on here? You've got a fucking fight on.' He turned on the TV crew. 'Get those cameras out of here!' Once he'd chased them out, he came back and said, 'Come on, son. Chin up. What the hell's the matter with you?' 'My wife's just had a baby,' I said. 'Great,' he said. 'We'll announce it after the fight. You okay?' I'm like, 'Yeah.'

Then I jumped on the pads and went nuts for five minutes. I looked awesome. Scary. But that was a stupid thing to do. I just blew all my strength out then and there.

Walking out to the ring, I found out that they'd stuffed up my music. It was supposed to be this really upbeat Paul van Dyke track. But they played the next one — a really ambient, soft breakbeat track talking about the reasons why we love someone; the sort of thing you have a pill and hug a friend to. So instead of getting pumped up and stormy, I drifted in on a fluffy cloud.

I stared at Bellin, trying to fire up, but it was like trying to start a car with a flat battery. As soon as the fight started, he hit me with a cracker of a shot and almost dropped me. That clicked me into gear. I boxed well, landing many blows to his head. He was coming at me all the time and I was moving onto the back foot and counterpunching, destroying him going backwards. You fight a boxer and you box a fighter, as they say. Bellin couldn't touch me. I lacked the oomph to knock him out, and he got cut into pieces. Ended up looking like the Elephant Man. His corner stopped the fight in the eighth.

I was the Australian champion and was like, 'Yeah, give me the belt. Let me go home.' I walked back to the dressing room, sat down and balled my eyes out. Nathan sat down next to me and put his arm around me.

Next morning, I was on the six o'clock flight home. Clint picked me up from the airport. I was in another world. He said, 'You've got to get flowers.' So we went and bought a huge bunch of roses. He dropped me off at home, said that he wasn't coming in, that he'd see us when we were ready, and gave me a big hug.

I walked in and saw that Tash was in bed. Then I saw Isaiah. I was speechless. I flung the flowers to the floor in Tash's direction and walked straight to him. I knelt down and looked at him for 10 minutes or more. I couldn't even touch him. I was just marvelling at this amazing little being we'd made. I was in awe. To this day I can't even describe it. There's no feeling like it. He was so beautiful. He was so perfect.

'Are those flowers for me?' said Tash, smiling. I came round. 'Hi, darling. How are you?'

I got into bed with Tash and my little boy and we talked and talked all day. For the next week, I didn't want to leave the house. Every time I had to go and get something, I raced out and raced back. I just wanted to hang out with my little boy.

# XXVIII

## The Honeymoon's Over

Getting someone to fight me was proving to be very difficult. Bill Mordey had wanted to back me and build up my profile through his Fox Sports boxing deal but, after watching a long chain of good relationships with his boxers turn bad, he decided he'd had enough. He was going to stick with charges he knew were loyal: horses. With Bill gone, I was forced to feed off scraps. I fought two bouts in two days for two grand a pop. Each lasted two rounds. I should have taken that as a sign that lean times lay ahead. But Tash and I had our hearts set on moving up to Mount Tamborine. We fancied we'd find a better lifestyle in which to start raising Isaiah. With the eight grand I got for knocking out Sam Leuii, the wheels were greased again, so we checked out a three-bedroom house that had amazing views of the coast, big verandahs, beautiful gardens and a saltwater pool. Seeing the house was supplied by tank water and gas, Tash suspected upkeep might be a hidden cost beyond the extra rent we'd be paying. But I was keen to forge ahead and we moved in. And so began the worst year of our lives. Being poor was quaint before we married; we were about to discover how devastating poverty can be.

After a month, reality began to hit us. We were only half an hour's drive from Surfers Paradise but lack of cash began to turn our moderate isolation into acute confinement. Soon my winnings had gone and the only regular income we had was a modest fortnightly government benefit. Even the smallest expenses began to hurt. Before long, we realised with dread that we were stuck. No money to move and struggling to stay on top of the rent. We'd dealt directly with the owners, who'd moved to England, and they'd call regularly querying the lag in rent and I'd have to plead our case for them not to kick us out — the money was coming, the money was coming. We ran out of nappies and had to use cloth ones. There were times when I'd scrounge around the house looking for coins just to get some milk. I missed training a few times because I couldn't buy petrol. It was such a shock to be fretting over such basic items, day in, day out. We borrowed 20 bucks here and there from family and friends but we reached a point where we were just too embarrassed to ask any more. We couldn't humble ourselves to ask again. It was so hard for me to feel secure in myself as a man. I was not supporting my family. We were not surviving.

Tash was angry about our situation. Boxing wasn't providing any solutions and she put pressure on me to get some money in. We thought so hard about our options but for me the bottom line was that I could not make boxing a part-time gig — I'd never get anywhere if I didn't make that my main concern, and that meant training three times a day. I contemplated going back to The Breakfast Bar, but I just couldn't bring myself to do it.

We made an inventory of possessions we could hock. It didn't take long — we had nothing. I considered doing a few jobs, not that I told Tash. I got offered a couple of things and I gave them some serious thought. But that would have gone against everything I'd committed myself to, and I wasn't going to slip back into that life and have to lie to my wife about where the money was coming from. One time I went to Damian's place to talk. I was in a bad way, confiding in him, saying that I just was not coping at all. As I poured my heart out, his wife, Caroline, began packing shopping bags with food. As I got up, hugged Damian and thanked him, Caroline handed me the bags and said, 'Here you are.' I began to protest but she said, 'I don't want to hear a word about it.' What do you do? My friends were giving us food? And nappies? I drove home heavy with despair and sick with worry. I felt so inept. I was beyond tears.

So many nights Tash and I just lay in bed and cried, asking ourselves, 'What are we going to do?' Man, there is nothing worse. I'd say to Tash, 'Soon, baby. It's going to happen, it's going to happen. This next fight. Everything's going to change after this next fight.' But it didn't. Fights came and went and the winnings were swallowed up by back rent and bare necessities. There was no relief. I had that terrible feeling of being the only one who really believed that my career was going somewhere. But I never, ever considered ditching boxing.

Tash, however, was more than down: she had postnatal depression. Many things worked to compound her distress, like the isolation and our money situation. Nothing was in walking distance from our house, so she couldn't take Isaiah to a park. I was out daily for training and had to take the car. Tash's family was beset by a series of crises, and contact with them was largely limited to phone calls. But the crux of it was that Tash was struggling to come to terms with being a mother. It hadn't been so long since she'd been independent and keen to establish a career. This potential and capability and ambition defined her; it was how she saw herself, how she would achieve her important personal goals. And while she had a beautiful, precious boy whom she loved and adored so deeply, she felt that she was losing her identity. She'd wanted to accomplish something in the world or the workforce that affirmed her as an achiever, something else to enable her to be a woman as well as a Mum. It was like she was watching something she feared run an inevitable course — and it was so confusing for her and made her feel extremely insecure. She'd wonder how, after years of being at home with a child, she'd ever establish herself in the workforce. She had no work experience in her field and she would come up with ideas about setting up a business at home. But when you are struggling to buy milk, even a simple home office remains a far-fetched fancy.

Tash was depressed for months and months on end. At times she even thought of leaving me, as she'd be eligible for more welfare money. That's how desperate she was. But she checked herself whenever she reached that point. Was our marriage really an act of folly? Had we made one huge mistake we'd now regret for the rest of our lives? No. We still loved each other immensely and were not about to let anything destroy what we had. We talked it all through so many times, reminding ourselves that we'd entered our marriage with the conviction to stick it out and swearing that we'd get through this together. We'd keep working at it and working at it, no matter what. We were not going to give up.

Then Tash got a letter from the government: they were challenging our eligibility for family support as they'd discovered I was a company director. The first thing I thought was that it must relate back to my kickboxing days, when Dad had set up a company to handle my earnings. But I was confused because the letter said I was the director. The only paperwork I'd ever signed was to set up the Moorooka gym and that company, I was sure, had been dissolved after I'd pulled out. So I rang Dad to ask him what this stuff was about. He got defensive. At first he said he didn't know what I was talking about. I explained that apparently I was the director of a company, but that that couldn't be possible because I hadn't signed anything. And he goes, 'What do you mean? You're not the director.' I said, 'Yeah, I am.' He said, 'No, you're not. I am.'

I realised then that we were talking about two completely different things, and that I had a major issue on my hands with my father. So I told him I had to make another call, then I'd get back to him. I got onto Brett, the old guy with whom I'd set up the gym. He told me he hadn't got around to dissolving the company after all. So I asked him to sort it out pronto. Then I got back on the phone to Dad.

I mentioned the gym. I said, 'Now that's what *I* was talking about. What are *you* talking about?' He said, 'I opened this company to handle your fight things.' I said, 'And you're the director of it?' 'Yeah,' he said. 'I'm controlling it.'

I couldn't believe what I was hearing. I said, 'You can fucking close that down right now.' Then he started with some bullshit about how I'd gone along with it. I told him that was a lie. He claimed he was doing it for me, but whether or not he had my best interests at heart was beside the point. I was an adult. I would never have asked, let alone agreed to, him stepping in and taking care of my business. I was furious. My earnings were none of his damned business. I decided that I had to get him out of my face once and for all. He'd been coming down to the gym to help me train and had been manning my corner during fights, which was all great, but he simply did not know where to draw the line. He was caring the only way he knew how — with that old white-knuckle grip. I said, 'You know what? I've had enough of this. I'm the boss.'

'Oh, really? You're the boss, are you? Well, you keep fucking talking like that and I'll see you on your doorstep.'

That was it — right there and then. It was time to sort this whole shit out for good. There was only one way I was going to be free of this man. I screamed down the phone at him. 'You know what, you prick? Fuck you! You've had twenty-four years wishing for this. And now you're going to get your wish. I'll see you on my fucking doorstep in half an hour. I'll be waiting. And you'd better come willing, because if you front, I will fucking kill you!'

I was slamming my fist onto the desk, shouting at the top of my voice. Tash came running in, wondering what on earth was going on.

Dad just shat himself and piped down completely. 'Just settle down,' he said. 'Settle down.'

But he was not going to get out of it that easily. I said, 'Enough of this! Enough! You're not standing over me any more, you're not controlling me any more.' He goes, 'I don't know what you're talking about, Paul. Just settle down. You're being irrational.' He had his softest voice on.

'I am making sense, and you know exactly what I'm fucking talking about.' Then he started arcing up again. I said, 'Don't fucking arc up at me on the phone. Get down here and be a man! You get your wish now. I'll see you in fucking 30 minutes. Get fucked!' And I slammed the phone down.

I sat there waiting, thinking, *What have I got here? There's an axe downstairs, knives in the kitchen* — mental notes of my weapon inventory. I had meant every word of what I'd said. I was ready to unload and no consequences mattered beyond the object of killing my father. Not jail nor Tash nor Isaiah. I was fit to kill my father. He probably has no idea.

The phone rang. It was Dad doing the old, 'Oh, mate. You know this is just ...' I stopped him right there. 'No, no, no, no, no,' I said. 'You've done it. You've done it. And now you've shit yourself. You ain't gonna lob round my place, are you? I'm not going to see you on my *doorstep*, am I?' And he started on with all this other crap and then his girlfriend got on the phone and started carrying on. I hung up on her and then he rang back again. I said, 'You know what? Just go and get fucked. I don't want anything to do with you. Fuck off. Have a nice life, mate.' And I hung up.

A couple of days passed and he rang me saying he wanted to sort all this out. We agreed to meet at Rod's place and I arrived ready to go him. Again he backed down. I told him to stay out of my life completely. I told him he was sacked, that he was not a part of my fighting career any more. And he was just like this little kid who'd gotten a clip around the ear and had his butt kicked. I lost all respect for him. All my life he'd been saying to Nathan and me, 'When you think you're ready, have a go.' In other words, 'When you think I'm not the boss around here, you just take your shot.' And when I finally called him on it, he wilted.

After that he'd ring me and start rows — now he was the one doing the shouting. He told me I was not that good a fighter, that I thought I was but I was kidding myself. 'You're just an average fucking fighter,' he said. I said, 'Fuck you. That's all you've ever told me all my life, you fucking piece of shit.' I said, 'Man, you were in front of me the other day. And now you wait till you get back in Brisbane to ring me and start screaming at me on the phone. You're not part of the team. You've just been tagging along, right from the word go.' And he made another feeble attempt to keep the relationship open, to hang onto me, as a fighting prospect, as a son. But it was too late for that. I told him where to go again and hung up.

That was it for me with him. I didn't see or hear from him for years.

\*     \*     \*

With money being a major issue, Rod and I had tried a few avenues to get sponsors to help me out. Our search led us to a car dealer named Greg Eastment. A former copper who'd boxed when he was younger, Greg was a keen fight fan. He'd seen me in the ring years before and was willing to meet us for a chat. I told him I was going to become world champion, but any boxer will say that. I told him about my training, my work ethic, my focus and my determination, and I guess Greg liked and respected me. Given the people he'd dealt with in his working life, he knew how to tell a genuine spiel from a phoney one. Before we wrapped up the meeting he said he'd like to help out. The offer he came back with floored me.

Greg called me in and told me he was willing to supply me with a new car. Tash and I had this crappy little Barina that had a big crack on the windscreen from when I'd punched it and windows that didn't work. I'd walked through a yard of gleaming vehicles and now here was Greg telling me I'd be driving home in one. Then he said if I needed to bring a sparring partner up to the Gold Coast and they needed to take time off work, he'd cover their air fare and wages. To round it off, he said that if I ever needed a hand with money to just let him know. In return, he wanted nothing. He said part of the deal was that he didn't want to cost me a cent. He didn't even want free tickets to my fights. He was getting nothing out of it but the satisfaction of helping me out. He and his partner knew sponsorship didn't work. What would be the value of me wearing their company name or logo during a fight staged in the US or interstate? None. He took me downstairs from his office, showed me a brand new V6 Mitsubishi sports edition and handed me the keys.

It didn't take long to test the new relationship. I was back there the next day bearing some bad news I dreaded telling Greg about: Tash and I had been in a major accident. A farmer, making a late bid for an exit off the freeway, cut across us and caught the front of the car. The impact flipped our car up onto two wheels and when it landed Tash, who was driving, could do nothing as we veered off the road and into a gutter head-on. The front wheels and suspension were destroyed. The farmer had no insurance.

Greg was shocked but he sorted it all out for us. The accident aside, I don't think he was aware to what extent his generosity had brightened up our lives. Meeting him was the high note of a very bad year.

The effort to get fights took me to London and Los Angeles. Bill Mordey set it up for Rod, myself and Bill's son Craig to visit a promoter there. Nothing came of it. Then I had a visit to the US, where I trained in Freddie Roach's LA gym and knocked out James Green in San Francisco. I'd hoped the win would lift me into the WBC's top ten rankings but I was having myself on. I realised I needed a promoter behind me — as a no-name fighter, I had little pulling power in any place other than Queensland.

I was offered the sort of contracts most hard-up boxers sign — a modest amount for the duration of your career. Great to put food on the table now but later, if and when you win a world title and your purses amount to millions, you'd still get little more than your original stipend while the rest would go to the promoter. Due return on his investment in you. But there was no way I was signing my life away for a short-term fix only to wind up in court trying to get myself out of one deal and into a better one. It was a very hard call considering our finances, but we had to hold out. I knew I was going to make it. Soon after I got home, though, I found that my confidence about the future of my marriage wasn't so high.

Everything was getting all too hard for me, so I looked to create an opportunity where I could get off my head and not think about the responsibilities of supporting a family and finding money while not being able to fight. On New Year's Eve 2001, I invited a few friends to our place for a party when I knew Tash wasn't up for it at all. I'd done this once before and caused a major row between us — Tash was still struggling with her depression and was in no mood to host a party. She was okay with the notion of a small gathering this time around, although I deliberately neglected to tell everyone that Tash had explicitly told me she didn't want any drugs in the house whatsoever. So, as I'd hoped, there were a few pills on hand and I necked a couple. Next thing I was off my face acting like an imbecile but I didn't care. In the morning Tash packed her bags, grabbed Isaiah and said, 'Later — I'm not living like this', and took off.

Tash went to her mum's place. She wanted me to spend some time by myself and get a taste of what life would be like without my wife and son. She also wanted to have some time alone to think about whether she really did want to leave on a permanent basis. I spent the day berating myself. *What the fuck are you doing? You're here again. You've done it again. Where is your wife? Where is your son? Is this what you want? Is it?* I was ringing Tash constantly, leaving messages, but she had turned her phone off. Eventually she answered one of my calls. It was the kick in the arse I needed. They came home that night.

Early in the year we escaped from Mount Tambourine and moved into a gated community in Robina on the Gold Coast. It was such a relief. Wayne and his wife and child lived here, so we were in good company and so relieved to be back in the land of the living. Still, it took Tash a couple more months to come good; she came to terms with herself and her new role, though, and we both felt relieved that we'd moved past a very real threat to our marriage.

While I'd seen off a string of fighters, my profile hadn't registered a blip beyond dedicated boxing fans. If the broader public doesn't know you, they're not going to be interested in watching you fight. Like it or not, boxers are in the entertainment business — and nobodies don't sell. In boxing, the world title belt is the sun around which everything revolves, and obscure fighters like me just float around out there in the ether. All boxers on the up want to tighten their orbits around that flame, and when they hit the top ten of the contenders list they start to be noticed and to feel the warmth of that golden dream of boxing — the title shot.

What confuses most people are the three-letter Scrabble combos world titles go by. It's a mess that continues to splinter with the introduction of super champions and interim champions who lend prestige to, and hence milk more money out of, non-world title fights. But the belts awarded by the governing bodies do matter, though they don't have equal cred.

There's a hierarchy of kudos. If, say, the WBC (World Boxing Commission) and the IBF (International Boxing Federation) are the Beatles and the Stones, then the WBA (World Boxing Association) is The Who and the WBO (World Boxing Organisation) on a good day, Small Faces. The rest are just covers bands. I wanted to win the WBC title first and foremost because that green belt is the most sought-after prize in boxing. I'd said from the start that I'd take on anyone. And I didn't want to go the easy route and beat up cadavers to fatten my record in the hope of getting a lucky-dip grab at a title. I'm not saying all my fights were hard — I took what I could get. But I honour every guy who stands in front of me. I give thanks to him for making me a greater person. You can't get into the ring and fight thin air to become champion. Each and every opponent helps me move towards financial security and provide a better future for my family and he provides insights as to how I can improve. I don't hate him at all. But the respect and repute you earn comes from the calibre and fame of the boxer you beat. And I had no big scalps to leverage off. So, since winning the Australian title, I'd been calling out Glen Kelly. After almost two years, he finally took me on. He no longer had much of a choice.

Kelly had risen to become the IBF's number four contender and finally achieved what he'd been aiming for — a crack at America's Roy Jones Junior and the cheque that went with the privilege. Jones didn't just have a belt — he had a wardrobe. Considered the best boxer of any weight for a decade, he had seven different titles branded with enough letters to write lofty prose. Kelly was a pulp fiction read for him. The gap in class was glaring as Jones carried Kelly and toyed with him before taking him out in the seventh. A month later, I won the OPBF (Oceania Pacific Boxing Federation) title. Kelly had a choice of retiring or taking me on to redeem himself for his humiliating display against Jones. The fight would reveal who was the best light heavyweight in Australia. At the time I said I believed I had the potential to be the best in the world. But talk's one thing — the ring is where you leave your business card. Kelly was my first chance to show that there was meat on the bones of my words. I'd had fourteen wins on the trot, twelve by knockout. And that's the way I wanted Kelly to go. That was his gift on offer.

From the outset I stalked him aggressively, leaving him in no doubt that I was not only strong but scary. I wasn't stupid, though — I respected Kelly's ability. I don't succumb to the folly of power, which in the ring corrupts by breeding careless thought. I knew that Kelly, like any opponent, could knock me out, but only if I lapsed to allow him. And I did not. This was the biggest fight of my life. I left nothing to chance, neither in training nor the fight itself. And once in the ring, I made Kelly's fear a reality — the worst he'd imagined about me before the fight was upon him in the flesh. I monstered him. Seconds into the fourth, I smashed him with a right that almost sent him through the ropes and from which he did not recover.

With that win, I moved into the WBC's top ten. I was poised for the next level — international. And I have Glen to thank for that.

# XXVIII

## *Hard Call*

On the face of it, Rod and I appeared to be a successful team. He was back in the game and training a boxer who was clearly making a charge for the world title. He was without question one of the closest mates I've ever had. Actually, he'd become more like a father to me. I would talk with him about everything going on in my life. We spent so much time together that we were as good as family. When it came to training, I'd long since lost my resentment over his verbal abuse — I responded to his barking tutelage and he was someone I wanted to work hard for, to make good his faith in me, to please. During our first two years together, he devoted his life to my career — everything he did was in my best interests. But he had his limitations, and as they became more and more pronounced I was forced to determine for myself what my best interests were.

As I've said before, a boxer's greatest asset is his strength of mind. It is your field marshal in the ring, your driver in the gym and your counsellor through wild fluctuations of hope and disappointment. For every fight I've had, there would be three that have fallen through. I guess it would be like piling all your energies, resources, passion and thought into one vital pitch or tender only to have it rejected outright. Again and again you have to start anew, as though that bid never failed, as though your

resources aren't depleted, your enthusiasm not jaded. I had my
downs but I had a great bunch of people around me at the
Boonchu gym from whom I took much-needed encouragement,
plus I had my own undying fire. I'd always regroup and refocus
with my head clear of precedent, which is what a boxer must do if
he's to make the most of those rare chances that eventually do
come. So he needs to have absolute confidence in the commitment
of his trainer and manager. It just doesn't work otherwise. After
two years together, my faith in Rod began to wane.

One pivotal sign that things weren't as they should be was the
Jorge Castro fight. Castro was a 36-year-old Argentinean warhorse
who'd had 143 fights and lost just 8 of them. You should never
read too much into records, but Castro's took some reading — and
from the videos I saw he took some beating, too. He was
positioned at five in the WBC rankings while I was at seven. We
were battling it out for the number two spot. I trained hard for
eleven weeks with Castro as my focus. I'd gone along with Rod's
suggestion that we promote the event ourselves, but I didn't have
a mind to seriously evaluate the risks involved.

I beat Castro comfortably on points, so I moved up. But the
night was a financial disaster. There was no local blackout of TV
coverage, so anyone who was half interested went to the pub to
watch the fight instead of forking out for our overpriced tickets.
Hardly anyone came and we lost a sickening amount of money.
Rod had been so cocksure about it all, but the proof lay in the
pudding. And this wasn't the first time. Rod had mortgaged his
house to promote the fight I had before Kelly. And credit where it's
due — the bout itself was a move to further my career. However,
he hadn't mortgaged his house for me — he'd done it because he
had no money and wanted to make some. I threw some cash into
the pot and we both ended up losing a bundle. Rod was a gambler,
not a grafter. 'Spend, spend, God will send' was his motto. But this
was my life we were dealing with, not some slot machine. I rued
my poor judgment in trusting his. Not only did I have to forego my
$60 000 pay cheque, Rod and I were now in debt to the tune of
$120 000. I was about to become a father again and here I was
moving one step forward and two steps back.

The birth of my daughter came six weeks later. And it was a day during which financial woes were rendered insignificant. I gained a beautiful daughter — but I almost lost everything I'd been fighting for.

Three nights before Aramea was born I had this dream in which everything went smoothly but then suddenly something went horribly wrong. Tash had to be taken to hospital in an ambulance — just for precaution, they said — and they wouldn't let me ride with her. I had to follow in another car. On the way we lost the ambulance somehow and once I got to the hospital a doctor approached me and handed me Aramea. I said, 'Where's my wife? I want to see my wife.' He said, 'That's what we have to talk to you about. Unfortunately, we lost her.' I reeled away, struggling to comprehend the unthinkable. I was shouting, 'Fucking *what*? She was fine in the ambulance! She was brought to hospital as a precaution!' Then I woke up to that awful moment when imagination bridges reality and I was briefly overcome with grief. That dream was so real — even thinking about it now chokes me up.

Come the day of the birth, I'd completely forgotten about my dream. Again we had a home birth and I helped deliver my beautiful little girl. But Tash lost a critical amount of blood in the process and turned bone white. The midwives laid her down and she was so weak she was barely conscious. She looked for all the world as though she was dying. The midwives were checking her blood pressure constantly but it was not improving. I was growing frantic. Not wanting Tash to hear me, I pulled one of them aside and said, 'You be 100 per cent honest with me — how much blood did she lose?' She said, 'I think we need an ambulance.' I was dialling as she spoke. I then called Mum to ask her to come and look after Isaiah.

Once the paramedics had loaded Tash I went to climb in, blind to everything but my wife's health. One of the guys put his hand on my chest. I said, 'Dude, with all due respect, you don't want to be touching me right now.' He said, 'Listen, Dad. Listen to me. Keep cool. Be nice and calm. You've got to have your wits about you for your wife here. Getting all aggressive isn't going to help anyone. What I need to explain is that you can't come with us — it'll be too much for your daughter. You need to take her and ride in the other car.' He said, 'Your wife's going to be fine. She's okay. We're just taking her to the hospital as a precaution.'

Once we were on the Gold Coast Highway heading towards Tweed Heads Hospital, I figured there'd be no lights to hold us up. Then up ahead I saw that Tash's ambulance had stopped in the middle of the highway. I started freaking. 'Why have they stopped? Why have they stopped?' The guy said, 'Calm down, Paul. If anything had happened they would have radioed me.' As it turned out a woman had passed out in her car. The paramedic from Tash's ambulance told my guy they had radioed for help and that he needed to stay and make sure the lady was okay while they went on ahead. My driver pulled off the road and got out.

So I was sitting there, trying to keep a grip, when all of a sudden the recollection of the dream hit me. I almost jumped out of the car to drag the guy back behind the wheel. It was all I could do to hold myself together, but I was telling myself that I had to be calm for Aramea. Then my phone rang. It was Rod. And I just went to pieces, sobbing to him about what had happened and what I'd dreamt. He told me I was just being silly. 'Tash will be fine,' he said. 'I'll come and meet you at the hospital.' Finally we got to the hospital and a doctor walked towards me like in the dream. My legs went on me and I almost collapsed and dropped Aramea. I was shaking my head going, 'No, no.' He said, 'She's absolutely fine.' And he led me to her.

I walked into the room and she wasn't fine at all. She looked in so much pain, the poor thing. The doctors were looking at her and poking at her. She just gave me this look, tears running down her face, and said, 'Help, babe. Help.' And that was all I needed. One of the midwives took Aramea and I'm like, 'Right — stop poking her!' And this one bitch was like, 'Oh right, tough dad, hey?' And we had a little exchange during which she said, 'You shouldn't even be in here!' I said, 'You'd better ring the cops and get plenty of them, because you're going to need them to get me out of here.' I was rearing to go. I didn't start calming down until they'd given Tash morphine for her pain.

266

I said to the doctors, 'Don't just do things. Explain to me what you're doing. I've got no problem with you doing what you're doing, just let me know what's going on. I don't want anything done without my approval.' They didn't like that at all but they kept me informed. I didn't care what they thought. I said, 'This is my *life* lying here. Do you understand that? My *life*, not my wife.' I was thinking, *Anything happens to her, God help the planet*.

Tash pulled through okay but the drama of Aramea's birth precipitated another. My mother was furious about what happened, first that we'd risked having a home birth and second that we'd had Isaiah present. Mum had seen all the blood everywhere and, admittedly, it was like a murder scene. But the reproduction of life was not something we felt Isaiah should be sheltered from. And he was fine. He was reading his books, including a children's book that explained childbirth quite graphically but nicely. At one point he was making a lot of noise and I hushed him, but Tash checked me. Just hearing him was soothing for her. Of course he was upset at his Mum being taken away on a stretcher but the experience hasn't scarred him for life. And with regard to the home birth — that was our choice. This was Tash's second and we knew we could call for help if the midwives became overwhelmed. We decided to do this being fully aware of the dangers. I don't believe that was being irresponsible. Mum didn't agree, and to her the outcome vindicated her judgment. The tension that had begun with her reaction to my rape then escalated over the next few months. Finally, I reached the point where I could no longer live with the animosity I held towards her. Enough was enough. I had to get through to her once and for all.

I went down to Mum's factory, where she made clothes and costumes, cleared everyone out of the building — including Wayne, now her husband — and locked the door. I said, 'Now, you're going to stay here and talk to me about this whether you like it or not.' And then we launched into a big screaming match until I finally got through to her. She didn't have to defend herself — I'd never been mining for her guilt. I wasn't placing blame upon her. I just wanted her to validate me and validate my feelings. That was all. We were both in tears and I grabbed her and said, 'I'm not blaming you.' I did not want or need for her to feel bad. I wanted her to hug me with motherly care. I needed reassuring, comforting, that maternal sanctuary that is the most important thing in a child's life. I never had her as a refuge in the wake of my rape and it was something vital I lacked. And with a long, quiet embrace Mum finally gave that to me. It was all I needed. I told her I was at a point where I no longer felt like a victim. I could even look at that event and take some heart. I had had a massive trial to battle through and, having prevailed, I knew I could get through anything else life threw at me.

Mum and I still had some niggles to iron out in regard to how Tash and I were choosing to live and raise our family. But she had to accept that we were going to be guided by our own beliefs and value systems, not hers, nor anybody else's. I had needed to be, for that one moment, a little boy finding comfort in his mother's arms. But, looking ahead, I wanted her to love and respect me not so much as son to mother but as a man and father who lived beyond her maternal influence. From then on our relationship did change for the better. I guess I had closure of sorts — the rape had ceased to overshadow my relationship with anyone.

I took a break after the Castro fight. I'd been training solidly for three years and, taking into account all the other dramas Tash and I had been through, I wanted to spend more time with my wife and help settle our lives after the arrival of Aramea. The fact that I was closing in on a title shot had brought sports management types out of the woodwork to try to sign me. Rod and I had spoken about it, but only in terms of what sponsorship money they could bring in. Then I was introduced to a guy called Geoffrey Schuhkraft. He'd founded International Quarterback, a leading sports management company, years before. After he left IQ he had to see out a three-year embargo before he could operate in the industry again. He'd spent a lot of time overseas and had come back to Australia with a new company, On International, and a new model for how to do things. I met him at Surfers for a chat.

Geoffrey didn't hit me with the big sell, saying, 'We can do this for you and that for you'. He asked me some interesting questions about my aims in life, what I was passionate about and how I wanted to affect the world. I had already started to think about these things, about life beyond boxing. I'd joined Tash at Paradise Kids and had seen that many of the boys who'd come through the door didn't have good male role models in their lives. Either their fathers had died or were absent, or the man of the house was beating up the mother. With some other guys I discussed the idea of starting up a boys group to give young blokes a different experience of what masculinity is. So myself, a psychologist and men from all walks of life formed a mentoring team.

Every boy wants to be a man but they don't really know what it means. When do you become a man? When you leave school? When you're old enough to drink? When you get your licence? When you become rich? When you can punch another man out? When you reach twenty-one? When you've rooted fifty chicks? When you've experienced a full array of drugs? And can you be a man if you're gay? Can you be a man if you're a bookworm? Such questions have nothing to do with character, with responsibility, with knowledge. The whole issue is a blur. Our concept of what it is to be a man is so confused as to be an enigma or, worse, a caricature. How sad, how wasteful, is that? Our society wants good men but provides no clarity, no landmark, no ritual, no guidance. Boys look to peers, to movies, to athletes — but mostly they look to the central man in their life: their father. And boys disillusioned with the father–son relationship will often devote their lives to defying their fathers, to being better than them or worse than them — harder, tougher, meaner. As I had learnt, rarely does that bring you happiness and inner strength — you live your life trying to prove who you are not not, rather than taking nourishment from who you are, from your sense of worth, to build meaningful assuredness instead of meaningless or destructive 'achievements'.

What is of utmost value is finding that true strength within you. You can't fake it with ego — you can fool others but not, if you take the time to reflect, yourself. Our concept of man is tied to ego. But the security of knowing who you are as a man consigns ego to its proper place — a tool that, relied on too heavily, breeds delusion. The most common word used to describe what is manful

— macho — is all about ego, nothing about depth of character. Ego can be a major stumbling block for men and boys, but it isn't necessarily a wild beast that needs to be tied — it can be a power source if employed in healthy balance. Boys need to fathom that being a man is not about being aggressive, sexist, homophobic, emotionally mute, overconfident and pig-headed. Such qualities have no business being used as reference points for manhood. We have evolved too much psychologically to allow boys to be so limited in their thoughts and feelings.

Our mentoring group was about building trust and rapport. We allowed the boys to be boys — we wrestled with them, controlled rough play with caring men, because that's one way boys test themselves in relation to men: they want physical contact. We'd do activities with them, using that time to talk with them and open up avenues of communication. And I didn't present myself just as a boxer — I was a man who could sew, cook, clean house and change nappies. Things I'd learnt from my mother and my wife. And, thank God, I was a man who could feel. The experience with the boys group had rammed home to me the enormous gap boys must span as they mature, and so many were doing it alone without guidance or encouragement, to the detriment of themselves and, perhaps in the future, others.

I didn't lay all this onto Geoffrey. But I liked that he wanted to sound out my deeper thoughts about my life and goals. I told him about my experience with Paradise Kids and said that I really wanted to extend that work to help men, to give men a different perspective on masculinity. I'd come a long way since I'd made a concerted effort to address my own issues. I'd come to know my emotions and felt so grateful for that. Far from the experience emasculating me, I felt empowered, strong in a holistic sense that mere physicality can't provide. I'd learnt that vulnerability is the bed of courage. I'd learnt that kindness is not weakness. I'd learnt that self-love, not pride or narcissism or arrogance, is a man's best friend whose priceless companionship is not easily won.

I felt I had a very real responsibility to break the mould my father was cast in and be a father I could be proud of to my son. I told Geoffrey I wanted to become the ultimate warrior, to win world titles in boxing and kickboxing. Then I figured men would listen to me. And I wanted to talk with other men about men's issues and emotions and feelings, and I wanted to address boys schools.

Geoffrey liked what he heard. He told me he wanted to manage me. I said I already had a manager in Rod. Geoffrey said he'd love to meet Rod and then spoke about his approach to endorsements. He didn't make any fantastic claims or do the hard sell or make himself out to be a really shit-hot operator whom I had to have on board. He did not make a move. He was very realistic. He was refreshing. For starters, he wasn't a crook. He'd had nothing to do with the shark-infested world of boxing. But he knew his stuff well. He did not try to impress me. But he did. I liked the guy.

I told Rod about my meeting. I was invigorated by what we'd discussed. Rod thought Geoffrey had filled my head with rubbish. He got on the back foot, insecure about his own abilities to manage me. I know he had to forget anyone but me — it would have hurt him to think that I'd consider taking on another manager. After they met, Rod warned me off giving Geoffrey the slightest in. He said that he was just trying to jump our train as we were nearing the big money stations. But I knew that wasn't what Geoffrey was about at all. I'd already made my decision — I wanted to work with this guy. And after he'd met Tash, whose endorsement I would not proceed without, Geoffrey came on board. He'd only take a percentage of whatever deals he brought to the table.

For my next fight, Geoffrey went to work. And man, did he announce himself. He set about hardballing the promoters, making demands and getting them. His upshot was: 'Paul is a professional athlete; start treating him like one.' He got me a bigger purse, better accommodation and money for publicity. He was an amazing negotiator — very fair and non-abrasive in meetings but strong about getting what we wanted. And all these guys were going, 'Who the fuck's this prick?' Their noses were way out of joint. I thought, *This is superb. This is what I want. I want to really turn boxing on its head so promoters can't treat boxers like shit.* The sport of boxing isn't organised so much as manipulated. Compared to other sports organisations, it's as straight as a mad woman's knitting. It can't even be referred to as an organisation. It's an ongoing gold rush thick with fools and exploited by bullies and grubs. I wanted someone who could cut through the double-dealing and the bullshit, someone who wasn't afraid to be a bastard, who didn't care whether or not any glint-toothed shyster liked him. Rod wanted to be everyone's mate; Geoffrey wanted more than anyone had ever bargained for. He demanded respect for Paul Briggs. He was professional and ruthless. He did his job for me and my family. And he did it extremely well.

The WBC light heavyweight division was becoming a shitfight, and one that threatened to bring down the WBC altogether. Roy Jones Junior was their main cash cow so they bent over backwards for him. Jones had returned from his heavyweight campaign and the WBC immediately allowed him to try to regain the light heavyweight belt he'd vacated, since claimed by another American named Antonio Tarver. I was the number two contender and was ordered to fight the Mexican Jesus Ruiz, ranked at eight, for the right to take on the winner of the Tarver–Jones clash.

I went about training as usual. A while back Rod had installed a gym on his property at Nerang, so I'd been spending my afternoon sessions up there instead of at the Boonchu gym. The thing was, Rod wasn't around much. Never one to hold the pads, as most trainers do, Rod believed I only had to be within earshot for him to train me. But now, for the most part, he wasn't even in sight. I was training for a major bout but I'd learnt nothing new from Rod to take with me. I was just getting fit doing 20 kilometre runs and hitting the pads. I was relying on my ability to hit and on my fitness. No Plan B, zero strategising with trainer, just an in-shape puncher backing himself, the type of fighter happy just to get a crack at a world title, hoping for a lucky blow to answer all his prayers. I had so much more potential than that, but I was not developing it with Rod, and certainly not, as was becoming more common, without him. He was off the clock, attending to this and that. In the lead-up to that Ruiz fight his mind was somewhere else. I began thinking I'd be paying him 20 per cent just to stand at the ropes come fight time and give his opinion.

That fight was almost my downfall. Ruiz was a solid piece of work — a good, hungry fighter who had his life on the line. If he lost he'd have to leave the United States and his chances of getting a title shot would be flung into outer orbit. In the second round I made the mistake of walking straight back from him and he caught me on the chin with a right that flew express all the way from his hometown of Guanajuato. I hit the canvas and immediately sprang to my feet. To look at me, the way I came after him straightaway, you'd swear his punch hadn't affected me. That was just what I had to make him think — that he'd landed a bomb to no apparent effect. But it had an effect all right. I did come back at Ruiz — all five of him. I concentrated on the middle one. It took five rounds for my head to clear after that shot. But I took control of the fight, using my stamina and left jab to cut Ruiz down, accrue points and win round by round. I said into the announcer's mike that I'd prevailed by way of a home-town decision, that I thought Ruiz had really won. In reviewing the tape, that was far from true. I'd boxed well — well enough, anyway. But, at the time, I felt like I'd been handed an undeserved victory. That said a lot about my mind-set.

We had a big meeting the next day at Geoffrey's Sydney office — me, Rod and my US-based agent, Sampson Lewkowicz, who'd been on deck since Castro and had done so much for me for nix. Sampson said we needed to get real and get me based in the States and hooked up with a high-profile trainer. Sampson asked Rod if he had any objections to being a co-trainer; Rod said no. Then Sampson got one of his candidates on the phone from America: Jack Mosley. Jack was considered to be one of the best, voted Trainer of the Year in 1999 and 2000 after steering his son Shane to the WBC welterweight title. Jack coached power-punching — a fast-paced, attacking style backed by the ability to land hard, telling blows as opposed to a more defensive style based on shifting, sniping and jabbing. His style suited me perfectly.

We chatted a little and I told Jack I was a hard worker, that I wasn't a lunatic, that I was going to be world champion and that I was ready to rip shit up. We didn't strike a deal then and there with Jack — he was an option, and a damned good one. After we spoke, though, the question on my mind was, *Where does Rod fit*

*in? He can't just be along for the ride. No boxer has a co-trainer.*
If Rod was to be relocated and set up and paid for being in the
United States, what did he bring to the table? Nothing that
Geoffrey or Jack couldn't cover better. This was business, nothing
personal. It was only personal in that it was the business of my
entire life. And I'd watched Rod lose sight of that. We had so far
to go and he seemed to think it was all in the bag. So much so, he
was sure that we were about to get rid of Geoffrey. A lot of
people's noses were out of joint because of the way Geoffrey had
hardballed them, and Rod believed that the relationship was
untenable.

But I was so annoyed with Rod because of his lack of focus that
I hadn't discussed anything with him at all. During the meeting, I
was stressing. I knew I was coming to a point of decision in my
career that I never thought I'd reach. I began to think I might have
to leave Rod behind. The thought sickened me, for as much as I
was pissed off with him, I loved the guy.

I flew home that night and in the morning I woke, sat bolt
upright and said to Tash, 'I'm going to have to sack Rod.' She was
stunned, but once I explained she supported me. He'd taken me as
far as he could — I was no longer prepared to leave my life in his
hands. I went around to his place and he was making coffee when
I arrived. He started saying that we had to do this and get onto
that. I said, 'Rod, it's over.' 'What do you mean, it's over? You're
not quitting boxing.' I said, 'No, I'm not quitting boxing.' Then it
hit him. Hard. He asked why. I said there were about 400 reasons.
He said, 'Can you give me one?' I said, 'I can give you all 400 if
you like.' We sat down and it was very emotional. We both got
upset. I loved the bloke but I was so hurt and angry that he'd lost
focus right when we needed to tighten up. I told him I felt like I
was with my old man again. He said, 'Well, you're doing the same
to me as you did to your old man.' I said, 'We're almost there and
you're getting complacent and sidetracked.' I said I wasn't
prepared to do it all by myself again. I said, 'Tash and the kids
come first and that's that. My first loyalty is to them.'

Everyone was shocked by my decision and I was accused of
being disloyal. It seemed somehow irrelevant that I was a

professional athlete aspiring to beat the best boxers in the world and needed to employ every resource at my disposal to achieve that goal. Where was it written that I should be blindly loyal to this man and run my career into an iceberg like the fucking *Titanic* and watch it sink?

Two weeks after I sacked him, Rod was arrested and charged with conspiracy to import one and a half tonnes of pseudoephedrine, the chemical used to make speed. He was one of five people cuffed over a shipment the Feds had seized in the Philippines that was en route from Shanghai to Australia. The local news were all over it and when they mentioned Rodney Alan James, otherwise known as Rod Waterhouse, former trainer of light heavyweight contender Paul Briggs, what did they show but me banging away on the pads. My wife, working at Paradise Kids, found her husband associated in this way with one of the biggest drug busts in Australia's history. That was bad enough. But what if Rod and I had still been together when they were busted and I was being investigated? People would go, 'Paul Briggs hasn't come good — he's into the same shit, only bigger and better.' That would have destroyed everything I'd strived so bloody hard to change and to create anew. Needless to say, I do not have an ounce of regret over my decision.

It seemed no sooner had I met Geoffrey than Tash, me and the kids found ourselves settling into a lovely house in Westwood, Los Angeles, and I was driving across the breadth of the city every morning to train with Jack in Pomona, on the eastern fringe of LA. But soon I was informed that, despite winning my world title eliminator against Ruiz, my next fight would not be for the title after all. I was ordered to fight the number three contender, a Croat named Stipe Drews, for the right to fight Tarver, who'd just avenged his loss to Jones in a rematch. Once and for all a win here would position me as the number one contender for the WBC light heavyweight crown.

For a while it seemed as though I'd be lucky to have a belt to fight for at all — a month out from the fight, the WBC declared itself bankrupt. Back in 1998, Jones had vacated the title to move up to heavyweight. Then he changed his mind: he wanted to stay at light heavyweight and he wanted his vactant title back. In the meantime, though, a German fighter had won the title fair and square. But the WBC illegally stripped him of it in their eagerness to please Jones. The German sued and, in 2003, a New York court ordered the WBC to pay him 33 million bucks. That stung enough for them to shut up shop. Their next move appeared to be to re-open down the road with some other three-letter name over the door. But they managed to survive after all. And while the goalposts were being shifted and removed, I was preparing for Drews.

I arrived in Sydney on the eve of the Athens Olympics in 2004 and fought Drews out at Homebush, the heart of the 2000 Olympic Games. What followed was the most awkward fight of my life. Drews was a six foot seven southpaw and he leant on his reach advantage from the outset, clocking up points with his jab. I had to try to get in close to nail him but it was proving tricky. I was well behind in the fifth. In the sixth I got to put my left hook to work. I dropped him twice. I dropped him again early in the seventh. He was halfway gone. That's when he got dirty: he kneed me in the balls, he tried to snap my neck, he headbutted me several times, he tried to elbow me. He knew he was losing so he decided that getting himself disqualified was better than being knocked out. He made a street fight out of it and for a moment there I just wanted to bite this fuckwit's cheek off. But I kept my cool and controlled the remaining rounds to take a unanimous decision.

This was not my best fighting display. I still felt I had so much more to offer. I'd just started up with Jack and I still had so much more to learn and refine. I was now the WBC number one contender; my next fight would be for the world title. Really, though, I had some serious work ahead of me. I couldn't wait to get back in the gym with Jack.

# XXX

## A Matter For God

Tash and I settled back into Los Angeles with a sense that our long-held dream was coming to fruition. At last, everything was on track. I had a big win under my belt, a sixty-grand cheque in the bank and a big-money world title fight looming — before the year was out, I'd be taking on WBC champ Antonio Tarver for half a million US dollars — win, lose or draw. Tash and I allowed ourselves to mentally bank the fight proceeds, if not entirely the win. We couldn't help it. To think of that fight and not of how that money would change our lives, clear our debt, ease our burden and shape our future would be like trying to sleep with our eyes open. Planning by payday was how we'd lived for years now. More than ever, though, it seemed that our devotion to my boxing career would really pay off. We could count on a little surety, and even indulgence, coming into our lives. Los Angeles was going to be our home for the next two years and we were both okay with that. That was time enough for me to win the world title, defend it, make a name for myself in the United States and get some big sponsors on deck. In quiet hours after training, I'd find myself online checking out whether I'd treat myself to a Merc or a Jag. I was leaning towards the Merc.

Everything began falling into place. Don King had stepped up to promote Tarver–Briggs and my share of the purse was set at

US$675 000. All King wanted in return was the right to promote my first defence, if I won, which was fair enough. Now the only thing missing was the date. In late October, it came — 18 December. I was looking at being the new light heavyweight champion of the world by Christmas.

I should have known it was too good to be true. As it happened, getting into the ring with me was not on Tarver's agenda. I can't say whether he and his advisers considered me easy pickings or an unnecessary risk. It's a moot point. I do know that I was no stranger to the guy — the year before we'd begun negotiations to fight, but we never heard from them after we sent them tapes of my fights. Tarver was an ageing boxer dining out on the celebrity foisted upon him for knocking out the great Roy Jones Junior; he was also a bloke hard up for coin and, given that he was thirty-six, his remaining paydays were retirement funds. When Glencoffe Johnson, another twilight dweller, also knocked out Jones, the match-up between the these two 'giant killers' — at least in their minds — loomed as the fight of the century. Problem was that the WBC had ordered Tarver to fight a mandatory title defence against me. But he refused. Instead of fighting me for US$2.2 million, he decided to fight Johnson for US$3 million in a bout sanctioned by neither the WBC nor the IBF.

When Tarver announced he was fighting Johnson, he was stripped of his WBC title. If he had chosen to fight me *and* Johnson, Tarver could have made more than 5 million in a few months as the WBC light heavyweight champ. Instead he opted to give up his belt for US$800 000.

There was more to it than that, though. In the wake of his victory over Jones, Tarver had burnt Don King. King had done a standard deal with Tarver — I'll promote this fight if you let me promote your first defence. After he won, though, Tarver reneged on the deal and King was pissed off. So there was no question who King was behind in a Briggs–Tarver bout. 'After Briggs knocks you unconscious,' he told Tarver, 'I'm going to stand on your throat.' King never got the chance — Tarver pulled out. And, for what it's worth, he fought Johnson on 18 December and lost.

For Tash and me, the impact of the Tarver fight falling through was immense. Suddenly uncertainty reigned over us yet again. I had no idea when I would next fight. Of course we knew this was the nature of boxing, but the effect of seeing the greatest and surest opportunity of my career being snatched away was devastating. Now I'd be fighting for the vacant title. But against whom? And for how much? And when? It was at this point that the novelty of living in Los Angeles, and the optimistic outlook of a two-year stint there, began to wear thin. All bets were now off and the dream that our financial breakthrough was imminent quickly transformed into the dread of accruing an ever-deepening debt.

To shore up our future, it was time to look at signing with Don King for a long-term deal. I went to Florida with Geoffrey and Sampson and we secured decent terms on a three-year contract. For my first fight — the vacant world title — we met King halfway at US$200 000. After we signed, Don King stood up, raised his arms and shouted, 'Yes! I've got Paul Briggs!' Tash, however, wasn't inclined to do cartwheels when I told her about the deal. In the space of a couple of weeks the value of my next fight had been slashed by two-thirds. Given the cost of living LA with two kids, and the rate at which our debt was growing, that 200 grand would only be a short-term reprieve.

King pulled a Polish boxer named Tomasz Adamek out of a scheduled bout in December. He told Adamek there'd been a change of plan and that he now was up against Paul Briggs for a chance at the vacant world title. Okay, so now I was going to fight this guy Adamek, the WBC number four contender, and get 200 grand. But when? When was I going to fight? When could I get this done? *When will I be world champion?* Without a date, everything appeared so indefinite again. Our lives lost that sense of purpose we'd held so briefly. Our existence was suspended — there was no certainty, no momentum, no direction. The *date*. That crucial slot on the calendar slipped once again into a roulette wheel blur and our lives could not take root until the ball settled. But the wheel just kept on spinning and spinning and spinning. It was enough to drive me crazy. And damn near drove us apart.

The disheartening turn of events began to take their toll at home, especially for Tash. Given the fact that I was always training and that we knew few people in Los Angeles, our social life was limited. And because Tash was ineligible for a visa, meaningful work was not an option for her. Freeing her time up a little so she could work was also not an option — we had no money for daycare.

The brightness we'd felt upon returning to LA began to fade as once again we had to prop our spirits up with wearying resolve. Doubt over the future made us question the sense of staying in the United States for two more weeks, let alone two more years. Then Isaiah began talking about wanting to go back to Australia, how he missed his home, his grandparents and friends. This may sound trivial, but it placed more pressure on us. We didn't want our boy to be miserable and we didn't want him to be moved around from school to school. And Tash was like, 'What am *I* doing here? What am *I* about?' People might say, 'Well, you married a boxer, deal with it.' But that's not what our marriage has ever been about. Our marriage isn't all about my career. Tash's role was never going to be simply that of a housewife. She was thrilled to be a mother but she'd never disowned her work ambitions. And with every setback in my career, the time she envisioned she'd be able to start making inroads into a career was put back once more.

Then I began feeling guilty because her life was on hold because of me. One thing I was sure of was that I was not going to stand by and watch my wife slip back into a depressive state again. And the way things were headed, this loomed as a real possibility. So in the space of two months, our upbeat two-year plan for living in the States, which had been entirely centred on my career, had morphed into a money-guzzling, soul-sapping, tension-laden, open-ended period of uncertainty. We were sure about little more than the fact that we were burning through cash. It was costing us US$10 000 a month to live there, and that was with cheap rent. With every week that passed, that prize money dwindled rapidly as our debt burden grew.

In mid-December the fight was set for 16 January. By then, though, we'd had a gutful. We just weren't prepared to struggle any more. We had built our lives to a comfortable level in Australia; America was somewhere we could live if we had to, but the imperative had gone. After the Adamek fight, we decided, we were heading home. This may be seen as me losing my edge, my hunger, that previously I would not have let such circumstances prevent me from finishing the business of not just winning that world title but capitalising on it. I don't care. The fact is that my life choices ceased to be confined by the narrow band of my own career interests long before then. I believe it wasn't a matter of losing hunger but gaining perspective. At the end of the day, my boxing career will come and go, but my family is constant.

In the weeks leading up to Christmas, Jack and I relocated to his place in Big Bear, Calfornia, to reap the benefits of high-altitude training, where your body responds to the reduced oxygen content of the air by increasing the production of red blood cells. Your fuel, so the theory goes, is effectively optimised. Once you are back at sea level, the supercharged blood gives your performance a boost. When I returned home to spend Christmas with my family, I learnt that the fight was being put back. It doesn't matter what the reason was. The date, 16 January, was gone and Don King was trying to get a new one for February, maybe the seventh ... And so the cycle started again. We started setting a fragment of hope against a strand of faith, to rebuild piece by piece what might yet prove to be another house of cards.

The news of the setback did get me down. But then I just tried to put it out of my mind and relax a little. Hell, I needed a break anyway. For almost five months I'd been driving over to Pomona to train and I couldn't just keep banging my head against a brick wall. So I managed to enjoy a lovely Christmas with my family. And I looked forward to seeing Stu and Diana, friends of ours who were coming to stay with us for a week or so before heading up to San Francisco.

One night during their visit, the perfect opportunity presented itself for me to run and hide from the pressures weighing upon me. I had been carrying a lot of guilt about putting my wife and children through such a destabilising period. I felt I wasn't delivering on my promises; I felt sick about us borrowing and borrowing to the extent that it didn't seem like borrowing any more. We were detached from the fact that we were spending money we hadn't yet earnt — we simply took whatever money was accessible. When I was actually going to make some money was once again anybody's guess. So when Tash and Diana went out to see a band called The 5678s, I found myself drinking vodka with Ben and feeling the door to an old room begin to open. I was only a little pissed, but I started to feel like I deserved a treat. I deserved to get off my head, to give myself some time out from the shit I was freaking about. Ben had some coke on him, so I thought, *Fuck it, it's Christmas, things aren't going my way, it's only for a night . . . Let's have a line, eh? Rack up, mate.*

After a couple of rails I'd become a completely different person, someone I'd never wanted to be again. That feverish appetite was unlocked; I had that mischievous delight of loitering on the cusp of abandon. I was poised to hook right in, to rack up fatter lines, to demolish the bag, to get more. But that self-aware thought checked the heady flush of coke racing through me. I took stock of myself. I thought, *This is ridiculous. I don't* like *how I'm feeling now. The cocaine is not comforting me, it's unravelling me. What's wrong with you? Are you twenty years old still? Are you unable to cope? Is your answer simply to cop out?* I proceeded to give myself a real arse-kicking. When Tash came home, I told her what I'd done and we discussed it calmly. She said, 'I thought you dealt with things differently now, babe. Obviously, you don't. As soon as the right circumstances present themselves, you don't see yourself as who you are — you see yourself as who you were.'

And as if Tash didn't feel the need to get out of it, to get into a head space where our problems and frustrations were not so incessantly present. Yet she didn't. She was strong enough to feel what she felt and deal with it. Then she returned home to find that her man had become a little boy again.

I had to think this through. Was I going to do something about this or was this behaviour pattern going to turn up time and time again? And where would that lead? Would there come a time when the kids would watch their old man run and hide from his problems, seeking refuge in pills, powders or bottles? Sure, I'd only had two lines of coke, but they were in effect a potent virus that had the potential to break me down and destroy my entire life. That was the truth. And I had to face up to it: I was a drug addict. Still.

I called Tim, a good friend of mine who cuts my hair. He's one of the most inspiring blokes I know. Man, has that guy done some super-hard yards. He's kicked cocaine and alcohol. He lives with being HIV-positive. Years ago, the person he loved had committed suicide. And he gets up and gets on with life every day and is one of the nicest, most charming blokes you'll ever meet. One day a week he goes to downtown LA and cuts underprivileged kids' hair for free. He has done this for nine years — doing all these whacked-out hairstyles for these kids — and has seen them grow up. Talking to Tim helped me put things in perspective. I said I wanted to look deeper into this problem I had. I told him I wanted to go along to an Alcoholics Anonymous meeting with him. He said that would be fine.

It was AA but it was for people dealing with all forms of substance abuse. There were all sorts of people there — really successful Hollywood types working through the same thing. Some had been clean for many years but still came for the fellowship and to offer inspiration to those who were struggling. The experience did help drive home some important messages.

I had to realise that drugs were no longer a part of my life. No manner of excuse — friends, special occasion, wins, losses — could be allowed to change that. I was fully aware of the excuses I'd used and I felt pathetic. It was like, *Oh, I know it's not me but, fuck it, I'll do it anyway because I can put it down to the fact that my fight's getting put back.* I seized onto something like that and made it my justification ticket. And if I continued? Maybe I would get to a point where I'd just go, *Ah, fuck it, I take cocaine, who cares?* Then I'd be all the way back where I was. *So what, it's only a little bit. Who cares? I don't need to justify myself to anyone. Fuck 'em.*

No. Fuck *cocaine.* Thankfully, the days of me bullshitting myself are getting fewer and further between. The fact is that I need to get coke out of my life once and for all. But that's much easier said than done. Staying off the gear completely will take some work. I know there will be those moments when hooking into a bit of charlie will seem like a harmless, fun indulgence, a refreshing lapse of vigilance to remind myself that I'm no saint. I know I can be seduced — but I do have faith that my incentives to resist are becoming more powerful. In recent years, drugs have played only a very small part in my life. One day soon, that part will be nonexistent.

We returned to Australia in mid-January. A February date had been set and then lost and now March was being explored. As we were preparing to leave, Tash learnt that her grandfather, to whom she was very close, was dying. She wanted to get home to say goodbye in person but he died just before she and the kids flew out of LA. I left four days later. I landed in Australia the day before the funeral and was glad just to play a small role by supporting Tash.

We were back in Australia but our issues were not left behind. While it was great to have the cost of living reduced, and family and friends close to us again, Tash and I were not seeing eye to eye. Never before had our lives felt so aimless and wearying and indefinite. Rather than the proximity of a world title fight opening up a clearer road ahead, the dispiriting weight of uncertainty hung over us more than ever. I was consumed by failure issues, that I had returned home and I wasn't the champ, that we were so in debt, and that ... it just wasn't how it was meant to be. Tash was completely over it. She'd had a gutful of this treadmill life that was all motion, no progress, an ever-extending hallway that was now testing the limits of us both.

Beyond her own concerns of what was becoming of our family, Tash was completely over me and my self-absorbed mind-set. She shut me out. She was sick of hearing about me and my problems. She was over me. Communication between us dried up. I knew what she was feeling — exhausted and frustrated and wondering how long we could continue to live like this. I resolved to be patient and wait until she was ready to talk again. Every morning I'd wake up and think, *Is she over it yet?* I knew I had to just keep supporting her. It was really tough, I can tell you. Eventually, thank God, the lines began to clear a little and we both got a few things off our chests.

We basically decided that boxing wasn't going to rule our lives any longer. Everything hinged on dates and it was too much of an emotional roller coaster for her. I said I was not going to let Tash in on everything about the boxing business. I'd share only what needed to be shared. There was stuff she didn't need to know about that she'd form an opinion on and react to when it had nothing to do with her, and her reaction would rouse some kind of emotional response in me. So as much as was feasible, we were not to keep our lives beholden to boxing. Having broken through this issue, the air cleared and we felt genuinely pleased to be home on the Gold Coast. Soon afterwards, I don't think a day went by that we didn't say to each other how lovely it was to be there.

Then something amazing, something absolutely beautiful, happened. I went to church and committed my life to God. In saying that, I can't help but wonder what your reaction is, whether there's some disappointment, some sense of hearing a broken record in the vein of 'Amazing Grace', some suspicion I've led you here and all the while kept a Bible behind my back. I say this because that's how *I* would react. My back would be up and I would read on, if I continued to read at all, in a state of high alert, the tripwires set for any bullshit religious con. Not so long ago, any suggestion that I needed a church to be close to my God reeked of arrogance and discrimination and conscription. But I'm not here to spruik the word of Jesus. I'm here to tell you what happened. And this was not something I planned. In some ways, though, it should not come as a surprise to you. I'd been digging away at issues about faith and spirituality for years. I mean, those sweat lodges were no day spa, Grandmother Windhawk no back-rub girl. To find meaningfulness and worth within myself was neither an easy nor short process. It has, though, been a journey that has given me great rewards in return for my efforts. I said to myself that day I swam in the water off Surfers Paradise, on the first morning I spent living with Wayne, that changing my life for the better required constant work. I have achieved some amazing results. But I'm far from done. I would like to achieve more.

My leap of faith began with an argument. Well, it was a discussion about faith between Tash and I that grew heated. There was nothing unusual about this — we'd been at it for five years, but we'd come to a place in our marriage where we could have a rational discussion without one of us getting our back up and it turning into a row. This time, though, things got a little feisty. Tash was talking about things and expressing them from a fully Christian viewpoint. Every 'Jesus this' and 'God that' irked me. I got defensive and I piped up with my own views, as though she'd expressly denounced them. For years I've accepted much about Christianity but have recoiled whenever I sense righteousness and exclusivity and superiority, as though all peoples, all faiths, all beliefs should kneel before the Lord Jesus Christ. Whatever Tash was saying, I just wanted to say things can be grey, they don't have to be black and white. I was not a churchgoer but I believed I was a good spiritual person striving to be better. Although Tash was attacking neither me nor my views, a frustration arose within me as though I'd been deeply offended, as though my beliefs and spirituality were being rendered inconsequential because I didn't find the glory of God through Jesus. Man, that word again! Soon enough, I was venting a headful of steam which incited Tash to counter in kind.

I ended up saying to Tash, 'I can't be this Christian guy you want me to be.' She said to me, with some exasperation, 'I'm not asking you to! I want you to be who you are. This isn't even about God, Paul. It's about you and your father.' Bam! Straight between the eyes.

I stopped myself from saying anything more. I needed to take some time out, calm down and gather my thoughts. I told Tash I was going to get the paper.

In the car I turned it all over in my head. What was eating me, exactly? I was so sick of this coming between us. And the more I thought about it, the more I realised it wasn't Tash and her words that were shitting me — it was me. The problem was me: I could see and admit that. I didn't want to commit to the Christian thing. I was arguing with my wife for argument's sake. It was all about me not wanting to conform. I'd been a Christian as a child and I believed I was so much more advanced because my spiritual understanding was not confined by Jesus or Christianity or any religion. It was just me and God. But deep down I felt there was something missing. I'd argue with Tash but I still felt hollow. Years ago, we'd agreed that we both believed in God, but we came at Him through different ways. The bottom line, though, was that we couldn't share in each other's faith. And I desperately wanted to. I knew that. Through my parents I'd seen the strength of a united faith in a marriage — their happiest times had been when they shared in God. I had hang-ups about Christianity because of the hypocrisy I beheld growing up, seeing my father claim to be devout and then cheat on his wife and beat up his children. He was the god of my universe then. And I had looked at him and thought, *The god of everyone's universe is like you — a hypocrite*. But now I was feeling sick of this discord with Tash and I wanted to resolve it. I stepped away from our argument and decided, *You know what? I'm over this, and the problem lies with me*. I needed to sort my shit out. What was I rejecting: Christianity itself or my father? I guess to some extent I felt that I was an ex-Christian. I'd rejected Christianity before, and if I was to return it would be on my own terms. But what, exactly, were my terms? They were defined by the memory of my father. Tash was right.

The need in me to find clarity on this God issue was so strong and deep, I believed no amount of my own rationalising could attend to it completely. I felt that the power to provide answers was beyond my consciousness. I guess you could say I was desperate. And I reached for help. In the car, I started to pray. I asked God to open my heart to Him. I said I wanted clarity in my mind, heart and soul. I didn't want this wall between my wife and I to exist any more. As much as I felt I knew God, I knew that I wasn't fully at peace with Him. I wanted to be, once and for all. I kept praying, saying, 'Please, Father, just pull the walls down around my heart. Please be with me. I want to feel You. I want You in my life. I don't want these hang-ups I have around You any more. I want to share in You with my wife.' And I found I was praying through tears. And I was like, *Why on earth am I crying?* But I was feeling such a great sense of emotional release, the tears were fitting. It was as though my long, hard vigil over some precious bounty had come to an end. As though I could walk away from ideas I'd held for so long as pillars of my self, great structures that defined and distinguished me. I had my own beliefs on God.

Now it seemed clear that they had served their purpose and it was time to move on. This particular war was over. I had neither won nor lost; I'd just surrendered.

I snapped out of this state before I got home. I walked in and said to Tash, 'I want to get baptised with you.' And she was like, 'Oh, that'll be nice', as though I'd suggested we make the most of this fine day and have a picnic. I said, 'No, I want to do it. I want to go to church next Sunday.' She said, 'Yeah, well, it's Easter — we'll go.' 'No,' I said. 'Not because that's what we do on Easter. I want us to go to church on Sunday as a family.' And Tash looked at me as though I was having a dig at her, because we'd just been arguing. I said, 'I want to go to church and I think I want to recommit my life to God.' She was like, 'Why do you always have to do this? First, we have an argument then you come back with this. Are you being a smartarse?' I just looked at her and she was like, 'Oh, baby. Wow! So you're serious?' I said, 'Yeah, something full-on's just happened to me.' That's when I realised I was different. I said, 'I'm sick of this being between us, babe.' And I left it at that.

As we got closer to Easter Sunday, I was waiting for these reactive feelings to come up and try to talk me out of my 'nonsense', but none did. Tash and I took the kids to a new church. It was one I felt comfortable with. You know, the Pentecostal hands-in-the-air type. I like that they're not so regimented and dour. And as soon as I walked in, I knew we'd come to the right place. I felt completely at ease.

They showed this clip from *The Passion of the Christ*. And my issue had long been with Jesus, the word Jesus. And I guess the film humanised him. It touched me — I saw him in a completely different light. Then Aramea took off and I went after her, then remained standing up the back by myself after she slipped away again and returned to Tash. After the service the pastor was walking around and he began asking, 'Is there anyone who wants to commit their life to God? Just put your hand up.' And he was looking at me as he walked along. 'We'll wait,' he says. And he was still looking at me. And I was thinking, *Put your hand up*. Then it was like, *No, you've done this before! You've been a Christian.*

*You've done the Christian thing.* And the pastor's gone, 'If there's someone here who's been a Christian before and done the Christian thing and just wants to come back to the Lord, just put your hand up.' I kid you not, *word for word* what had just gone through my head. This was too much. I raised my hand. *What are you doing?* I chided myself. And he went, 'Thank you.' It was as though he'd been waiting just for me.

I walked down the front and could see people going, 'That's Paul Briggs', and I was freaking. I was so nervous. I felt like a little boy again. When the brief ceremony was done, I felt a hand on my shoulder and Tash was standing there with tears running down her face. She couldn't believe it — she'd had no idea that this was going to happen. Nor had I! But she'd been praying for such a thing for five years. Not that I'd be converted or get saved, but that we could share this together. I really had no idea what I was doing — all I knew was that I was opening my heart up to God again. I wanted Him to be part of my life and for it to be known. No longer was it going to be me going, 'Yeah, I've got a relationship with God but it's a personal thing.' That was my cop-out. As I returned to my seat, these men were watching me and I could *feel* them thinking, *I can't even believe you're here, let alone doing this.* There was this big Maori bloke looking at me and his eyes were lit up so joyously. I'll never forget it. He had this smile on his face from ear to ear. I felt so proud and so humble, and so very, very happy.

About a month later, I got word that the wait was over. After five false starts, a date had finally been set. On 21 May 2005, I was going to fight for the WBC light heavyweight title in Chicago. I'd been keeping in good shape on the Gold Coast, and I loved being back training and sparring with Wayne. The guy has such a presence about him. And in the ring I was reminded of how much more hunger and savage intent Muay Thai fighters give off compared to boxers. There's such an intense kill-or-be-killed urgency in Thai boxing. It's often all-out war from the bell, whereas boxers tend to feel each other out and deploy more patient, strategic — but ultimately no less brutal — campaigns. As

I packed my bags to leave for Los Angeles and hook up with Jack Mosley, I was thinking about how I must retain that edge and ferocity I'd become reacquainted with through Wayne. And in my luggage I packed a Bible. These two sources of inspiration might seem incompatible, but they aren't — and that's what I love about fighting. The rush of nerves. The heightened, totally alive sense inspired by battle is like a drug. When I'm in the ring, I feel like nothing else exists in the universe but me and the force flowing through me to do what I'm doing. There's a feeling of oneness, of me being connected to everything. It can be so powerful. Nowhere have I felt closer to God than in the ring.

Not every time, though. And while I'd packed my Bible and my Muay Thai mojo for a journey to Chicago and glory, turns out that I was bound for the brink of hell.

# XXXI

## *Becoming A Champion*

Seven weeks out from the fight, Jack and I headed up to Big Bear Lake, a small alpine resort a couple of hours' drive out of Los Angeles. The place is popular with LA-based boxers — Oscar de la Hoya and Jack's son Shane, for instance, have built houses there, complete with fully equipped gyms. It's not hard to figure out why: you get the rewards of high-altitude training and seclusion from the big smoke while not having to forego mobile phone coverage and Blockbuster Video — there are a lot of hours to kill in camp.

The pre-fight camp has always had a degree of mystique about it. The boxer disappears for a couple of months until the date draws him out of isolation, and what happens during his absence is only glimpsed or guessed at by those beyond the inner circle. My lifestyle at Big Bear wasn't Spartan, just low-key, but there's definitely something monastic about the rigours and dedication of camp. You're removed from your familiar world and your entire being is devoted to one aim in life. It goes far beyond mere training. This camp, however, was something out of the ordinary. It exposed me to an incredibly deep and exacting experience — a religious experience, you could say — which was the last thing I was expecting when we arrived and got ourselves settled.

Jack and my sparring partners set up in the Mosley house. I rented a small log cabin that had wagon wheel chandeliers and snowshoes, sleds and a big white deer head hung on the walls. A massive TV took pride of place in the living room, complete with a DVD player and a hundred mind-numbing channels of cable. Did I ever give that DVD player a workout. Boxers in camp are major couch potatoes — intense workouts are followed by long periods of idleness. By camp's end I'd churned through so many movies that I was about to start a second lap of Blockbuster's shelves. That said, the fight and my readiness for it never left my thoughts for long. It was an obsession I never felt inclined, let alone permitted, to shrug. One day, though, it was suddenly swept from my mind by an event of stunning force.

No matter how determined you are to lock yourself away and focus on a project, no matter what measures you take to remove all possible distractions, the mind can't be so neatly corralled. Many times in my life I've wanted to switch off my brain because of its incessant activity. But its strength has been my saviour, helping me through rape, drugs and violence, and then driving my reform. And sometimes I wonder if I'm now too emotional, that where once I was unreceptive to tender feelings I'm now almost a soft touch, an emotions junkie. As an example, I watched my favourite film, *The Notebook*, for the ninth time in camp. And I still cried. Getting in touch with my feelings has not been a slide from fortitude to feebleness, though — I've gained so much knowledge and power by opening up and being vulnerable. 'Weakened' is the last word I'd use to describe the result. When I think of the man I am now compared with the person I was, I feel so incredibly fortunate. And my strength of mind has played an enormous role in that growth. That I can never shut it down has become something I accept as an asset, despite the occasional inconvenience. But out of the blue, on one of the first days of camp, I found my mind locking onto something I didn't want nor expect to be going anywhere near while I was in camp: my rape.

Out on a run, I began to dwell on what happened 21 years back. To be specific, I was thinking about the guy who raped me. As always, powerful and distressing emotions rose up from within. I thought of all the pain I'd gone through — injuries of my own doing as well as his — and, for the first time in my life, I didn't become consumed with anger and sorrow. I reflected on what I remembered of this bloke and found myself entering fresh emotional territory. What began as a degree of compassion became a state of absolute forgiveness. To my amazement, I found myself *forgiving* the guy who raped me with all my heart and soul. And I'll say again the words I never thought I'd utter: I forgive him. I was so churned up by this phenomenon that when I got home I felt unusually drained, like I'd completed an odyssey. Over the following days and weeks, as my new mind-set remained an unchallenged conviction, the enormity of what I was going through began to sink in. With the help of many a prayer, I came to believe to the depths of my soul that the suffering born of my rape was finally coming to an end.

For most of my life I'd never wanted to forgive: I wanted to be angry. I wanted people to know how much I was hurting. Such rage drove me to a world kickboxing title and, once retired, found an outlet in arbitrary violence. I bore such consuming hatred towards this man that I conjured up many twisted acts of torture by which I could exact my revenge. I believed that by inflicting cruelty upon him, my suffering and pain would cease. I can now accept and embrace that period of anger, but the truth is that it held me back. Having chosen to break the cycle of hatred, having chosen mercy, I have come to feel that a significant part of my trauma has been dealt with. Through forgiveness, I've depleted much of the power that this dreadful experience held over me for the past twenty-one years. Through forgiveness, my deepest wound began to finally heal.

The flow-on effects were sad and joyous at once. Memories of my childhood started coming back. I recalled that Christmas more fully. We had a real Christmas tree and it was so big that once, when it fell over, it half destroyed our lounge room. I remember Nathan and I snuggling under a doona with our cool babysitter — Christine, I think her name was — to watch *M*A*S*H*. I remember Dad pulling a loose tooth of mine out with a pair of pliers, and even that ranks as a fond memory because it fills a small hole in that period of childhood I'd erased. So many pieces have since come back to me.

To say this was a breakthrough doesn't do justice to the profound impact of the event. For the first time in my life, I felt so at peace with myself, so whole. I was attuned to a sense of passage: I felt as though I'd finally broken clear of a violent storm. It was that distinct. I was free. I harboured no trace of anger concerning my rape, no hatred. And rather than feeling weak and powerless, I felt charged and liberated and light of heart. This guy, or at least his essence, ceased to exist with me any more. I had released 'him' with no parting spite or loathing — *Just go, man, be on your way. Wherever you are, if you're still on this planet or not, be on your way.* Up until that point, I would have shunned such reconciliation as treachery. It was anything but. I came to realise that dispelled with all the fury, resentment, bitterness and malice that I'd clung to so vigilantly was my own burden of guilt — for the rape itself and for all the evil I'd done, unknowingly or otherwise, in its name. In forgiving my nemesis, I forgave myself.

This was in many ways a rebirth. There was the shock of emotions being played out followed by a sense of alienation, of having to readjust to seeing and feeling the world in a fundamentally different way. Then there was a pleasant wonder, a relief and the absolute joy of realising that the shadow across my soul had finally lifted. This doesn't mean I'll never speak of my rape again; I'm sure I will. Nor does it mean that the recollection of it will never again move me to deep sadness and discomfort. But I am no longer a victim, a captive. My wound was at last allowed to begin healing. All I have in me is love — and, really, nothing else matters.

Maybe this was not the right time and place for me to be experiencing such a monumental inner shift. But what can I say? You can't stop *being*. You can't simply place your life entirely on hold, especially when you've actively set yourself on a particular path. In recent years I could never have been accused of allowing my life to merely happen to me. By making better choices in my life, I'd opened myself to better fates. I'd been working to find peace and redemption for years and I could no more schedule the timing of their arrival than pause the movement of the sun. And why would I ever want to delay this event? I'd strived so much to attain peace and I feel utterly blessed to have found it. I feel blessed to have had the gift to persist with all my work. I know there are other people who have and will remain trapped by their abuse all their lives. That saddens me. How many are suffering in silence, living in hell and, quite possibly, inflicting hell upon others? I shudder to think, because so few victims find the voice to speak up.

If I can inspire one person to talk, to seek help and so begin the journey of reclaiming their self-love and richness of life, then I would be the proudest man on earth. But as for the timing of my own healing, all I can say is that the time was right, no matter where I was, no matter what the circumstances. This was so much bigger than fighting for the light heavyweight world title. I felt that, regardless of what happened in the ring, if I had to go over to Big Bear to finally break free from my rape then I was every bit a champion. I have emerged from a 21-year war victorious. I *am* a champion for getting to this place within myself. The world title belt itself is a trinket compared to the prize this personal victory has given me. In the broader scope of my life, a fight may well hold very little of lasting consequence. And you know what? I was looking forward more to my daughter's birthday party than the world title. I couldn't wait to be back home to take her out and get her hair done and buy her a little bracelet and enjoy the day with her. This was more important to me than winning the world title. As I have said before — and as this camp experience had made all the more clear — boxing is what I do, my family defines who I am.

While it may seem I'd drifted into some flower-petal head space, that I was preparing myself to lose, I trained with commitment and intensity. I won't say my emotional upheaval had no effect on my physical and mental state. Of course it did. After one particularly draining episode, where I recounted the story of my forgiveness and its effects to a couple of mates who joined me in camp — the first time I had spoken about the experience with anyone other than Tash — I sparred like a drunk. But beforehand and afterwards I was sharp and hard and very much on track to becoming world champion. I was dropping a sparring partner every day with powerful rips to the body. Three weeks out from the fight we had to replace one that I broke, and of the two left one was nursing a busted rib and only stayed on after being assured I wouldn't hit him with body shots. Everyone was convinced I was going to snap the Pole in half.

A typical session would be to do twelve rounds of sparring — six rounds each with two partners — then two rounds of continuous punching on the heavy bag, two rounds of rips, two rounds of jabs, then two rounds on the speed ball. Twenty all up. I'd throw up by about round fourteen. But whenever I felt my energy waning, I'd grit my teeth and yell 'WORLD CHAMPION!' and I'd find extra reserves and push through. When my arms were leaden and my muscles searing — 'WORLD CHAMPION!' When my shoulders were screaming for mercy — 'WORLD CHAMPION!' When my entire body was a miserable chorus of protest — 'WORLD CHAMPION!' And on I went. On I went.

After a session in the gym I'd head back to my cabin to rest, eat and basically chill for the rest of the day. At the time I wasn't sure that doing just one session a day was the right way to go. All my career I'd trained twice a day, right up to fight day — but everything seemed to be going well and I was taking Jack's lead. I felt terrific and I'd think, *If I feel this good at altitude, how charged will I be at sea level?*

Even though I was hidden away in the mountains, I had a phone and hence was still involved in the concerns of life outside camp. One day, Tash was having a really tough time handling the kids and she said she wanted me to come home. Of course this was out of the question, but I felt terrible and, after I'd hung up, prayed for her to find strength. She did. At last she put her foot down with Isaiah, who worked the Dad-free zone like a pro. Even Aramea was in on the act and the pair of them would double-team Tash. Thankfully, Tash took the matter firmly in hand. She rang me back, saying sweetly, 'Did you pray for me, babe?' Then there was Sampson ringing me a week out from the fight to say the WBC needed a copy of my health report urgently — like, within two hours — or else I couldn't fight. *What? Why hadn't they got this before? Why this panic now? I don't need this shit!* And there were debt issues that, as much as I tried, I simply couldn't forget about. Almost all of the money I'd get from the fight was going to be used to pay off debt.

But what occupied my mind most was Tomasz Adamek. About six weeks out from the fight, we'd met in Chicago for the initial press conference. The main event King had put us under was a heavyweight clash between American Lamon Brewster and Andrew Golota. This was why we were going to fight in Chicago — Golota's Polish and there are more Poles in Chicago than any city besides Warsaw. Adamek was the entrée to the Golota main.

When we met, Adamek struck me as being more a sportsman than a warrior. He seemed to lack any real intention to do me harm. I didn't leave thinking that I had his number, but I did feel all the more confident that he'd faced no one like me, a fighter who'd be in his face and hitting him very, very hard. He had a clean record — twenty-eight wins, no losses and twenty knockouts — at the expense of no-name Poles, mostly. And from what I'd seen on video, he fought like a bean-counter — a guy to whom punches are numbers, who keeps a fastidious eye on the balance of each round's ledger. I saw that he'd won his fights easily — but his opponents appeared to have been coaxed from hospice beds and went down with their gloves dry, dampened neither by Adamek's sweat nor blood. To Adamek boxing seemed to be a demonstration sport, his bouts the showcases of a very good technician, but they were about as visceral as algebra. However, I never write an opponent off. I knew there was every chance this guy would rise to a level I'd not yet seen. I had little doubt his full courage would come to the fore. And I was sure he was going to need it. Just as I was sure it would not be enough.

I won't say I never entertained a moment's doubt, because I did. There were instances when I feared I'd lose. I remember that the day I left Australia, after I'd given a farewell press conference in Sydney, doubt overcame me. The conviction of many people that I was a sure thing was based purely on the fact that I had some runs on the board and this Polish guy was just a name in black type below mine on the rankings list. The closer the fight got, the more Tomasz Adamek materialised in my mind as a man I must oppose. At a point where many people were underestimating his calibre, I swung the other way. *He could be so much more than we are giving him credit for*, I thought. But that, again, was a natural fear of the unknown and its stay was brief. Once I'd arrived in the States, my old reckoning was firmly in place: *Disregard those fears you conjure up; get face to face with the guy,* then *we'll see what we're afraid of.* And after that first meeting in Chicago, I knew I had nothing to fear from Tomasz Adamek. But I didn't quite know what to make of him, to tell you the truth. He was so quiet and indifferent and blank. He'd strike you as being enigmatic if he had a hint of personality. He was this Eastern European stoic, and you can never tell what lies beneath with these guys. But bringing it down to brass tacks, I was convinced I could take everything he had and that my all would be too much for him.

We got to Chicago a week out from the fight. It was a long week, just hanging out and waiting when all I wanted to do was get into the ring. Jack and I let our momentum slip — I ran every day but we did pad work rarely. This was crazy, now that I think about it, but at the time I didn't see fit to start directing my preparation. It was not like I felt we'd suddenly lost track; I still felt absolutely confident that I would win.

Coming into a city to be swamped by all the fight hype highlighted the tranquility of the camp. Suddenly it was all bustle and movement, going here and there, dicking around with hotel rooms, tides of people wanting to get their photos taken with you, and people around me being constantly anxious about what I was doing, what I wasn't doing, what I should be doing, what I shouldn't be doing, what I was thinking about, what I wasn't thinking about, what I might be upset about ... Everyone close to me was doing their best to appear calm and relaxed but you could feel the static, that contained agitation that dared not be displayed for fear of getting the boxer out of sorts in any way, shape or form, as though I could be somehow thrown by the discourtesy of a sneeze. The tension was understandable — we were all approaching a day we'd waited nine uncomfortable months for, during which our faith had been sorely tested and our hopes cruelly teased.

At last the day of all days was upon us and I'd have had to have been inhuman not to feel the slightest bit daunted. There was so much riding on this fight. Not only my career, my finances and the livelihood of my family but people like Geoffrey and Sampson had staked so much, personally and professionally, on me winning. I didn't feel the weight of expectation as an unreasonable burden. I am a boxer. This is what I do. No, I walked to the ring thinking my time had come at last. I was ready to rip shit up.

Entering the stadium, it was like a sea of screaming Poles had parted before me and now they bobbed overhead, hurling abuse at me and booing me like some villain who should be strung up on the spot. Ah, the roar of the crowd. The noise was incredible and invigorating. There were around 20 000 seats sold and Polish bums occupied most of them. Don King had done well. All week he'd buttered up Chicago — 'Chi-ca-go! my kinda town' — and hammered home the Polish angle. He'd talked tirelessly about how Andrew Golota was ripe to knock Brewster out, even though Brewster was one of his fighters whom, in other breaths, he lavishly hailed as the black Rocky. It was beautiful stuff. King the master salesman was in full, effortless flight and, as though every word might snag him a ticket, he gave as much time to, say, a no-name journalist from Polish radio as he did to major television crews. It wasn't a huff and puff act, a long-winded con job. It was a lengthy stroll through the park. King doesn't turn it on so much as stretch it out. What you might see as a blustering soundbite is merely one unremarkable fragment from his unceasing flow. The guy gave everyone — not just those holding microphones — the time of day, and for Don King the day is long and leisurely and active. But at the end of that day, he'd better have made a good buck. And he was paying me 200 grand for this fight while Adamek was getting 30. He'd invested in Paul Briggs. The time had come to see some return. And I was going to take pleasure in giving it to him, at the expense of Adamek and every single member of his overnight fan club.

The first round was like most first rounds — a feeling-out process. At long last Adamek was before me, and, as expected, he got busy with his crisp combinations. No question, the bean-counter was a good boxer. As usual, I started slow but introduced myself to Adamek as not only a fighter with power but someone who wasn't going to be quite the easy target he'd expected. From his pre-fight comments I knew that he believed I was slow and very hittable. My improved body movement was proving otherwise. Still, the first round was his. But we were away and there was plenty of time. Or so I thought. By the end of the second round, to my utter shock and disbelief, I was on my way out.

A head clash produced an inch-long cut above my left eye. Not so bad in itself, but the amount of blood that poured down my face made me think the cut was severe. The ref stopped the fight immediately so my cut man could stem the bleeding but by the end of the round a steady flow had resumed. When I sat in my corner, the cut became my preoccupation. I felt absolutely gutted and so rueful that this unexpected setback had been sprung on me to make my mission all the harder. At the start of the third, I'd forced the cut out of mind and reset my focus onto the fight. I knew I was now two rounds down and I went on the offensive and staggered Adamek. But I didn't capitalise on the split-second opportunity my assault created. Rather than jump on him, I stood back and watched him recover. It was the first sign that my mind was drifting.

As the rounds progressed, the blood continued to flow. I grew angry with my corner. Why couldn't they stop the bleeding? I zoned out. I switched off to Jack's words — nothing he said could rouse me. My mind went wandering, and man, the places it went. *I'm fucking cut!* I'd wipe blood from eyes, from my cheek. *Fucking cut!* My left eye was flooded and my sight blurred against the best boxer I'd ever faced. Adamek stayed diligently on the job, throwing good combinations to rack up the points. But, protecting my cut, my guard was tight and many of his blows found my gloves and were hence worthless. And the punches that did connect only confirmed what I'd thought all along: he couldn't hurt me. The punches I landed, on the other hand, showed clearly that I could hurt him. We weren't in the fight long before his nose was rebroken — he'd busted it three weeks earlier in training — and his face was steadily growing deformed.

Yet the cut stole my focus. I took it as another lash of ill fortune. I'd waited nine months for this fight, for this validation, for this defining career and personal breakthrough moment. Never had there been a more important fight for me and now look at what was happening — my mind was off somewhere else and my body was on autopilot, lacking the zest of improvisation, the head for strategy, the ferocious drive, the clarity of motive, the goddamn basic killer instinct to seize any breath of a chance to destroy the man seeking to destroy me. I was still very much in the fight, though, landing some telling blows and countering Adamek's steady assaults to quell the roaring Poles into respectful and uncertain silence. Yet I had somehow lost the wherewithal to throw combinations greater than two. Could I not count to four? It was like I'd had a lobotomy — I couldn't let my hands go. Every short explosive effort drained me. For all my training, I was running out of puff. From the fourth round onwards, I didn't even want to be there.

I began to think of Rod, of all people. I guess because he was connected to my financial predicament. Under his management I'd begun to lose money rather than make it. And it so pissed me off to think that from 200 grand US I'd bank about 8 Aussie.

I'm fighting a guy in a ring in front of 22 000 people and this is the sort of stupid shit that's going through my head. Why Rod? Because of the debt, but also because he was someone I trusted, a father figure, a huge support to me who ended up drifting away, leaving me to handle it all by myself. And here again I had that awful sense of abandonment; that, once again, my corner was letting me down. I needed to be snapped out of this sinking mind-set, but Jack did not have the words. And I kept bleeding and bleeding — at times my face was masked in blood — and I could not clear my mind.

In the eighth I caught Adamek with a terrific straight right that stunned him. His legs buckled and he looked as though he'd drop, although he stayed on his feet. Again, I stood and watched. Now, of all moments, when I'm losing on points, when I need to knock him down if not out, when I must surely step up the pressure on him and let my hands go, I seemed to go all Good Samaritan, as though I'd be more inclined to offer him a hand than unleash an onslaught. It looked like I'd figured I could afford to let him recover, that I could afford to wait. God, it was even seen as a sign of confidence, that I had him where I wanted him, that it was all a matter of time before I'd create a better knockout opportunity, all part of the plan. But there was no such plan in my muddled head. I was throwing punches and expecting them to be knockout blows, as opposed to throwing punches to set up the knockout blow.

I have said before that the mind is a fighter's greatest asset. I have said how a losing fighter finds himself up against more than his opponent as his own spirit begins to work against him. This is what happened to me. I had wanted to leave by round four but I was never going to quit. The moment I was cut I was lost; what should have been no more than a concern became the watershed of my mind's unravelling. At least I showed an abundance of courage, if not wits, in that fight. The crowd was on its feet for the final rounds. They gave us a standing ovation at the final bell. People were left with the potent impression that I was every inch a warrior, for I was so clearly thriving on heart more than anything. But heart is not nearly enough at this level.

I was in a daze when they announced that Adamek had won the decision. His tearful elation was the first sign of emotion I ever saw from the guy. It was a lonely walk back to the dressing room. My existence had suddenly become surreal yet oppressively bleak. Like the death of a loved one, a loss of such magnitude is met with resistance by the mind. And not only mine but the minds of so many people who had helped and supported me. My inner circle were all but speechless and deeply upset. I was shattered. I'd let them down. I cried in the arms of a few. I bawled in the arms of my wife. But there was little consolation to be found. The solitude of boxing is never so pronounced as when you lose. Instead of flying home world champion, triumphantly facing an upbeat press conference, feeling that sublime sense of victory and achievement, and anticipating the money that the belt could now start to earn for me at last, I'd be returning to Australia a gutted nobody, a loser, just another Aussie slugger who'd had a crack and lost. It was all a bit much for him. What a disgrace.

I saw Adamek when we went to be checked out by the doctor shortly after the match. His face was grotesque, as though it was host to several rampant tumours. 'You hit very hard,' he said.

'Yeah,' I said. 'Can't wait for the rematch.' But his attention was gone. Then he goes, 'What? What?' as the doctor was examining him, thinking I'd addressed him. 'I didn't say anything, mate,' I said. I looked at the doctor, who indicated that Adamek was off with the pixies. I'll give that guy his due — he beat me well. I had no reason to object to the judges' scoring. He was the best boxer I've ever fought and he showed he had tremendous heart and will. All credit to him: he proved himself to be a fine warrior after all. And he was now the WBC light heavyweight champion of the world. But I don't think he'll forget me in a hurry. He left the United Center and went to hospital. We both did, actually. I had my eye stitched up and returned to my hotel to have a few subdued drinks with my wife and friends. He spent three nights in his hospital bed.

# XXXII

## *Who Will You Say You Are?*

In the days and weeks that followed the loss I thought about that fight ad nauseam. I thought about the healing experience I'd had in Big Bear. And I considered how my anger and hatred of men had driven me to a world kickboxing title. In uprooting that dark seed, had I cast out my instinct, my relish, my reflex to go for the kill? I believe there is an element of truth in that. To some extent, I sacrificed that title fight for the cause of being a better man. And I am happy with that, for I was on a mission much bigger than a world title. The guy who raped me tortured me for a matter of minutes; I tortured myself for twenty-one years. Now — thank you, God — that chapter of my life is closed.

And so a new one opens. I have moved to a much better place in regard to my abuse, but the truth is that I am still not healed. At least I know that my healing is under way. For only now am I living without the anger that has possessed me for much of my life. That I can think of the guy who raped me and not grow hot with rage is a sign that I have changed in a fundamental way. Countless times I have thought of cutting him into a thousand pieces alive. Not any more. Now all I am dealing with is me, and the many issues relating to my abuse that have grown inside me over the years. And, yes, they can still bring me to periods of debilitating sorrow.

I don't know when, if ever, I will be done with my rape. Maybe never. But I'm okay with that; I will keep working at it. I have come so, so far that I feel blessed and proud. I love who I am, and for me to say that is a minor miracle.

I am adjusting to a new life in which anger is not my crutch. The cycle of anger, very much like crying, can be a comfort mechanism. To go through the process of feeling your anger build and then venting it explosively delivers a payload of relief. It also gives you the feeling that you are doing something, expressing something, acting it out. Violent demonstrations of anger validate the injured, the hurting, the disconnected.

Recently, I had the most intense episode of anger I'd experienced in a long while. It was sparked by something trivial — Tash telling me about a night out she had with her girlfriends. But that whole day I'd been feeling vulnerable and insecure and I was looking for something to get pissed off about. Tash had done nothing wrong but I seized upon something in her account as the trigger I'd been seeking. And this anger rose quickly within me like a rampant flame. My rage had no valid source — it just fed and fed upon itself. I got so worked up I couldn't sleep. I was *seething*. I didn't want Tash to know what an intense state I was in, let alone why, so I got out of bed and went and sat down on the lounge to let it pass through me and to observe what was going on. I swear, it was like I was peaking. I was truly in an altered state. I could feel whatever was going on in my body — my hormones surging, my blood hot, my lungs working like bellows — as distinctly as I would had I dropped a pill. Eventually, it passed and by morning I was in a sedate state that was damn near post-coital.

After this night, I realised how much anger had been such an addictive drug for me. There were so many times when I overreacted and resorted to violence suddenly and with extreme prejudice. It was like being constantly doused in petrol — only the slightest spark was needed to set me off. Anger would engulf me and I would be so consumed by it and so blinded to all other sensibilities that I wouldn't, couldn't, feel anything else. But there was calm after the blast. Whomever I'd injured, whatever I'd destroyed, I'd feel sedated. But I realise that, like drugs, anger served as a suppressant, helping me to block out feelings I didn't want to acknowledge, let alone know what to do with.

More than anything, anger has been the biggest struggle of my life. It's been my most resilient, deep-rooted vice. I'm lucky enough to have now reached a point where I don't attack someone when I get angry. I process my anger as a feeling rather than releasing it violently. I can now reflect on and apply perspective to my intense emotions. And in a sense that is harder than acting on them, because it makes me face my vulnerabilities, those things that unnerve me. For a moment, violence seems an appropriate response. But it will ultimately be seen for what it is — impotent and ruinous, the creator of little more than remorse.

Anger stems from fear — the fear of not knowing how, or being unable, to cope with your feelings. Many men don't know what their feelings are, let alone how to handle and process and express them. It's *hard* to address your deep feelings. It can be confronting, confusing and despairing. But the consequences of not addressing them can prove damaging to oneself and, often, to others.

I'm a sensitive man. This is a revelation I'm still learning to live with. I'm no longer this unfeeling hard nut, and it disturbs me greatly to think of how I have treated people in the past. I'm such a different person now. And, might I say, that's only because I have striven to effect change within myself.

I'm still on a mission to become world champion. Now, though, for the first time in my life, I'm fighting for me, not because I'm angry with anyone or anything. I have a flame burning within me that is as intense as the one I possessed when I was thirteen, when I vowed to become a world kickboxing champion. The difference is that now it's a pure flame, not one burning on the dirty fuel of anger. I'm no longer a damaged individual but I'm still a warrior. I'll fight because I want to fight and because I believe I am the best light heavyweight on the planet. And no, I'm not forgetting I lost to Adamek. That loss will be a prelude to my ultimate success.

For so long I had envisaged a whole new life for me and my family after Chicago, with me as champion. And that is actually the case, though in a different way than I'd expected. I may not be world champion yet but I am free, and I am a champion who fought long and hard to win my spirit's liberty. As for whether I still possess the fierce will to destroy men in the ring, I have no doubt that I do. I know it. I actually feel a huge relief for the passing of that bout, for now I feel truly ready. I know that sounds like spin, but I'll prove it to be otherwise. I will be world champion — that is more clear to me now than ever. There was so much for me to take out of my loss to Adamek. And it will make winning that green belt all the more sweet.

But while that belt is a personal goal I hunger for and will strive for, but there are bigger challenges ahead for me. The reason I'm telling my story is not so people will glorify my ring exploits — it is for people to hear me. And by people I mean men. In a broader sense, beyond my own family's welfare, I hope my achievements in the ring will prise open the stubborn minds of men to ideas I have about masculinity, to listen to me talk of valour, honour and responsibility. I'd like to show them a fresh take on masculinity, that it's not something rooted in physicality and ego but in vulnerability, self-love and noble values. To have power is one thing; to have power and the emotional wisdom to wield it responsibly and honourably is another thing entirely. Yes, I am a Christian now, but I've been a man who has embraced God for years. And whether or not you believe such a person as Jesus ever existed, think of the man He is said to have been. Now, who thinks of Jesus — or at least all that he is said to stand for — as being an icon of masculinity? Not many people. To me that is sad. The torrent of gung-ho, aggressive and vacuous male role models steamrolls over qualities such as kindness and gentleness and caring. They are seen as weak, disdainfully feminine qualities a man should avoid like rattlesnakes. I say the opposite. I say women are lucky. Generally speaking, they are closer to their emotional centre of gravity. They seem to be born with an emotional maturity that men inherently lack. So unless we develop this asset ourselves, we will never acquire it. If men made the effort, they'd realise what powerful, enriching rewards are to be had by tapping into their emotional wisdom. To do so is to become more of a man, not less. I think one of the greatest gifts a man can give himself is to learn to understand and process his feelings.

Also, I hope to encourage people to act, to not just accept their fate as something they can't influence. I have broken the mould in regard to my father. I was once on track to being like the worst of him; now I reflect only the best of him, as a man and as a parent. I am all that he could be. And I want this to be clear: I don't hate my father. I love him. As much as I have wanted to change him, I realise I cannot — that is not within my powers, nor is it my responsibility. I love my father over and above everything. He was the father that I needed to have for me to be who I am today. I'm everything good that my father was. I don't believe he was a bad father intentionally. I'm sure he was doing the best job he could with what he knew. It's far easier to cite bad parenting than it is to define good parenting. I have learnt both from Dad — what to be and what not to be as a father. But I still have to be mindful of making the effort to get out of my comfort zone as an individual and a parent and spend time with Isaiah and Aramea. Continually. Time slips away so quickly. Before you know it, your children have grown up and you haven't made that effort to spend quality time doing what *they* want to do, not what *you* want to do. And you will know it as pain, as regret, as guilt, as failure. As far as Dad and I go, I don't feel the need to have him in my life. I can love him from a distance. In relationships, you have to set boundaries — what you are prepared to accept and what you are not. The power to change rests in his hands, not mine.

I have also broken free from the hell my rape caused. I have steered myself away from a path leading to jail, addiction and death. I have worked at my marriage to a woman who is the queen of my world and our love is more passionate than ever. We still have some humdinger rows and the occasional stand-off but that doesn't change the fact that we have built something that is so precious to both of us.

I can't believe how our marriage continues to grow richer as we travel through life together. But Tash and I invest in our marriage. We want to live it consciously.

My existence at the moment is like some fantasy I might have conjured up in my youth. But this is no fantasy — this is real. This is my journey. And while I have completed a major part of it, I look forward to the next and to finding out how I can maintain the process of effecting meaningful change. For my life is a work in progress. I'll never stop seeking to make myself better.

Life's not about the goals you set. It's about the gold you can mine from your journey towards those goals. What can you pull out of it to make yourself freer, more whole, more real? These will enable you to live a more free, more full and more genuine life. Get real with yourself. Take responsibility. I profess to have taken full responsibility for the last twenty-one years of my life. Me. No one else. I'm responsible for everything I've ever done, everything I've ever said, every pill I've ever popped, every hurt I've inflicted upon others, every hurt I've inflicted upon myself and every time I've abused myself, and every time I've failed to love myself. Each was a choice that I made. There is no right and wrong, only what serves you and what does not serve you. Your life is already so unique, so special. You've experienced things that I and no one else will ever know because that is your life. And when it comes down to it, who will you say you are? That's what it's about — for every man and woman to look at their life and say, 'Who will I say I am? What have I done with my life? What have I done with my experience? What have I chosen to bullshit about? What have I chosen to change and colour and twist?' No, get real. Who do you say you are? Who are you, really?

I am a drug addict, I am a good father, I am a good husband, I am a good boxer, I am a man of my word, I am a Christian who will challenge Christians to think outside the square, I am a man who will challenge men to better themselves, I am a man who is still capable of doing the bloody deeds of my past but will never again choose to, I am a man whose temper can be raised by my children but who will never allow it to overrun me and hurt them, I am a warrior who holds in my hand a sword that one day will only be carried in my heart, I am a man who is no longer imprisoned by my past, I am a man who has gorged on revenge only to starve, I am a man who embraces love and sensitivity and understanding and acceptance and forgiveness and who rejects judgment, I am a man on a journey through life that with God's grace will continue to be as enlightening, humbling and fruitful as it has been up until now, I am of God and have the power to create my own universe, I am human and thoroughly imperfect and I love my imperfections, from the spare tyre I develop between fights to the wonky teeth I once strove to hide.

I am a spiritual being enjoying a physical experience. And what a priceless gift that experience has bestowed upon the spirit of me, Paul Darius Briggs.

Gregor Salmon was born in Adelaide on 6 October 1965 and shot through ten days later. Being the youngest recruit to join an army family, his movements were subject to an authority higher than his parents. The Salmon unit was dispatched to Malaysia and endured a weary campaign in Watsonia, Melbourne, before being deployed to a dusty fibro outpost on the Sydney southwestern front, known as Ingleburn Army Camp.

After high school and university, Salmon embarked on an aimless sortie around the world that he passed off as geopolitical reconnaissance. He got a taste of magazine publishing in London and returned home armed with a reference from *GQ* and great expectations. Offered the role of sub-editor on *Fishing News*, Salmon leapt. Having served a few good years in magazines, he joined the online uprising. No soldier of great fortune, he currently writes freelance, filing from his bunker in Paddington, Sydney.

The effort he put into this book is sincerely dedicated to the memory of Ben Smailes, a gem of a soul who made the gods stoop to larceny.